CONQUISTADORS
in
North American
History

D1431524

Also by Paul Horgan:

Things As They Are, A NOVEL

CONQUISTADORS
in
North American History

by Paul Horgan

A FAWCETT PREMIER BOOK

FAWCETT PUBLICATIONS, INC., GREENWICH, CONN.
MEMBER OF AMERICAN BOOK PUBLISHERS COUNCIL, INC.

TO
WITTER BYNNER

CONTENTS

IV. TO THE NORTH

V. FRUITS OF CONQUEST

VI. THE NORTHERN KINGDOM

VII. THE LAST CONQUEST

PREFACE

Soon after the making of the Spanish empire in the New World began with the island discoveries of Columbus, the great colonial effort moved to the mainland of *Mesoamerica* to put down roots. Its growth and flowering were prodigious, rapid, and full of both splendour and horror, whether in the branch that grew toward the southern American continent, or to the northern. This book traces the path of Spain in the northern continent.

That which spread its bounty and its shadow to the north seemed to carry a continuity of design not to be found in the movement toward South America. New Spain and Peru, while they reflected a common parent culture, were divided by geography and a separation of authority. But New Spain and the thrust toward North America were never divided—and until the settling of Spanish power and hope in the northern kingdom of New Mexico, they were united as expressions of the lingering energy of the man who above all others seeded the daily actualities of Spanish life in the New World—Hernando Cortés, the Lord Marquess of the Valley of Oaxaca. The conquest of Mexico was his, and the lifelines to the north grew out of what he had implanted in *Mesoamerica*. First he conquered the great Aztec city of Mexico, and then his successors sent their soldiers, friars, families and governors northward, where he would have gone himself, if the play of power and the spending of his years had allowed. In a sense, though he dies a little more than halfway through this chronicle, Cortés, as the progenitor of colonial North America, provides a unifying thread of character and style until the end.

For the foreground of actual events and in the use of direct quotations bearing upon these, I have relied, as my bibliography indicates, upon published documents written by participants or witnesses. Though I acknowledge it later, I must cite here also the remarkable historical value of the details of Aztec life and the conquest of Mexico recorded in both Aztec and Spanish from Aztec testimony by Fray Bernardino de Sahagún shortly after the Spanish victory under Cortés. These, in the extraordinary new translations from the Aztec by Dr. Arthur J. O. Anderson and Professor Charles E. Dibble, have placed at the disposal of the student a new rendering of the direct testimony of the defeated peoples of Mexico, and I have with respect attempted to enrich my account of the conquest with the Indian as well as the Spanish record of experience. To bring the reader closer to the Aztec, I refer in quotations in my text not to Fray Bernardino but to anonymous Aztec chroniclers or historians from so many of whose memories he compiled through a decade of the mid-sixteenth century his account of their own ways of life and the circumstances of the conquest as their traditions recalled these.

I state my gratitude also to Rev. Fray Angelico Chavez, O.F.M., who has generously shared with me certain of his historical resources and granted me the benefit of his professional advice.

In earlier works of my own—*Great River: the Rio Grande in North American History* (1954) and *The Centuries of Santa Fe* (1956)—I have previously touched upon some phases of the historical movements which I treat here, though in different proportions and with other designs. Necessarily I consulted some of the same sources for those works and the present one. If any readers of both should find bits of the same information in them, this will explain their recognitions.

In the retelling of historical events few authors have managed dimensions and proportions to the satisfaction of all readers and critics. For my own taste, there is comfort in hearing from a single delightful authority two arguments in favor of generous treatment of historical detail. I quote these with pleasure which is quickened by the fact that the book from which I recall them is the capstone of the literature of Spain, and as such crowns the national temperament and style to whose colonial expression my pages are devoted.

". . . Historians," says the author in *Don Quixote de la Mancha*, ". . . usually relate matters so concisely, that we have scarcely a smack of them, leaving the most essential part of the story drowned in the bottom of the ink-horn, either through neglect, malice, or ignorance."

And later, when Don Quixote says to Sancho Panza, "Pray thee tell it concisely, and like a man of sense, or let it alone," the reply comes, "I tell it to you (quoth Sancho) as all stories are told in our country, and I cannot for the blood of me tell it any other way, nor is it fit I should alter the custom."

P.H.

Center for Advanced Studies,
Wesleyan University.

I have gained nothing of value to leave to my children and descendants but this my true story, and they will presently find out what a wonderful story it is.

•

Often, now that I am old, I stop to think about the heroic deeds that took place then, and it seems as though they happened only yesterday. I say that what we did could not have been accomplished except that all of us marched with God.

—Bernal Díaz del Castillo

Thanks be to Thee, O Lord, Who hast permitted me to see something new.

—Juan Ponce de León, on seeing Florida

I

DISCOVERER

History knows of no man
who ever did the like.

—*From the epitaph of*
Columbus in the Cathedral
of Seville.

i.

THE LIGHT

WAS THAT a light? Standing on the sterncastle he looked
again through the darkness of ten o'clock at night. The
ship was in considerable movement, for it had been a rough
day—the roughest, he noted, of any they had met during the
whole voyage. To see a distant light one should be still. He
saw it again, but it was "so obscured," he said, that he could
not be sure he was seeing the first sign of land. He called to
Pero Gutierrez, who had left his post as butler of the King's
dais in Castile to come on the voyage.

"There seems to be a light," said the Lord Admiral, indi-
cating where. "Watch for it."

He called also to Rodrigo Sánchez of Segovia, the King's
accountant whose duty it was to keep books on all wealth
that might be found—gold, jewels, spices—to insure that the
Crown would receive its royal fifth share. The Lord Admiral
told him to watch, too, for the light. Sánchez came to look.

"There!"

Gutierrez saw it, and so again did the Lord Admiral. It
showed once or twice. It was like the light of a small wax
candle which was raised and lowered. From where he stood
Sánchez could not see it, and said so.

What was it? They thought it might be a torch in the hands
of fishermen who raised and lowered it in their work. When
it vanished in the darkness so suddenly, they thought perhaps that it was a light being carried from one house to
another. Nobody knew. Word of it went through the ship. It
had shown so briefly that few were sure it was a sign of land.

They had been at sea for just under five weeks. Only the
Lord Admiral knew exactly how far they had come. The sailors were doubtful. But his own confidence was so great that
even before sailing from the Canary Islands he had given
orders to all ship commanders that there would be no night
sailing after passing a point seven hundred leagues (or something over two thousand miles) from those islands.

Now he changed his orders. After sunset, when the sailors gathered together in each ship, as in every nightfall, to chant the prayer to the Queen of Heaven, after which they went to their cramped quarters to sleep, the Lord Admiral signalled that the course was changed from west south west to west. There might be danger of running aground in this, and he warned all to keep a sharp lookout. But there was also hope, for by running straight westward they might sooner see land, and he changed his orders to meet what all longed for. They ran before the wind at twelve miles an hour. The full-blown sails of the three caravels looked like the cheeks of the winds made visible on old maps. To the man who should first see land, said the Lord Admiral, he would immediately give a silk doublet, over and beyond the reward promised by the King and Queen—a grant of ten thousand maravedis a year for life, or about a third of a seaman's pay.

Few slept that night, watching for land and daylight.

ii.

THE LORD ADMIRAL

THEY SAID of him, Christopher Columbus, born in Genoa, and now in the service of King Ferdinand and Queen Isabella of Castile and Aragon, that he "was affable . . . though with a certain gravity," and that he was "a skilled man, eloquent and a good Latin scholar, and very glorious in his affairs," and that he was "a learned man of great experience" who did not waste his time in manual or mechanical tasks, which would hardly suit "the grandeur and immortality of the wonderful deeds he was to perform."

He stood taller than the average and was sturdily made. His eyes were lively in his ruddy and freckled face. His hair was "very red." He wore a hat with a wide brim turned up like a bowl. Over a doublet with full sleeves and knee breeches he put a cloth-of-Segovia poncho which hung down fore and aft and was open at the sides for his arms. His straight sword with a basket hilt was slung by straps from his girdle. He could be "graceful when he wished, irate when he was crossed." One purpose ruled him, and he pressed forward with it in all works of preparation, persuasion and deed. It was his wish to discover what was unknown about the world.

"To this my wish," he wrote, "I found Our Lord"—he was a deeply religious man—"most propitious, and to this end I received from Him a spirit of intelligence. In seamanship He made me abundant, of astrology"—by which he meant astronomy—"He gave me enough, as well as geometry and arithmetic, and of ingenuity in mind and hands to draw this sphere and on it cities, rivers and mountains, islands and harbours, everything in its right place. In this time I have seen and studied all writings, cosmography, histories, chronicles and philosophy and other arts."

He read the Greek, Egyptian, Roman and French geographers, and he gathered travellers' tales wherever he could from mariners who had sailed farther than he. He had a copy of the first Latin edition of the travels of Marco Polo, and pondering it, he marked its margins with his comments. From the idea of the table-top world of the Middle Ages, the advanced cartographers of his day were coming to see the world as a sphere, and the Lord Admiral understood and agreed with them. The pleasures of theory were important, but if a man was given to action as well as thought, they led straight to testing in the world. A most pressing concern of his time was to find a direct sea route to India. The Lord Admiral Columbus like others was concerned with it, but his solution of the problem was like nobody else's. It began in his mind, as an intellectual concept.

At the end of his book, Marco Polo wrote, two centuries before Columbus, "I believe it was God's will that we should return, so that men might know the things that are in the world." On Marco Polo's testimony, India, China and Japan were vast and rich beyond measure. Gold, silver, and jewels were the familiar items of value. The king of Malabar wore so many gems and pearls that they were worth more than a great city. Another chronicler, writing to Columbus, declared that the royal palaces of the east were immense, one river alone had two hundred palatial cities with marble bridges along its banks, and the palaces of Japan were covered with solid gold. Beyond these, spices abounded in the east, and were needed in quantity by Europeans to make palatable the meat they ate which was often spoiled in slow transfer from slaughterhouse to table. Well: in a single "very noble port called Zaiton . . . every year they load and unload a hundred large ships laden with pepper, besides many other ships loaded with other spices." For Columbus, his view of the shape of the world must hold the secret of how to find a direct sea route to the Indies which would make useless the overland animal caravans of the Polo family and all who had gone eastward after them.

As early as June, 1474, Paolo the physician of Florence was writing to Columbus, "I perceive your noble and grand desire to go to the places where the spices grow." Thinking of where the Portuguese had gone by sea, far south along the coast of Africa, Columbus asked himself why, if men could sail so far south, they might not be able to sail to the west, far enough to find land. If they could, must not such land be India? He had read in Seneca's treatise on the elements, winds, earthquakes and comets, the statement, written in about 63 A.D., that "A ship may sail in a few days with a fair wind from the coast of Spain to that of India." There was no proof of this so far, but the idea was not so new as to seem absurd. Columbus knew of men before his time who swore they had seen land west of the Canary Islands, and once in Madeira, an "unknown pilot" who lay dying told him how his ship had been driven by storm to an island far westward in the Atlantic sea. Moreover, there had once been cast up on the shores of Ireland a corpse whose features were clearly oriental which must have come across the Atlantic from Cathay.

Rumor seized upon all evidence, however small, and to many men brought only idle wondering. But as for others, a son of Christopher Columbus said long afterward, "from small matters some draw substance for great deeds." For Columbus believed "that since all the water and land in the world formed a sphere, it would be possible to go around it from East to West until men stood feet to feet, one against the other, at opposite ends of the earth."

He spent the better part of two decades bringing his theory to the test. The hardest part of this task was to find the backing for it which he could not supply himself.

He first approached King João of Portugal, and "offered to discover the Indies." So grand a confidence carried with it certain conditions. Columbus required honors, titles and riches in return. The King put him off, meanwhile sending in secret a ship of his own to carry out Columbus's plan and take the Indies for himself. Such royal treachery deserved its end: the King's mariner returned with nothing to show but his own incompetence and happy ridicule for the vision of Columbus.

Portugal held out nothing but sorrow for Columbus. Now widowed, he left Lisbon secretly, in 1484, taking along his son Diego, and proceeded to Spain where he started all over again to lift his great plan to the attention of princes, appealing to King Ferdinand and Queen Isabella.

Columbus was a son of his time, the dawning Renaissance, when the spirit of discovery in all of man's arts and sciences was breaking across the European world. But the new spirit was not fostered everywhere in a spontaneous recognition of its power for growth. Seven years passed without action by Ferdinand and Isabella upon the plan of Columbus. While he waited for them to act, he made overtures to Henry VII of England and Charles VIII of France—but these came to nothing. But finally, when the King and Queen had completed the old Spanish design of expelling the Moors from Spain, and establishing unity for the Spanish kingdoms and peoples, they acted at last to approve the expedition to India. After early objections, they agreed to the personal conditions of Columbus, by which he became a nobleman with the address of *Don*, and Lord Admiral of the Ocean Sea, and viceroy and governor forever of all the islands and continents which he would discover. They agreed further that these powers would descend to his heirs forever, and that he should retain a tenth of all the wealth he should find, and that he should receive all the salaries of his separate positions as admiral, viceroy and governor, and that he should himself appoint or remove all officers of his own government in India, and that those other officers appointed by the Crown to represent the royal interests would be chosen from lists prepared by him.

He knew the art of dealing with princes. Having told them what he would do, he assured the King and Queen that it was what they themselves ordered him to do.

"Your highnesses," he wrote, "took thought to send me, Christopher Columbus, to the said parts of India, to see those princes and peoples and lands and the character of them and of all else, and the manner which should be used to bring about their conversion to our holy faith, and ordained that I should not go by land to the eastward, by which way it was the custom to go, but by way of the west, by which down to this day"—a day shortly before he was to sail—"we do not know certainly that any one has passed . . ."

He promised to keep a journal, day and night, of the whole expedition. Now royally commissioned, he went rapidly ahead with his preparations. Included in his equipment were letters

from his King and Queen addressed to the Grand Khan of
China, who ruled all lesser kings of the Orient.

iii.

THE VOYAGE

THE FLEET made ready in the harbor of Palos, where for
weeks men and supplies were brought together. The Lord
Admiral had three ships. All needed caulking, and he watched
the caulkers at work while the ships were careened in the
shipyards. He thought they did a poor job, and they knew it.
To avoid having to do their work over, they ran away. To
his regret, now and later, he had to accept the ships as they
were.

On Thursday night, August second, 1492, the commander
and all his men went to the church of St. George in Palos.
There they confessed their sins and received Holy Com-
munion. The unknown lay ahead and it would be well to meet
it in a state which would render danger less terrible. Long
before daybreak, the Lord Admiral went on board his flagship. Half an hour before sunrise, he gave the order to up
anchors, and in the grey light of sky and water, to a salute
from the shore battery of lombards, he sailed "with very many
supplies and with many a seaman, on the third day of August,
of the same year, on a Friday." Setting his course for the
Canary Island possessions of Spain, he said he felt it "very
fitting that I should forget sleep and give much attention to
navigation, because it should be so. And these things will be
a great labour."

The armored Spaniard wore a visored helmet, with a neck-
piece, called a casque. The admiral's ships—caravels—looked
like casques floated upside down in the water, higher at stern
than at bow, and with masts higher than their lengths.
Santa Maria, the flagship, was rated at a hundred tons' burden.
She was fifty feet long, eighteen feet wide, and carried stone
ballast, like the fleet's other vessels. *Pinta* was smaller, at fifty
tons, and *Niña* still smaller, at forty. They carried three masts,
with immense square sails on the mainmasts.

With him in the flagship the Lord Admiral carried 39 officers and men. In *Pinta*, Martín Alonso Pinzón commanding,
there were twenty-six, and in *Niña*, under Vicente Yañez
Pinzón, twenty-two. Each ship bore a pilot, a navigator who
was also first officer, and a surgeon. Most of the seamen
came from Palos, and the officers were sons of leading families there. Three sailors were criminals released from life-
imprisonment to serve out their sentences in the dangers of
the expedition. Four foreigners were in the roster—a Vene-
tian, a Portuguese, and two Genoese, one of whom was the
Lord Admiral. Among the men was one who spoke Arabic.
He was expected to be helpful in conducting conversations
with the Chinese and Japanese. The men were paid in gold—
seven dollars a month for seamen, fourteen for officers, and
four dollars sixty cents for cabin boys, or gromets.

In their small sugar-loaf hats, their slashed doublets of
Segovia cloth or leather, their spikes of dagger and sword,
their ballooning knee breeches and rough-skin leather boots
or shoes, they were hardy and simple, for the most part.
Their sun-ripened faces with sharp dark eyes showed to the
world various tempers and characters, but in one matter they
were all of one mind. This was their faith in God and the
proper expression of it through their religion. No other expression of all life could possibly be accepted. They took their
belief with them as the most natural of possessions. They were
prepared to bestow it upon others as the greatest of all gifts,
and if it might not be wanted, then they would offer it again
with sword and torch—not for cruelty, as they saw it, but in
ultimate mercy. For the rest, after much they had heard, they
were prepared to become rich, if they lived, and if the Lord
Admiral's lands were as he said they were.

Though not all were content. Beating southward for the
Fortunate Isles, as Ptolemy called the Canaries, Cristóbal
Quintero, who owned *Pinta*, and Gómez Rascón were "exas-
perated at the voyage," as the Lord Admiral said. He had
noticed before sailing from Palos how they had been "inclined
to oppose and pick holes" in the enterprise. On Monday,
August sixth, three days out, the rudder of *Pinta* jumped
from its gear. At some risk, it was repaired. The Lord Admiral must conclude that Quintero and Rascón were responsible for the breakdowns. *Pinta* continued to steer badly. She
shipped water. He might replace her with another caravel
when he reached The Grand Canary.

But when he reached the Canaries he undertook full repairs

of *Pinta,* and he had *Niña's* rigging changed from lateen to
square sails, whose greater area would take more wind. He
remained there from August ninth until September sixth.
While the refittings proceeded, he listened to vehement reports
by "many honourable Spaniards" of the Islands who swore
that each year on their voyages they saw land to the west of
the Canaries. All evidence in support of this theory was important to the Lord Admiral. Preparing to sail again, he took
into the ships new stocks of water, meat and wood. Sailing,
he ordered a new course—west: no qualifying directions of
north or south: but due west, in full accord with the plans
he had worked out for so many years through books, maps,
and the testimony of other mariners. In the latitude of the
Canary Islands, the prevailing winds blew to the westward.
The Lord Admiral proposed to go with them.

Others would prevent him, if they could.

On the first day out of Gomera a caravel from the island
of Hierro signalled him with a warning. Three Portuguese
caravels were beating about the westward course "to take
him," under orders of King João. The Lord Admiral concluded that this menace could be traced to "the envy which
the King felt because he had gone to Castile." Despite a
continued calm the fleet passed safely by the interceptors. At
three o'clock in the morning on September eighth the calm
broke with winds from the northwest, and shipping great seas
across the bows, making slow progress, the fleet bore to the
west again. On the following day the Lord Admiral recorded
an advance of fifteen leagues.

Thinking of how long the voyage might have to be, and of
how time and the unknown could work on men at sea, he
resolved to log fewer leagues than he made each day. So,
actually sailing farther than they knew, the crews might come
to land sooner than they could properly expect.

In his log he kept record of both great and small events. At
night, on September fifteenth, there was a mystery. "They saw
fall from the sky a marvellous branch of fire into the sea at
a distance of four or five leagues from them." In the next
day, the "air was soft and refreshing . . . the sea smooth as a
river." The Admiral said that the only thing missing was "the
singing of the nightingale." The wind held steady to the west
for many days, and the crewmen feared that "no winds ever
blew to carry them back to Spain." And then they encountered a head wind. If this slowed their progress it was also a
blessing, as the Lord Admiral saw, for the men were "much

excited" with relief to know that a homeward wind could yet be had.

Soon after, the sea was smooth enough so that many sailors went swimming. They saw schools of gilded fish. At sunset in the same day, a great hope broke forth from *Pinta*. From her masthead she threw out a standard, and from one of her gun-ports she fired a lombard. Captain Martín Alonso Pinzón mounted the sterncastle of *Pinta* and "in great delight called the Admiral, asking for a reward from him because he had sighted land"—the ten thousand maravedi life income prom-ised by the sovereigns. At sunrise and sunset, by order of the fleet commander, all ships closed upon the flagship, when with mist clearing, all could see farther.

Hearing this report of land, the Lord Admiral kneeled down and gave thanks to God. In *Pinta* all prayed with their captain the *Gloria in excelsis Deo*. The crew of *Niña* went up the rigging to look, and all declared that they saw land to the southwest. The Lord Admiral agreed that he saw it twenty-five leagues away and changed his course to approach it. All night long and into the next afternoon they sailed in a smooth sea—"like a river" with "breezes sweet and very soft" and the men swam again, but there was no land. What they had seen was a cloudbank. They resumed the course due west. A chart was sent back and forth between the flagship and *Pinta* on a rope. To mark the passing time, a sand glass was turned over every half hour day and night.

The greatest ship of the fleet was no larger than a small house. Three dozen men filled her completely. Her bow was round and blunt and it buried itself in every wave. She rocked like a bowl. Her heavy canvas pushed her down into the water as well as forward. In the trough of a moderately heavy sea even her high sterncastle would be lost to sight, with only the misted sails showing above. Sailors knew the emptiness of the ocean, where through low clouds the light closed and opened so swiftly. After a bright instant of sunlight which lifted the spirits, how quickly hope could die when the clouds closed again over the watery wilderness. In the spin of wind across wave the men knew a lost sameness. When somebody was bewildered or directionless, he would say in a common ex-pression that he was "all at sea." Not knowing where they were going, the sailors of this fleet held the ocean doubly empty in their minds and unchanging, with the little casque-like ships cockling and leaning over their own bows against ridge after ridge of waves, on and on, it must seem forever, and all the same.

What abided with them in their land longing were the power and vigilance of the Lord Admiral. "Christopher Columbus," said an early Churchman in a famous *History of the Indies*, "in the arts of navigation exceeded without any doubt all others who lived in his day." The sailors in his ships who knew his seamanship called him "divine," and the days passed straining to the westward, while all watched for signs of land.

On Thursday October fourth a gromet on the flagship saw forty birds together skimming the waves often catching water with their webbed feet. They were petrels. He found a small stone out of the ballast and threw it at the birds and hit one. Two boobies flew by. A frigate bird came to the rigging, and they saw a white bird "like a gull." The wind freshened during the night, and they made eleven miles an hour, and in the day they advanced fifty-seven leagues, but for his men the Lord Admiral recorded forty-five. Many more petrels appeared above the calm smooth sea, and many flying fish sailed into the ship. There was mystery in a bird far out at sea, and an even greater one in fish that went like birds in short arcs of flight.

At sunrise two days later, as the ships were closed together for sighting exercise in the lifting mist, *Niña,* small and swift under her great canvas, sent up her standard to the peak and fired a lombard, declaring land. Again the fleet pounded through a day to nightfall without coming to any shore, though the Lord Admiral believed that they might "sleep on land" that night, for a great flock of birds came over the ships from the north, flying southwest, as if to find land, or perhaps he thought, to fly "from the winter which was about to come to the lands whence they came." He remembered that "most of the islands which the Portuguese have held had been discovered through birds," and since these birds flew southwestward, he ordered a change in course to the same direction, to be tried for two days.

Monday, October eighth, the following day, brought another suggestion of land—breezes fragrant with scent wafting over a calm sea. Drifting vegetation "seemed to be very fresh." Many land birds were about. A night later the darkness over the ships was alive, and "all night they heard birds passing." If they were near land, still they saw none, and "here the men could bear no more," but the Lord Admiral spoke to them, encouraged them, and added flatly that complaints were to no avail, since no matter what, "he was going to the Indies and must pursue his course, until with the help of Our Lord, he found them."

That he must find them, he was sure by all means—his philosophy, the charts he had studied and extended, the currents of the winds, the kinds of fish he had seen, the flights of birds, the drifts of branches in the sea, the perfume of land on the air, the objects worked by men which only today, October eleventh, Thursday, he had seen in the tumbling of the roughest sea of the voyage. The mystery awaiting its answer then gave him the vision of the light which must only come from a shore.

As the gromet turned over the half-hour glass at midnight, the fleet rode forward under a moon just past full. Jupiter was rising in the east, behind the ships. They sailed in close formation. Every man awake was a lookout in the strong moonlight. *Pinta,* lighter than *Santa Maria,* stood out ahead of her. At two o'clock the wind carried a long cry from the forecastle of *Pinta.* Rodrigo de Triana, who came from a suburb of Seville, cried,

"Tierra! Tierra!"

They looked. Six miles to the west, as the Lord Admiral reckoned it, lay a long shore on the moonlit horizon. The man who cried out "Land! Land!" was the first Spaniard to see the New World. Thirty-three years later he lost his life to it, in another expedition.

The Lord Admiral ordered all sail taken in, except mainsails, and all the rest of the night, the ships "kept jogging" back and forth in sight of land, waiting for the daybreak of Friday, October twelfth, 1492, when safely they could come to shore.

iv.

NEW WORLD

AT DAWN they saw a coral island about thirteen miles long. They sailed toward it. Ruffled combers proclaimed the pres-

ence of reefs all along her seaward side, and indeed, on her
leeward side for all her shore except for one and three quarter
miles. Through that gap in the breakers the Lord Admiral took
his fleet into a shallow bay and anchored in five fathoms of
green water facing the broad curve of coral sand. The island
was six miles wide. It lay in the twenty-fourth parallel of
latitude and the meridian of 74° 30′ west of Greenwich.
What was it named? Whatever its name, the Lord Admiral
named it San Salvador. It lay "in one line from east to west"
in the latitude of the island of Hierro in the Canaries.

On the sands they "immediately saw naked people." Lowering a boat, and taking with him from the other ships his two
captains, and Rodrigo de Escobedo, the secretary of the fleet,
and Rodrigo Sánchez de Segovia, the King's accountant, and
some armed sailors, the Lord Admiral crossed the lagoon and
touched shore. He carried the royal standard and the others
carried the banners of the Green Cross which was the fleet's
flag, bearing in addition to the cross the crowned monograms
of the King and Queen. When they landed they saw bright
green forests and little streams of water and many kinds of
fruit.

Awaited by the island people who gathered in growing
numbers, the Lord Admiral, addressing the witnesses from the
ships, took possession of the new land for his sovereigns
according to the prescribed legal process, with its pronounce-
ments of the Crown, its prayers, and its tenure across time.

The island people watched.

They were naked as when they were born. How beautiful
they were, "with very handsome bodies and very good faces."
They were as gentle, generous and trusting as they were beautiful. They bore no arms, and not knowing what a sword was
they curiously clutched a Spanish blade and cut themselves.
Some bore old wounds, and explained that these were given
by invading people from other islands. The Lord Admiral
decided that the invaders were mainlanders who came to take
these people as slaves. They said their island was called
Guanahaní. Some of the people were painted in various
colors, including black. How intelligent they were! He believed they understood all that was said to them. They would
make excellent servants, and surely they would readily become
Christians. They indicated clearly how they believed that the
Lord Admiral and his men had come from Heaven.

He bestowed gifts on them—little bells of copper or brass
such as men at home tied to the feet of falcons the better to

trace the flight of these gaming birds, and those little cones of metal which bound the ends of laces or thongs, and little caps of red cloth, and little necklets of blue beads. With exquisite civility the islanders accepted these as treasures. Such lovable people should be known at home, and the Lord Admiral proposed to bring home six of them who could meet the King and Queen and learn Spanish. As for animals, he saw none, except for parrots.

Later in the day, when the staff had returned to the ships' boats, the islanders swam out to see them alongside, and took delight in the strangeness they saw, and so did the crewmen. On Saturday, the next day, they saw from shipboard how more people came through the trees to the beach and then how they came to the ships in canoes made from long tree-trunks. The Lord Admiral could not help remarking on their comeliness again. They all had fine, broad brows, and large, lovely eyes. They had handsome straight legs and no fat. If a canoe turned over, the paddlers went with it, swam neatly alongside it and righted it and then bailed it out with gourds. Now they brought things to give in trade—"balls of spun cotton and parrots and spears and other trifles" and among these the Lord Admiral looked closely for gold.

All he saw was a small golden ornament worn in the nose by some of the islanders—Indians, as the men must call them, since this was the first land of India which they had reached, just as the Lord Admiral had said they would. Now he asked where the gold came from, and the Indians indicated that they came from an island to the southward, where the king had much of it, and large utensils made of it. He asked them to take him there, but they would not. He thought of Japan, the great island which he must find next. The Indians said there was land also to the north, but it was from there that attackers came. The Lord Admiral resolved to go to the southwest, "to seek the gold and precious stones."

The visitors stayed on board all day. How easy they were to get along with. They gave all they had for the smallest trifle—a broken dish or glass cup. Some dived off the ship and swam to shore with these treasures fearing to lose them if they could give nothing in return. Their gentleness continued to amaze. How easily they could all be captured and returned to Spain; or fifty armed soldiers could control them in their own island where they could be "forced to do whatever may be wished." At nightfall they returned to shore in their canoes, leaving the Lord Admiral to consider his next move. But he knew: "I wish to go and see if I can find the island of Japan."

He spent Sunday the fourteenth coasting along the island of San Salvador in the ships' boats. He saw Indian villages from which on seeing him the people came forth "calling us and giving thanks to God." They brought him food. Later he landed and found a splendid piece of high ground where a fort could be built. He saw the most beautiful stands of trees that he had ever seen. Then, and in many later days, he recorded the loveliness of the new lands, which never ceased to enchant him. Every new place was lovelier than the last—"the singing of little birds is such that it seems that a man could never wish to leave this place; the flocks of parrots darken the sun . . . it is a marvel. There are, moreover, trees of a thousand types, all with their various fruits and all scented, so that it is a wonder." He saw good harbors and many rivers and fine mountains and great serpents and more than once he would come upon dogs that could not bark. Above all, throughout his journal, he celebrated the people of this first island and all others. He told the King and Queen to "believe that in all the world there cannot be a people better or more gentle." Full of love and without greed, they loved "their neighbours as themselves." They had the softest voices and they always smiled. They touched the Spaniards and kissed their hands and feet "wondering at them." Their generosity was as sweet as that of children, giving whatever they had for any scrap without noticing how little they received, and with significance the Lord Admiral reported to his employers that the Indians would do the same-"with spices and gold, if they had any."

He could stay there forever, but he had set himself a limit of two days at San Salvador. Japan beckoned. If by chance he should miss that great island, the Lord Admiral, knowing well his fifteenth-century maps, felt sure of coming instead to China. Early on Sunday afternoon, October fourteenth, keeping on board seven of the islanders as specimens for the sovereigns, and opening with every thrust before the wind a great new world for all centuries to come, the fleet set sail for Japan.

II

CONQUISTADOR

Oh! what a troublesome thing
it is to go and discover new
lands—the risks we took it
is hardly possible to exaggerate.

—*Bernal Díaz del Castillo.*

i.

THE CAPTAIN GENERAL

TWENTY-SEVEN YEARS after the Lord Admiral Christopher Columbus sailed on for Japan and instead found Cuba, a powerful expedition based on that island came to the mainland of the Americas to stay.

Its leader was born in Medellín, in the province of Estremadura in Spain. He was seven years old when the Lord Admiral had made his first discoveries of the new world islands. Before he was sixteen he was a law student at the oldest university in Spain at Salamanca. He soon found that the life of book and brief was not for him. At seventeen he returned home, and a few years later he presented himself at San Domingo in search of the active life.

In 1511, at the age of twenty-six, he sailed for Cuba over the Lord Admiral's now well-established seaway. Going in the train of Cuba's new governor, Don Diego Velásquez, he soon found himself the mayor of the new Cuban capital city of Santiago, where his taste for fine living kept him short of funds, despite his valuable holdings in lands and Indian slaves.

In successive years, small probing ventures were directed against mainland America from Cuba. Coasting expeditions along Central America brought back reports of savage people and fine harbors and scattered specimens of gold work. In 1518 Governor Velásquez thought to found his own fortune with the riches of the lands across the great gulf west of Cuba. To dissemble his private aim, he announced a major public expedition to colonize the new lands for the Crown. There resulted a scramble for the post of Captain General in command of the enterprise. It ended when the Governor, believing he could manage him, gave the command to the mayor of Santiago, who was called Hernando Cortés. Soon, but not soon enough, the Governor knew his mistake.

The Captain General Cortés at once assumed the style as well as the duties of his new power. He added plumes to his hat, and around his neck he hung a gold medallion and chain, and over his stocky, powerful body he threw a velvet cloak heavy with knots and braids of woven gold. A soldier who enlisted under him and who later wrote a chronicle of the enterprise, said he looked "a gallant and courageous Captain."

He needed both qualities to meet the intrigues which promptly developed against him. When the Governor was urged by his relatives to revoke the appointment of Cortés, Cortés never left his side, swearing that he would soon make him "a very illustrious and wealthy man." But it seemed wise to hurry all preparations, and the Captain General, with embraces and speeches, took leave of the Governor, sailing from Santiago ahead of schedule, and steered for the port of Trinidad, where all the people came to welcome his fleet of eleven ships.

At Trinidad the expedition was overtaken by orders from Governor Velásquez, who had finally had second thoughts. The Captain General was to be relieved of his command and returned to Cuba—if necessary as a prisoner. The fleet was to return home at once. Under persuasion by the Captain General, who could beguile and threaten in the same tone, the officials at Trinidad failed to arrest him, and the "matter was quietly dropped," said the chronicler of the expedition. In ten days the fleet sailed for Havana, for final recruitment and provisioning.

Once again the Governor sent in a rage to demote the Captain General, and once again to no avail. "If," said the chronicler, "in the town of Trinidad the orders of Velásquez were slighted, in the town of Havana they were absolutely ignored." The Captain General wrote to the Governor in maddening respect, quite as though he were not disobeying orders, and told him that he meant to set sail the next day, and "that he remained his humble servant."

In Havana the Captain General completed the official organization of his command. Here he created his personal household, and began "to be treated as a Lord."

This came to him by right of nature as well as position. His bearing was lordly yet genial. He used his charm both as a gift to bestow and a weapon to wield. He could endure all which his soldiers endured, and more. His mind was quick as lightning, but his more important thoughts were never known unless he meant them to be, and this only for a purpose which he allowed to break over lesser men like light. His imagination was powerful, and he was equal to it in his acts. Even under difficulty, if he wanted a thing to come true, he seemed able to compel it to do so. If most men were governed by events, it seemed the other way round with him. His face was pale and his expression usually serious, though he could be wonderfully cheerful, especially in adversity. "Mild and grave," his eyes were rather small, and so were his other features. He was black-haired and he wore his beard thin. Those of a great horseman, his legs were somewhat bowed. In anger the veins of his throat and temples swelled visibly, and in greater anger, he would refuse to speak. He remembered his Latin from Salamanca, wrote well, and was even "something of a poet." They said that in his younger days he was "wild about women," and "a scar that appeared through his beard came from one of these affairs." He had a devotion to the Blessed Mother of God, and to Saint Paul and other saints. "God pardon him his sins," wrote the chronicler, "and me mine."

At Havana he took a census of the horses of his expedition, beginning with his own, "a vicious dark chestnut horse." The horses totalled sixteen, which was all that could be bought to take along, and, like Negroes, they were "worth their weight in gold" to the expeditioners. The final muster was passed some days later when the fleet made rendezvous at Cozumel, an island of sapphire water, white beaches and tall palms, off the mainland of Yucatán.

The Captain General counted five hundred and eight men at arms, including thirty-two crossbowmen and thirteen musketeers. In addition he had a hundred crewmen, two chaplains and two greyhounds. His armament included four falconet cannon with a two-inch bore to discharge a shot weighing a pound and a half, and several brass guns, with a good supply of powder and ball. He ordered spare bolts and Valencian cords to be kept with each crossbow and he commanded the crossbowmen to hold regular target practice.

One of his severe problems was that of establishing communication with the native people whom he meant to find, who would speak their own outlandish tongue. At Cozumel a marvel occurred by which he went a long way toward solving the difficulty of how to talk to Indians.

ii.

THE NEW CONTINENT

EIGHT YEARS earlier a party of Spaniards—seventeen men and
two women—were shipwrecked near Cozumel and taken
prisoner by the Indians. Now only two men survived. The
Captain General heard of them and at once sent to ransom
them. One came—Jerónimo de Aguilar, dark as an Indian
and dressed in rags. At home he had studied for holy orders,
and all he now had left of his old life was his devotional
Book of Hours. He explained that his surviving companion
refused to leave his Indian wife by whom he now had three
handsome sons. For himself, Aguilar was overjoyed to be restored to his countrymen, and at once put on the proper
clothes which the Captain General gave him.

What of the country and the towns of these Indians? asked
the Captain General.

Aguilar knew nothing of these—he could only tell of his
work as a slave, for in his wood cutting and water hauling
and digging in the corn field he had never been farther than
four leagues away from his place. But he did know the Indian
speech, and when the fleet sailed on, he went along to be
their "useful and faithful interpreter."

After eight days they came to the Tabasco River, where
they found the river banks and mangrove forests "swarming
with Indians" who were prepared for battle. Through Aguilar
the Captain General spoke to their chiefs who came near in a
canoe. He assured them of his peaceful intentions, but they
said they would fight if the soldiers landed among the trees.
The chronicler knew the place—he had been there on an
earlier expedition, when there had been no trouble with the
people. Now a fight must come.

A battle of two days opened on the following morning
after Mass on the ships. The Spaniards fought their way upriver and through the forest by a path that led to the town
of Tabasco, where twelve thousand armed Indians awaited
them. The opposing battle cries arose—"Saint James!" from

one side, "Alala! Alala!" from the other. Cannon, muskets and crossbows took effect against arrows and fire-hardened spears. Gaining the center of the town, the Captain General took advantage of a lull in the combat to execute legal possession of the place in the name of the King of Spain.

A great tree stood in the court at the center of Tabasco. Going to it, the Captain General drew his sword and made three blazes in the tree trunk as a mark of claim. He called out that if any should dispute this right of possession, he would defend it "with the sword and shield which he held in his hands." The act was recorded by the Royal Notary to establish its legality. All of the watching soldiers approved except for certain adherents of Governor Diego Velásquez, who "chose to grumble" that the new place was claimed for the King of Spain instead of for the Governor of Cuba. But Cortés knew where lay real authority, and by his loyalty to a higher power he claimed its support for himself now and thereafter.

The people of Tabasco challenged his claim and continued the fight. Through the following days in thicket and swamp and village the Indians attacked and were thrown back by the soldiers. The skirmishes were rehearsals for what might come deeper in the mainland. In thickly padded armor which made them sweat under the tropic sun, the Spaniards demonstrated the power of their arms and knew that though outnumbered by hundreds to one, they could prevail. After much fighting on foot, the Captain General ordered the cavalry horses to be landed from the ships in the bay, and himself riding at the head of the mounted soldiers, led them into battle under orders to aim their lances at the faces of their naked enemies. Little bells hung from the breastplates of the horses' armor. When the mounted troops suddenly bore against the Indians, they turned and lost themselves in the swamps and fields. They had never seen horses before and believed that horse and man were all one animal.

Two soldiers were killed, and over eight hundred Indians. It was time to dress wounds. Cutting the fat from a killed Indian the soldiers used it with a red-hot knife to cauterize the wounds of their comrades. It was time, also, to make good the victory by pacifying the Indians under the name of the Emperor Charles V, King of Spain. Through Aguilar the interpreter, messages went to the defeated chiefs, who gradually losing their suspicion came to treat with the Captain General.

He received them gravely, even reproachfully.

How could they have made war? he asked them. Had he not come promising peace to them? It was their fault that battle had come, and now he really felt that they deserved to be executed, with all the people of their towns. Still, they now came asking his pardon, and he was sure that his Lord and Emperor would have him be merciful, and forgiving, and if they would render homage to the Crown, and be of good will, then the Captain General would receive all into the royal service. But they must beware, for some of his cannon were still angry at the Indians for giving battle, and if the Indians did not render their submission, he was afraid that a cannon would leap forward and kill them.

At this instant of the conference, by a secret command, one of the falconets was touched off, and made such a roar and sent a cannonball "buzzing over the hills" with such a noise that the chieftains were appalled: all the Captain General said was true, then.

Through Aguilar he told them not to be afraid, for already he had commanded that no harm come to them. More at ease, the chieftains continued the discussion, and Cortés saw from this success how to handle the native people to advantage.

On the following day came chieftains from all the country around, bringing gifts: quilted cotton cloth, and samples of worked gold, and—such was their custom in making gifts—women. The cloth would do to wear under Spanish armor. The gold, which promised more to come, was worked into objects of adornment. There were four crowns or diadems of gold, several golden lizards, and two ornaments resembling little dogs, and five golden ducks, and some golden earrings, and two golden masks with Indian faces, and two golden sandals, and a few trinkets besides.

Where did this gold come from? asked the Captain General.

The Indians pointed toward the place where the sun went down, and answered.

"Culúa. México."

Nobody knew what these words meant, and "paid little attention to it," stated the chronicler, though later an Indian made it clear that "México" was far distant. "México," he said again.

As for the twenty women, one among them was the daughter of a chieftain, a noble lady with many vassals. Her intelligence was lively, she was beautiful, she was trustworthy, and she bore herself with a natural authority so that all Indians obeyed her "without question." She was willing to serve as an interpreter, for Aguilar could speak with her in the Tabascan language. But what was more useful—she could speak also the language of the land which lay ahead, Mexico; and through her, the Captain General quickly saw, he would be able to reach the minds of the next people he must find. He would speak his thought to Aguilar, who would give it to her, and in her turn, she would make it plain to the Mexicans. She was worth more than all the gold put on the ground before the Spaniards. Soon Christianized, she was called Doña Marina. The Captain General eventually gave her to one of his captains.

Now he ordered the defeated Indians to return to their towns, which they did. He next required them to abandon their idols and sacrifices—he knew they killed men as an act of worship—and instead to become Christians. They agreed, asking him for a statue of the Mother of God which he showed them. They erected a small chapel to house it, and then two of the ships' carpenters made a "very tall cross" which was erected by order of the Captain General. The people made their submission to Cross and Crown, and the day now being Palm Sunday, they watched as the Captain General, with his chaplains and soldiers, marched in procession to the chapel, and kissed the cross, after which the chieftains brought ten fowls to him, and much baked fish and cooked vegetables.

Take care, he said, of the holy image and put flowers on the crosses, and keep the chapel clean and well-kept, and then, he assured them, they would have "good health and bountiful harvest."

He took his men aboard ship that night, with their new women, and in the next morning, he set sail along the coast, staying close inshore all the way. The coast led the fleet northward in a great curve. It was the western shore of the vast gulf west of Cuba—the Gulf of Mexico. The pilot Alaminos knew from his earlier scouting voyage with Juan de Grijalva how four days away they would come to a small palm-crowned island called the Isle of Sacrifices, for there the earlier expeditioners had seen altars fresh with the blood of Indians given to the sun a little while before.

Near this island, and about a thousand yards offshore, a great reef reached north as far as they could see. It made a chain of white combers in the shoreward roll of the blue

tropic waters. A passage through the reef made way to a wide,
curving beach protected by another island close inshore. In
due course the fleet took the passage and cleared the reef.
There, with the assault of open sea storms broken by the offshore reef, and with protection under the southern face of the
island against the gales out of the north—the "northers"
which seamen knew to be fearsome when they came—the
fleet came to harbor on Good Friday, 1519, the day of the
True Cross, whereby they named their new port Vera Cruz.
The protective island offshore they called San Juan de Ulúa.
The Captain General ordered all royal standards and pen-
nants aloft on his ship.

In pleasant weather the air was alive with strong crystal-
clear breezes, and the deep blue color of the water in the
roads shaded lighter to emerald just before it broke into white
surf. The sailors, the soldiers, of the fleet gazed shoreward.
The beaches were not very deep, but they were smooth and
gradual, and beyond them lay sand dunes grown with salt
grass and reeds. The harbor's arms reached north and south
in great open curves. Inland, palms and other jungle growth
showed on the uplands. The sun was bright upon everything,
and the eye could see great detail at far distance.

Within half an hour of dropping anchor, the fleet saw two
long canoes put out from shore, bringing the first people of
the new land which later he named New Spain, to see the
Captain General Hernando Cortés.

iii.

PORTENTS AND POWERS

DEEP IN THE land new to the Spaniards, but older than
memory to the nations of people who lived there, the most
lordly of their cities was Tenochtitlan—the city of Mexico.
Here ruled the Emperor Moctezuma, in his immense fan-
shaped crown of precious feathers and under the timeless
burden of a promise whose origin was lost in myth. It was a
promise that the rule of Mexico would one day pass to the
supreme god Quetzalcoatl who after creating the life of the

land had disappeared into the direction of the rising sun, but who would at last come again from the rising sun, according to prophecies kept alive through the generations.

Ten years before the first coasting expedition of Juan de Grijalva, a series of eight portents visited the Aztec nation of Mexico. Aztec chroniclers recorded these; popular tradition passed them on for years.

The first portent was a fiery tongue which appeared at midnight and reached from the earth to the "very heart of the heavens," making the night as bright as day, until the sun rose, when it vanished. But the sign lasted a year, and when it appeared, the people shouted, breaking their cries of dread by striking their open mouths with the palms of their hands.

The second portent was again fiery, but in a different form. Fire without cause broke out in a temple of the god Uitzilopochtli, war god, and when the guardian priests cried out for help, and worshippers brought water to halt the fire, it burned only the more fiercely, until the whole sacred house was destroyed.

In a third portent, a bolt of lightning out of a faint drizzle destroyed another temple. The facts that there neither heavy rain fell nor thunder sounded were considered disturbing.

In a fourth, a comet appeared in full sunlight, divided itself into three parts, and spread from west to east, "as if sprinkling live coals," causing an "uproar" among the observers.

In a fifth, the waters of the lake at Mexico about the city suddenly foamed up "with a cracking sound," though no wind stirred. The lake entered houses and destroyed them.

In a sixth, a woman was moved to wander about by night lamenting and crying out, "O, my dear sons, we are now about to go!", and again, "O, my beloved sons, where shall I take you?" People were shaken by her.

In a seventh, fishermen caught and brought to the Emperor Moctezuma one day a strange bird like an ash-grey crane. It had a round mirror on its head, and in the center of the mirror was a little hole. The Emperor looked through this and to his dismay saw—though it was only a little past noon—the stars and the constellation of the Fire Driller. Then he looked again, and beyond the stars he said he saw a mass of people armed for war and riding upon "deer." Turning to his soothsayers and counsellors, he asked if they saw the same? But when they looked, the vision was gone.

In the last portent, many men of monstrous form were seen, bearing two heads on one body. Certain of these were taken to the Emperor, but when he looked at them, they vanished.

It seemed sure that strange matters were preparing, filled either with the possibilities of dread, or with the unspeakable honor and joy of the return of the Creator. It was for the Emperor a time of troubled caution.

One day he received reports of a single great ship at the eastern shore of the land, and he sent stewards to investigate whether this might be the vessel of Quetzalcoatl. They went, taking gifts which at first they would present as though in barter, until they could know more about the newcomers. Reaching the ship, they kissed the prow in courtesy.

"Who are you?" called the sailors—they were the men of Juan de Grijalva in 1518—"and where do you come from? Where is your home?"

"We have come from Mexico."

"If you really are Mexicans, what is the name of the ruler of Mexico?"

"Your Lordships, his name is Moctezuma."

An exchange of gifts followed, and—acting very little like gods—the Spaniards sailed away. In all haste, the stewards returned to Mexico to give their news to the Emperor. Once again he must consider whether the matter in hand was divine or human. He concluded that it must be human, and ordered his stewards, repeating heavily for emphasis, to say nothing to anyone of what they had seen.

"No one shall let a word of this fall; no one will say a word he should not; no one will spread news of this. Keep it only to yourselves."

But in the following year—under the Aztec calendar it was toward the end of the year Thirteen Rabbit—Spanish ships were again seen standing at the eastern coast, and once again there was speculation and wonder in the Mexican city. The Emperor sent for five emissaries and said to them,

"It is said that our Lord has at last arrived. Receive him. Listen sharply. Bring back what you hear. Now see what you are to take him."

And forthwith he showed them the glorious raiment of Aztec ceremony—a mask of turquoise mosaic representing a serpent's maw, and headdresses and corselets and fans and ornaments of exquisite workmanship in the rarest of brilliant feathers, picked out with gold, and necklaces, brassards and leg ornaments of precious stone and metal, and warriors' clothes of ocelot fur, and a turquoise spear thrower, and sandals paved with obsidian, and other splendors highly valued by the courtiers—"the array of the gods." These were loaded into great baskets, and slung on wooden poles, to be carried to the coast by fast runners.

"Go!" commanded the Emperor, "linger nowhere! Pray to our Lord the God, and say to him, 'Thy servant Moctezuma hath sent us; behold what he offereth unto you, for the God hath come to reach his wretched home in Mexico.'"

For the strangers were at the coast to stay, and the portents were surely now confirmed. The Emperor could only wait to hear what his ambassadors would learn. Meanwhile, he could neither sleep nor rest. No one dared speak to him. Whatever he did seemed done in vain. He sighed often. "He was spent," said a traditional Aztec historian of those days, "downcast. He felt delight in no savory morsel, joy, or pleasure." He was heard to say, in what must seem great uncertainty whether it was god or man who came from the direction of sunrise,

"What will become of us now? Who in fact is ruler here? Alas, until now, myself."

He said his heart was in torment, as if pepper water ran through it, until it burned and smarted. "Where," he implored, "where, in truth, O Lord, may we turn?"

Many days must pass before his informants could go and return. When at last they were again at the palace, he was asleep. They asked the guards to awaken him. But when he awoke, he would not receive the ambassadors in his quarters, but sent them to a temple, where Indian captives were held in supply for sacrifice. He would hear the ambassadors there.

"Have two captives dusted with chalk," ordered the Emperor. It was the first act in the ritual of sacrifice. Then he met his ambassadors, and before he would let them speak he ordered that the chalked captives be sacrificed. Priests at once slashed open their breasts, uprooted their hearts and sprinkled the ambassadors with their blood to sanctify and purify them after their journey, which had taken them into "perilous places," where they had "looked into the faces and heads of —and had truly to spoken to—the Gods."

Then the ambassadors were permitted to tell what they had seen at the eastern coast.

iv.

THE ENCOUNTER

THEY SAID some dwellers at the coast took them in a small boat out to the ships anchored by the sheltering island in the harbor. Seeing them draw near, the men on board called down.

"Who are you? Where do you come from?"

"From Mexico," they replied.

"Perhaps not," said the men on board. "Perhaps you only say that. Perhaps you mock us."

But the ambassadors insisted, and soon the sailors drew their boat to the ship by hook and then put down a ladder and they went on board. Each came forward to the commander who stood among the others and bent down and kissed the planking before him. He was the Captain General Hernando Cortés and his men were Spaniards, among whom were a few blacks. The ambassadors said to him, in reverence,

"May the God listen: for Moctezuma, his subject, makes this prayer to him: 'The God has suffered—he is travel-weary.'"

With this, they said, they began to clothe the Captain General with pieces of the "array of the Gods," beginning with the turquoise mosaic mask of the serpent's maw. They added the quetzal feathered fan crown and green stone ear ornaments like small serpents, and two necklaces, and a feather cloak, and the obsidian-paved sandals, and arm and leg bands, and a shield of shells and gold. The rest of the godly vestments they laid at his feet as the most rare and beautiful of their possessions. When they were done with this, they said, the Captain General asked,

"Is this all you have to give me? Are these your only greetings?"

They replied,

"This is all we brought, O our Lord."

They were at once put in iron shackles by command of the Captain General. At another word from him, there was a tremendous noise, with fire and smoke, from a brass tube on the ship—it was, they later learned, the Spanish lombard cannon. Hearing it, the ambassadors fainted dead away, one by one, and fell to the planking. When they awoke it was to know that the Spaniards were giving them wine and food. As they revived, the Captain General said he knew by rumor how brave, how strong were the men of Mexico. He proposed to discover this for himself.

"I would see and test how strong and powerful you are," he said. With this, he gave them Spanish leather shields and steel swords and lances, and said, "Early tomorrow morning, at dawn, we will fight and try our strength against each other to see who is the stronger."

No, said the ambassadors, they had not been sent to fight—only to bring their ruler's reverences and greetings. They must not disobey him.

"No," said the Captain General, "it must be as I say. I want to see and marvel at your powers. In Castile, we are told how powerful you are. Early tomorrow morning, you shall eat. I shall eat. Then be ready for combat."

They said he let them go after that, and they clambered down the ladder. In the boat they went so fast that some paddled with their feet. Once on shore, they raced inland, over the dunes, across the sandy plain beyond, into the jungle on the slopes that began to rise away.

Without pausing to rest, and hardly to breathe, they came to the Emperor "quite by night."

Listening, the Emperor was lost between marvelling and trembling. Yet he must know more. Those gods—or those men—what were they like?

The ambassadors had more to tell.

The Spaniards covered all parts of their bodies—only their faces were revealed, and these were "very white." Their eyes were "like chalk," and some men had yellow hair, some black. Their beards were long and the hair of the black men, the Negroes, was close to the head and curly. The men clothed themselves in metal. "They covered their heads with iron." Swords, crossbows, shields, lances—all were of iron. Their food—this interested the Emperor greatly—was like the food of lords—"very large and white," not heavy and doughy like the Indian tortillas, and it tasted somewhat sweet, "a little honeyed."

They had huge dogs, with "ears doubled over; great, hanging jowls; blazing eyes—fiery yellow; thin flanks, with ribs showing." The dogs were "tall and fierce," and went about panting with their tongues dripping and hanging out. They were spotted "like ocelots."

They had other creatures, which seemed as "high as rooftops," and on the back of these the Spaniards rode. The only thing the ambassadors could compare these creatures to were deer, and so spoke of them as deer.

But most amazing of all was that tremendous effect of thunder, with fire and smoke—the lombard. They repeated that they were deafened by it, overpowered. The smoke smelled "very foul," indeed, a "fetid odor which wounded the head" to smell it. On being discharged, the lombard cast forth a round pellet which if it struck a mountain made it crumble and fall apart, or if it struck a tree made it splinter and vanish "as if someone blew it away."

Listening to his ambassadors, the Emperor Moctezuma "was filled with a great dread, as if he were swooning. His soul was sickened, his heart was anguished."

Believing he was hearing of gods, who must be welcomed, he yet must discover if they were men, who could be defeated.

He sent for his magicians and soothsayers, who would cast spells and try to bewitch the Spaniards, as men could be overcome. At the same time, new messengers went forth with Indian captives to be sacrificed in the presence of the Spaniards as in the presence of gods, whose food must properly be sprinkled with blood. No spells availed, and when the Spaniards saw food sprinkled with fresh human blood, and smelled it, they were "sickened and revolted," and turned away.

The Emperor's uncertainty and terror grew as the Spaniards strengthened their foothold at the sea. Doomed feelings seemed to enter into him and to reach from him to those about him. "He was weak," said the Aztec historian, "was no longer fired; was incapable." He "could only await the Spaniards—only steel his heart and tax himself."

Removed from the great ceremonial square at the center of the city which contained the official palace where he held state, the Emperor kept a private house with gardens. It lay a mile or so to the southwest of the great square, and he now retreated to it, crossing many canals and odd waterways. Coming to its terraces and deep roofed open rooms and its patios with trees, scented bushes and private chambers, he "resigned himself" to whatever he might soon see and marvel at.

v.

THE SHORE

THE MEXICANS who came to grasp the hand of Cortés in peace presently found that they would never be able to let go, even in war. He had come to stay. Affably receiving his native visitors he would give them food and drink and glass beads, assuring them that his arrival among them was their good fortune. Many of them returned to their inland trails "well content," imagining that they were still free.

The Captain General set up a shore camp, which later was to be reestablished as the seaport of Vera Cruz about forty miles up the coast in the harbor of Point Bernal, with a chapel, and a fort armed with his brass falconets, in the dunes.

Ambassadors from the interior kept coming bringing gifts that grew richer with each visit, and taking away the dazzling rubbish of glass and metal brought from Spain. Their lord Emperor—the Spaniards caught his name as Montezuma, which became their usage and that generally of the world— still desired to know all he could about the newcomers. His messages continued to be cordial, urging them to ask for anything they required. Since he must know for himself all he could discover, he sent artists to paint their likenesses and to draw their ships, sails and horses, even to two greyhounds.

The Captain General demonstrated all that was wonderful and new. He showed off the cavalry in mounted manoeuvres and he ordered salvos from the falconets, which at every blast stunned the Mexican observers. All was recorded by the Emperor's painters in long scrolls, drawn either in clear, explicit line in black, or painted in flower-like colors, on coarse cotton cloth. A formal art, intended to convey exact information about real sights and objects, it was also stylized, and when Europeans later saw such works, they were put in mind of the miniature illuminations in the manuscripts of the monastic or courtly painters of the late Middle Ages. By every means the nature of the newcomers must be reported to the Emperor.

That helmet, said one of the Mexican ambassadors on an early mission to the coast, on that soldier there? The Emperor would surely be pleased to see it?

The Captain General ordered it given to the ambassador, saying,

He would like to know if the gold they had in Mexico was the same as that he knew in Spanish rivers? Let the helmet, then, be filled with grains of native gold and brought back to him so that he could forward the gold to his great King. Meanwhile, he would send a fine Spanish armchair to Montezuma, who should sit in it when he came to see him.

A week or so passed.

Native women baked bread and cooked fish and fowl for the Captain General and his staff, while the common soldiers had to hunt or fish or forage for themselves in the tropic glare of the sand dunes of the coast.

"And then one morning," wrote the Spanish chronicler, a column of more than a hundred Mexicans, led by a great chieftain, who oddly enough looked like the Captain General, appeared over the dunes carrying grand burdens.

They came to the Captain General, kissed the ground before him, reverenced him with incense smoke, and made polite speeches. Then at a signal from "the other Cortés," as the Spaniards called the chieftain, the Mexicans unrolled mats on the sand and covered these with cotton cloths, on which they began to lay forth gifts from Montezuma. It was all true, then, and the New World was a vast treasure house, for the tokens of good will sent by the Mexican lord were glorious wonders of beauty and value. "With delight," the Captain General received each one.

The first was a great disc six feet high, representing the sun, with many designs carved and modelled in it, the whole of pure gold. The next was a larger disc all of silver representing the moon. The Mexicans gave more—twenty golden ducks, "beautifully worked and very natural looking," and dogs, monkeys, deer, tigers and lions of gold, and many precious necklaces, and golden scepters, and headdresses of plumes caught in gold or silver, and marvellous skulls carved in rock crystal, and robes of brilliant feathers, and more than thirty loads of rich cotton cloths.

And here again was the soldier's helmet which the "other Cortés" brought back filled to the visor with newly mined gold, which showed the Captain General how rich were the mines of Mexico.

The ambassadors paid many compliments, saying that their Emperor knew all about the battles at Tabasco, adding that one day he would like to meet the commander of such valiant men as the visitors.

For the present, however, they said, their Emperor ordered the visitors to remain where they were at the seaport.

At this setback, the Captain General "kept a good countenance," and in his turn bestowed gifts upon the Mexicans— a pair of shirts of Holland linen for each ambassador, and some blue beads. And then he spoke of what he most desired, which was to meet the Emperor Montezuma. How, he asked, how could he ever face his own great King if he should fail to meet the ruler of the Mexicans? His King had sent him to meet Montezuma. He would go anywhere to meet him and do whatever he ordered.

The ambassadors agreed to take this message to Montezuma, but repeated that the interview was unnecessary. They left, taking with them such gifts to Montezuma as the Spaniards, with their meagre stores, could offer—an engraved Florentine glass cup, three shirts of Holland linen and "other things."

A few days later, during which two ships of the fleet explored the coast, the ambassadors appeared again bringing more gifts and reporting how gratified their Emperor was at the gifts of the Spaniards.

And the interview?

The Emperor ordered that no more be said about it. Nor should any more messages be sent to Mexico.

It was evening and the bell for vespers rang in the Spanish camp. The soldiers went to their knees and chanted the *Ave Maria* before the cross.

What were they doing? asked the Mexican ambassadors. Why did they humble themselves before a strange tree cut "in that particular way?"

The Captain General knew his opportunities. He said to one of his chaplains that here was the ideal moment, as the Mexicans had brought up the matter, to speak to them of religion. He turned to them and gave them a discourse "so fitting to the occasion that no good theologian could have bettered it."

The Mexicans understood everything through Doña Marina and Aguilar, and promised to repeat it to their lord.

Moreover, said the Captain General, they must give up their abominable practice of human sacrifice to their idols. Let them put away their bloodthirsty gods and set up in their place this image of the Holy Mother of God with her Divine Infant, which he would give to them, and then let them see what blessings must follow. The ambassadors departed with the Madonna.

One morning a while later the Spaniards awoke to find that not an Indian remained in camp. All had gone away during the night, ordered to do so by Montezuma. They were to have no further relations with the strangers who tried to destroy the gods of Mexico and abolish the proper worship in which living youths were daily sacrificed.

The essential terms of the Spanish invasion and the Mexican resistance were stated. They were opposed to each other in the end on religious grounds. All other differences might have been composed. Through the spring and summer of 1519 the Captain General worked to overcome the obstacles that would keep him from confronting the Emperor Montezuma.

vi.

INLAND

WITHIN HIS OWN command he faced enemies who kept their loyalty to Governor Velásquez. The Captain General wooed them with words and with gold—"that solvent of hardness," as his chronicler called it—and brought them over to his side. There was a threat to his sovereignty when an expedition sent by Governor Garay of Jamaica anchored in the new harbor founded by the Captain General. He seized and stripped a shore party from the Jamaican ships which having been scared off sailed away.

On a number of reconnaissance missions his soldiers made contact with Indians, some friendly, some resistant. It was of the greatest interest and importance to him to find that certain Indian towns were hostile to the Emperor Montezuma. The Captain General at once exploited their positions and exhorted them to rebel. Wherever he went he showed his strength and tempered it nicely with his robust charm. It was not long until Montezuma himself was sending new ambassadors to him, with still more gifts. The Emperor must have still further news of the Spaniards, which the Captain General was happy to send.

One day a ship arrived from Cuba with word that the King had recognized Governor Velásquez as the proper colonizer and lord of Mexico. It seemed expedient to the Captain General that he send messengers straight to Spain, bypassing Cuba, to lay before the King the grandest of Montezuma's gifts, to prove who it was who first came to Mexico, and how he had possessed it in the name of His Majesty. A ship was fitted out and the messengers departed. At the same time, old followers of Governor Velásquez planned to seize one of the ships of the fleet and send word to Cuba warning the Governor to intercept the Captain General's embassy to the King. The plot was discovered and the plotters imprisoned.

As the army was soon to move into Mexico—the Captain General never thought of not going to Montezuma—there were dangers to its rear if ships remained, and a seaside garrison, to communicate with Cuba.

The Captain General resolved to dismantle his ships to prevent treason behind his back. Calling a council of his trusted men, he described the dangers he thought about. His case was persuasive. There seemed only one thing to do, and he waited for his friends to propose it, for he preferred not to propose it himself. Finally, said the Spanish chronicler, "we, who were his friends, counselled him, although others opposed it, not to leave a single ship in port, but to destroy them all at once, so as to leave no source of trouble behind."

The decision was made. Others had shared in it, which relieved the Captain General from sole responsibility to pay for the ships if payment were ever asked. Announcing that all the ships were unseaworthy, he ordered them beached and stripped. After Mass one morning, in the presence of the assembled army, he made a speech, quoted Caesar on crossing the Rubicon, and told all of their duty which lay ahead.

Learning from Indian chiefs of the best road to take toward the city of Mexico, and leaving a garrison of a hundred and fifty men at the fort by the harbor of Vera Cruz at Point Bernal, the Captain General moved inland on August sixteenth. Within two weeks he was at war with the people of Tlaxcala.

vii.

To Mexico

BRINGING HIS TROOPS away from the sea, he began within a mile or so of the beaches the continuous climb which would bring him to the heart of the new land. Indian trails might do for people travelling on foot, lightly laden, but mounted men, and foot soldiers heavily armored, and supply carts, and hauled artillery, needed more generous passage. The army soon found that it must make its road ahead for most of the inland thrust.

In great ridges and waves of land first densely clothed in jungle, later thickly matted with scrubby bushes and cactus bearing every sort of thorn and spine, the continent rose in vast terraces toward the eastern and central uplands of Mexico. The army, hauling and hacking and burning its way, passed a succession of landscapes which seemed to be repeated again and again—jungle slopes, deep, placid valleys with small streams, sudden escarpments falling off on either side of spines where the trail must go, and entry upon immense vacant plains defined by distant mesas and mountains. They saw mountains for the first time—three screens of them at different veils of distance—after first coming clear of the jungle, and they would always thereafter see mountains in some quarter of their new world as they marched upward toward still higher slopes and plains and valleys so wide that each could take three days or more to cross.

In the submarine light of jungle passages, as at Jalapa, they saw now and then great clusters of flowers—gardenia, olean-der, azalea, tavachín, bougainvillea with its red violet glory which was like the color worn by bishops, and they inhaled fragrance of heavy sweetness, and farther on they saw Indian towns where grapes were trellised, and they knew the sensa-tions of headiness which came in breathing mountain air when not used to it.

In such a land even a considerable town of several thou-sand Indians could be lost to sight until you were right upon it; and even then, its central structures, made of the same rock as that which lay all about, seemed to belong more to the land than to people.

Every town had its pyramided temples at whose crowning altars human sacrifices were held. In one town on the inland march the Spanish chronicler estimated a pile of human skulls carefully disposed. He concluded that they represented more than one hundred thousand sacrifices. "I repeat again that there were more than one hundred thousand of them." Elsewhere he saw in one pile more human thigh bones than he could count. The Spaniards knew by now that the Mexicans ate human flesh on occasion. How much there was to learn about Mexico. In an unexpected protection, they learned one day from Indians that they were regarded as gods and that therefore they could not be killed.

Yet battle came, first in skirmish, then in force, on September second against Tlaxcalans armed with broadswords and lances and crowned with plumed headdresses. In this battle a mare was captured. The Indians learned of her animal nature when they cut her open. A horse, then, was not a supernatural creature. The battle was resumed three days later with messages from enemy chiefs ringing in the ears of the soldiers—how their hearts would be torn out and offered up to the gods of the pyramids, and their flesh served up at a victory banquet. Four hundred Spaniards engaged an Indian army so great that even a random shot from a musket found its man. A cloud of stones flew from the Indian slings, and their arrows came so thick that where they fell looked like the floor of a threshing bin. With lances, shields and broadswords hardened in fire the Indians attacked again and again. But the Spanish cavalry, supported by musketry and swordsmen, prevailed against them, and the battle waned when the Indians left the field, retiring in good order.

The soldiers went to their camp and thanked God. They buried their dead deep in a room of an underground house built by the Indians, and to preserve the belief that they were immortal, they "threw much earth over the top of the house, so that they should not smell the bodies." Then they "doctored all the wounded with the fat of an Indian."

A third encounter fell in the nighttime. Indian priests, professionally knowing the nature of immortals, declared that the powers of the Spaniards left them at night, and that then would be the time to drive them away forever. But the Spaniards kept up their patrols and guards and repulsed the effort.

Some days later the Tlaxcalans opened peace talks, and
soon revealed that they had given battle only because they
believed the strangers to be friends and allies of Montezuma.

How was this? They were not allied with Montezuma?

No. He was their bitter enemy, he sent warriors against
them, he captured their young men to feed his gods, his men
ravished their wives and daughters.

Here was an opportunity not to be missed. The Captain
General seized it. The peace negotiations which followed took
many days, and much of advantage to the Captain General
was revealed in their course.

For one thing, an Indian town or nation which lay ahead,
Cholula, was allied to the Mexicans and Montezuma, and
therefore was considered an enemy by the Tlaxcalans, who
would help the Spaniards to fight against it. The Cholulans
were "very wicked," said the Tlaxcalans, and "they are our
foes. They are as strong as the Mexicans. They are friends of
the Mexicans."

"Where is Mexico?" asked the Spaniards. "What is it like?
Is it still distant?"

It was a "very good place," declared the Tlaxcalans, and it
was not far distant—an unencumbered traveller could reach it
in perhaps three days. It was built all on water, said the Tlaxcalan allies. The Captain General learned more of the great
city across the mountains than he had yet known. There were
bridges and canals between the houses and streets, and people
went by canoes as much as by walking. The houses had flat
roofs which by raising parapets could easily become fortifica-
tions. The city rose from the center of a large lake, or rather
from waters where two lakes met. Three main causeways led
over the water to the city, and each causeway had five breaks
in it spanned by bridges. If any single bridge were lifted nobody could enter the city by that way. It would be difficult to
take such a city by force, if the Spanish magic or strangeness,
or the belief in them as gods, or their commander's terrible
charm, should not permit it to be taken in peace. To a Spaniard the project seemed "a hopeless enterprise," and yet the
more it seemed so, the more determined to press on were the
soldiers who had seen golden sun and silver moon and all the
other treasures of Montezuma.

But first the Cholulans must be met and conquered. The
Tlaxcalans ceased to be enemies and became guides, gave the
Spaniards all they required, and ended by delivering over their
maidens to the soldiers.

The march was resumed and now passed across the great recumbent desert shoulders of mountains which after many more heights and hidden rises sprang to towering vision against the burning blue sky. One such was the Cofre de Perote—the Casket of Perote, so named because its pinnacle looked like a great treasure chest. Farther to their left the soldiers saw the awesome splendor of the volcano Orizaba, whose vast cone wore its robe of snow the year round. They passed across hard valleys of lava, like scatters of excrement from hell, and then were rewarded by a long delivery from their rocky travel when they came to the plains of Perote, where immense flat reaches of mountain meadow and pasture were easily crossed with all the heavy gear of the armed column.

The city of Cholula lay in a dusty plain. Its temples of stone blocks rose above the wandering course of a river. Beyond in the sky, like other temples, were two more mighty spectacles of rock and snow—the twin volcanoes of Ixtaccihuatl and Popocatepetl. Their cloud images hovered above them and sometimes descended to obscure them. From the valley of Cholula they seemed too high to cross. But Mexico lay beyond. The Captain General continued his march. Cholulans met him on his way, bringing chickens and tortillas, and accompanied by Indian priests who wafted incense upon the Spanish leaders.

When later the soldiers came to the town, they saw great throngs on the flat rooftops watching their entry. For two days the army was made welcome; and then curious events began to happen. Cholulans suddenly kept their distance and refused food to the army. Ambassadors from the Emperor appeared with a rude message—the army was not to advance to Mexico, for there was no food there to give the soldiers. Indian allies discovered that the Cholulans had dug pits with sharpened stakes in them on which horses would be impaled if they should fall through the flimsy covers set over them. Complicated treacheries were all about, and finally the Captain General demanded that the temple priests of Cholula tell him what lay behind the sudden change of attitude.

The truth was, they said, that the Emperor Montezuma could not decide on which was the right policy to pursue—now he sent orders that all honor and aid be given to the strangers, again he would forbid them the approaches to his city. The latest was that his principal gods had advised him to send twenty thousand warriors to ambush the army, and destroy it but for twenty soldiers who were to be saved to be sacrificed on the altars of Cholula.

The Captain General took counsel of his officers, and as soon as his plan was ready, opened warfare against Cholula, in their own city, among their own temples. Manoeuvring swiftly, he trapped the principal nobles, priests and warriors in their temple yards, and gave them a blow they would "always remember, killing many of them, so they gained nothing from the promises of their false idols." Tlaxcalan allies joined in the battle and once at large went on to pillage the town and take slaves. It was a swift and decisive victory, and the Captain General crowned it with a stern admonition to the Emperor's ambassadors that henceforth he was to be treated with proper respect. He also commanded the Tlaxcalans to give up their loot and to make friends with the Cholulans, which evidently they did. He was once again ready to press ahead up the great mountain approaches.

One of the volcanoes was throwing out fire. None of the soldiers had ever seen anything like it. A few climbed to its top and felt the mountain shake under them and saw fire, ash, and hot stones thrown above them. When they reached the crest—it was Popocatepetl—they looked down into the infernal lake in the crater, and then beyond it, they saw a greater sight. It was the city of Mexico, twelve or thirteen leagues distant, with its white facets shining in the sun. The soldiers brought back visions of their goal to their comrades.

Between the towering snowy crowns of the volcanoes, Ixtaccihuatl to the north, Popocatepetl to the south, a wide saddle afforded a pass over the mountain barrier at an altitude almost three miles high. The Captain General took his army over it through straw-colored meadows. Pines climbed the ridges on both sides of the army's encampment at the pass and clouds came and went so near that they cast no shadows but only enfolded all. When the atmosphere was clear, under the intense blue sky to which they felt so close, the soldiers, with their Captain General, saw for the first time far, far below them, the vast valley of Mexico, with its lakes from which rose dark humps of scattered mountain islands. Cloud shadows passed like moving stains of ink in the shapes of continents across the maplike world which the army looked upon from the viewpoint of eagles.

From here the descent could be taken by way of two roads. Both looped back and forth on the immense slopes, falling a little lower with each turn. The Emperor's agents came to the

Captain General and urged him to take a certain one of these trails. It led, they declared, to Tamanalco, a fine town in fief to Mexico, and see, they said, how well it had been cleared for the army. The other road was far more dangerous, they insisted, and indeed, to save the army from its perils, the Mexicans had placed impediments across it to make it impassable—thick plantings of maguey, and felled mountain pines, and rocks. This road led to Chalco, a town not so large or hospitable as Tamanalco.

The ambassadors were too eager—and the Captain General had already learned from allies how the Mexican forces were lying in wait for him in newly dug trenches along the cleared road. He took the army down the slope along the road of obstacles and snow fell on the column as it left the high camp in the pass. Allies hauled away the maguey and the felled trees and the army took its descent with braced steps and careful footing through the hot light and the cold shade which in turn the mountain put over them as they struggled lower to the plain.

On the slopes they were visited by fresh deputations from Mexico, who brought gifts and a proposal.

The gifts included neckpieces of gold.

"Like monkeys," the Aztecs observed, the Spaniards "seized upon the gold. It was as if only then they were satisfied, sated, and gladdened." The soldiers "thirsted mightily for gold; they stuffed themselves with it, and starved for it, and lusted for it like pigs."

As for the proposal—the Emperor sent congratulations to the Captain General on his newest successes, and then made an offer. He proposed to pay an annual tribute to the Spanish Crown in an amount to be agreed upon, provided the Spaniards advance no nearer to the capital city of Mexico. Anything, he seemed to say now, anything to keep them at a distance. He hastened to add that his only concern was to spare the strangers further hardships in passing through mountains and hazards to reach him. He must let them know that certain allies of his had sprung to arms to prevent the Spanish advance. He must inform them again that even if they should reach the city there was no food to give them.

The Captain General replied with splendid courtesy, yet he could not help mentioning how strange it seemed that the Emperor "could be so changeable, sometimes saying one thing and then sending orders to the contrary."

As for the offer of payment—for what he had already re-

ceived the Captain General would presently repay in good
works the value of all tribute. But being now so close to his
goal, he would only be derelict in duty if he failed to carry
out his mission and proceed to the capital, there to explain to
the Emperor why he came, which "must be done in person."
In the matter of the food—whatever the scarcity, he and his
soldiers were, he said, "men who could get along." He was on
his way to the great city and the Emperor should accept his
coming "as a good thing."

The Captain General could only conclude that a ruler who
could plead was already defeated. In the end, following the reports of the hardy advance of the small Spanish army, with
their thousands of Indian allies, over every obstacle of jungle
and rock and plain and duplicity, the Emperor suddenly gave
in and sent words of welcome, saying that since they must
come, he would receive them in his city.

From this change of heart following upon passionate pleas
and transparent objections, the Captain General learned much
about the ruler he intended to confront. He continued his
march out upon the vast floor of the dusty valley of Mexico.

"They came stirring up the dust," said Aztec history, and
added that seen from afar, the Spanish swords and lances
"moved in a wavy line like a water course."

The army arrived at the shores of the lakes south of the
city, and followed along in the golden air of autumn toward
the towns of Ixtapalapa, Xochimilco, and Coyoacan, never
relaxing their guard, day or night.

For they knew from many warnings what might await them
if once they entered the capital. One such warning told how
they would be taken, and held, and fattened in pens, until
they were plump enough for eating after their hearts had been
ripped out of their ribs to throw their blood upon the idol
with every last beat.

"I don't know," said the Spanish chronicler, "how I can
carry so much in my memory, except that I have had to tell
about our war experiences so often that I can see myself as we
advanced, my beard always over my shoulder."

As they came closer to the two connected lakes from which
the capital rose, they were met by new delegations from the
Emperor, richly robed and full of addresses. At last one
morning they came to a broad causeway which led from
Coyoacan straight north to the city of Mexico. The soldiers
felt that they were entering into an enchantment in a legend,
"on account of the great towers, and pyramids and buildings

rising from the water, and all built of masonry." They looked at each other and asked whether the things they saw "were not in a dream."

Far within those walls and towers that shimmered in air and shallow lake, the Emperor of Mexico awaited them as the greatest mystery of all.

viii.

THE MEETING

STRETCHING FROM the south across the lake the causeway was ten feet wide. It led into the city through watch towers. At a certain point the road was broken and the lake waters flowed through the gap. Over the gap was a bridge made of long wooden beams which could be taken up or put down. These were now down, to accommodate the procession which came to the city on November eighth, 1519.

As observed by the people of the city, four mounted soldiers came first, the advance guard, who rode back and forth and from side to side in constant motion, peering everywhere among the people, into the side streets, up to the rooftops. "They proceeded examining everything." With them were the greyhounds, running ahead, sniffing everywhere, and "ever panting."

The bearer of the royal standard of Castile came next, marching alone. He performed the ceremonial manual of the banner, "waving it back and forth, making it circle, and tossing it from side to side." In golden yellow and scarlet, its royal castles and lions came alive in the breeze. The flag "would stiffen and raise itself like a man," said the Aztec report, "it would smartly curve, fly up in turning, and billow."

Now came swordsmen, with bared blades, and carrying shields of wood and leather. After them marched the cavalry, mounted, in quilted cotton armor, with their swords hanging from their saddles, all jingling and clattering, and the horses, under both spur and rein, sweated and frothed. The heavy stamp of their hoofs on paving or wooden planking sounded to the people like the casting of great stones upon the ground.

The crossbowmen, in cotton armor which reached to their knees and seemed "very thick, very hard, very dense, like limestone," came next, shouldering their crossbows, and bearing their quivers slung under their arms. Their helmets were plumed.

After another squadron of cavalry marched the footmen with harquebuses, shouldered, and then, at the heart of the procession, in full armor, on his armored charger, rode the Captain General, surrounded by his staff and personal standard bearers. Behind him swarmed his Indian allies in their thousands, crouching in their dancing steps, and shouting against their beating palms. They were armed with their own weapons.

The Captain General could see ahead down a street two miles long another procession coming to meet him. To the music of two-toned drums and conch shell trumpets it advanced through lanes of flowers—magnolias, sunflowers, popcorn flowers, cacao blossoms—and on each side of the avenue at the base of what the Spaniards saw as "very large houses" marched a hundred Mexican lords, barefooted, and robed in court dress heavy with embroidery and precious metal.

Down the center, moving slowly under towering brilliant feathers that waved to and fro in grace like weeds in water currents a litter was borne, attended on each side by two great lords, one of whom was brother to the Emperor. Within the litter rode the Emperor Montezuma, robed like the others, except that he wore sandals with golden soles paved in jewels. All wore flowers and necklaces and feathers and wreaths.

Having crossed the bridge, the Captain General dismounted. Accompanied by Doña Marina and Aguilar as his interpreters, he went forward to meet the Mexicans. The litter was put down and Montezuma was assisted from it by the two lords who moved forward with him. In a rapid ceremonial walk, he reclined against their supporting arms as he came. Over him was borne "a glorious canopy of green parrot feathers." Attendants swept the ground before him and put down matting for him to tread upon. None of the court dared to look at his face.

As they met, the Captain General put out his arms to embrace the Emperor.

No!—indicated the attendant lords, preventing his touch upon their master. Instead, the Mexicans "made the ceremony of kissing the ground," and the Captain General said,

"Is it thee? Art not thou he? Art thou Montezuma?"

"It is so," replied the Emperor, "I."

At this he made "a great reverence" to the Captain General, drew close to him, and stood firm.

Then in speech which was like prayer—for the Emperor seemed publicly disposed toward belief in the Captain General as the god Quetzalcoatl—he said, according to the Aztec account of the meeting, these things, among others:

"O our Lord, thou hast suffered fatigue; thou hast spent thyself. Thou hast arrived on earth; thou hast come to thy noble city of Mexico."

Doña Marina listened, and the Captain General waited for her to translate these words for him.

"Thou hast come to occupy the noble seat and mat," continued the Emperor, "which for a little time I have guarded and watched for thee . . . I do not dream that I see thee and look into thy face. Oh, but I have been troubled for a long time. I have looked into the unknown whence thou hast come —the place of mystery. For the rulers of old have gone, saying that thou wouldst come to instruct thy city, thou wouldst descend to thy mat and seat, thou wouldst return. And now it is fulfilled; thou hast returned. . . . Arrive now in thy land. Rest, Lord. . . ."

The Emperor ended his welcoming prayer. Doña Marina translated it for the Captain General. When she was done, he told her what to reply for him, speaking, as the Aztec said, "in a barbarous tongue." She gave his words to the Emperor:

"May Montezuma quiet his heart and not be afraid. We love him greatly. Now our hearts are satisfied, because we know him and have heard him. For a long time we have wanted to see him and to look upon his face. Now that we have seen him and have come to his home in Mexico, at leisure he may hear what we have to say."

The Indian lords came forward to greet the Captain General, and the Spaniards came close and walked about the Emperor and examined him. From his own neck the Captain General took "a collar of pearls and glass diamonds" and clasped it about the neck of the Emperor. The Emperor's brother took the Captain General by the arm and led him along the street into the city. Presently a Mexican attendant brought the Emperor a cloth containing something. He took from it two collars made of colored shells from which depended eight golden shrimps eight inches long "and executed with great perfection." The Emperor placed these about the neck of the Captain General and resumed his march through the streets to the "large and handsome house" which he had prepared for the Spaniards. There he left them, saying,

"Here is your house and the house of your brothers."

Their thoughts were racing with the new after their "bold and lucky entrance into the great city of Mexico." Wonderful and strange, all they had seen crowded upon all they remembered of their own way of life. Golden shrimps. An emperor so great nobody could touch him or look upon him, who could not walk alone. Houses "well made of cut stone, cedar, and other fragrant woods, with great rooms and patios, all plastered and bright," shaded with cotton awnings. Orchards and gardens giving forth scented air. And here and there mosaic pictures on the walls "that provided food for thought," for they showed blood sacrifices and wild magnificent idols and glorious animal gods.

Taking up their quarters by companies, the soldiers placed their artillery "conveniently," and established the order of the guard. Food was ready for them—"a very sumptuous native meal"—and they fell to hungrily. Of all the mysteries, one made them wonder the most: how could all have been so easy for them on that day?

"Thanks," said the chronicler, "to Our Lord Jesus Christ for everything."

ix.

THE USE OF HISTORY

LATER THE SAME DAY, the mystery was somewhat explained when the Emperor returned to talk to the Captain General. He brought gifts—the usual gold, silver and embroidered cloths which he distributed "with a grace that gave him the appearance of being in every way a great lord." He then seated himself on a dais near another on which sat the Captain General, both in golden chairs, and with the aid of Doña Marina made a confession which moved the listeners greatly.

For a long time, he said, his people had known that they were not native to Mexico, but had come from the direction of the sunrise far away. Their lord of that time left them to return to the sunrise. Long later he came to them again to take them home with him, but by then the people had made their generations here, and were not willing to go. He departed again, but they knew that one day his heirs would return to conquer Mexico as their rightful domain.

Now his heirs must surely be here again; for the Mexicans had heard the Captain General say everywhere how he came on behalf of his lord the king who ruled at the sunrise, and who knew all about the Mexicans.

"Therefore," said the Emperor, "you may be sure that we shall obey you and recognize you as the representative of this great lord of whom you speak." The Emperor spoke earnestly. "In this there will be no deception . . . all we possess is at your disposal."

The Spaniards heard him say,

"Rejoice and rest, since you are, then, in your own rightful place and your own homes. I know all that befell you coming here, and I know the dreadful things people have told you about me. Believe only what you see with your own eyes. Those treacherous people of mine who deserted me to fight alongside you against me—they told you I have houses of gold and all I have is made of gold and I am a god, or pretend that I am. Well. The houses you see are of lime, earth, and stone."

As for being a god, the Emperor lifted aside his robes to show his body, and touched his arms and his breast and belly with his hands, and said,

"See: I am flesh and bone, like you and everybody. I am mortal and tangible. Look how they have lied to you. Of course I have some things of gold which my ancestors handed down to me. These and all else I possess are yours whenever you like."

The conquest appeared to be finished and done with, so soon, and so simply. The Captain General in his turn confirmed all that the Emperor had told him. Between them, they made use of history.

"I especially confirmed," wrote the Captain General to the King of Spain, "his belief that it was Your Majesty whom they were expecting."

The Mexican Emperor rose to take his leave with further polite speeches. All was in order—he had provided corn and grinding stones for the soldiers, and chicken and fruit, and Indian women to cook for them, and had even sent grass for the horses. As he went, members of the Spanish staff escorted him to the street, but there the Captain General halted his own men, ordering them to remain in their quarters. The Emperor had made him a gift of Mexico, and had acknowledged him as the conqueror out of the east. Well and good. Yet it was wise not to venture forth freely until, he said, "We know better what to expect."

It was not long until he knew.

By messenger from his port of Vera Cruz the Captain General received within days the news that on orders of the Emperor the Indians were to rise up and kill the Spaniards of the garrison at the seacoast, for fear they would continue using Indian allies against him. At the village of Almería the Indians attacked a Spanish detachment from Vera Cruz, captured a soldier, wounded the chief magistrate and six soldiers, and killed a horse. Keeping his calm and masterful countenance, the Captain General moved to counter deceit with precautions. The first would meet a particular danger.

Since all passage to and from the city must go by the bridges and the causeways a distance of two miles or more in any direction from the city in the lake to the opposite shores, and since all passage could be cut off by opening the bridges, he ordered immediate construction of two ships of the brigantine class. Built ostensibly for pleasure cruising, these ships might also be useful in case of forced, sudden retreat. Work went forward, and he meanwhile affably gave audience to many delegations of Mexican lords, and paid court to the Emperor, and with a heavy smile received his kindest attentions. Almost as if casting a spell against adversity, the Captain General, knowing what he knew, thought it wise to tell the Emperor through interpreters that neither he nor any of his soldiers "ever got tired from anything."

x.

THE EMPEROR
AND THE GODS

THE SPANISH CHRONICLER often had opportunity to observe the Emperor. He said Montezuma "knew all of us well, and our characters." The soldiers returned the compliment. Montezuma, they saw, "loved pleasure and song," and showing the "grace" of "a great lord," was "very festive in his princely manner." About forty years old, he was a man of good height, slender and finely proportioned. His skin was "not very dark," and he kept himself beautifully clean with a bath every afternoon. In his narrow, pleasant face, his eyes were vivid and lively. He wore his hair just long enough to cover his ears, and he showed few whiskers, and these were dark and sparse.

Ordinarily he dressed simply in a cloth headdress shaped like a diadem, a cotton mantle across his shoulders, and a waistband with an ornamental breech clout. For events of state, his wardrobe provided a wonderful variety of robes, jewels and ornaments. Aztec history noted fifty-four different capes of the most marvellous beauty—feathered in every gradation of color with plumage from hummingbird, parrot, duck, eagle, and some bordered with formal designs of eyes, others bearing flower, animal or bird images, and many jewelled. He had thirteen breech clouts of ceremony, each different in ornamentation, and all showing such variety as designs of foliage, butterflies, simple stripes, in embroidery, and some bearing the empowering likenesses of eagles or ocelots. The two great warrior clans of the kingdom were those of the eagle and the ocelot, and warriors—including the ruler—went clothed from head to foot in imitation of their chosen animal persons. The warrior's head was revealed through the open beaks of the eagle, or the wide snarling maw of the great fighter cat.

When he danced, the ruler was able to present himself in any number of magnificent combinations of costume and jewel, while his drummers, with two-toned drums and the long ground drum, gave the beat with rubber hammers. His jewels included golden ornaments for the lip—pendants or labrets—and nose rods, ear pendants, necklaces, brassards, calf bands, and head bands. But again it was the plumage of the rarest and most brilliantly colored birds which gave the highest interest to the costume, and when the gesture of head, arm or hand was elongated and made a thing of the air by feathers, a union of the elements of earth, air and fire seemed to result. One headdress of the Emperor—the fan crown of green, blue, red and brown feathers studded with gold— stretched from side to side as wide as his extended arms could reach. If wearing this waving splendor he should make an inclination or turn his head, the simple gesture was magnified into a scale which could only seem significant.

When fully costumed for worship, or dance, or war, the Aztec lord resembled a creation of formal magnificence, with hardly a suggestion anywhere of the human figure within all the panoply except for the movement it could provide. The impersonator of reverence, or delight, or death-giving terror became something quite other than his usual small-figured, earth-colored, embodied self. So in evident strangeness and splendor, he rose above the mortal certainty and limited condition of a man and presented himself to the view of other men and of women as an elaborately shaped edifice of symbol and power. Only within the flaring jaws of eagle, serpent or ocelot might his familiar and fallible humanity be observed— for there in deep shadow cast by his headdress was his small heart-shaped face with its color of smooth clay and its generously chiselled lips and its brilliant eyes set like black stones in white water, through which spoke his familiar human belief, desire and will.

To amuse the Emperor his courtiers arranged ball games for him to watch—there were many ball courts in the city. Everyone placed bets on their favorite teams, and the stakes were golden ornaments and jewels. He sometimes sang, and at other times, others sang to him, and recited proverbs to him, and told him pleasantries. When he moved about, his chamberlains preceded him making his way, and no people were permitted to come out of their houses to see him, and none could face him. With his gentlemen he practiced target shooting with bow and arrow or sling, and on occasion wonderful acrobats and jugglers performed for him. Their tricks were "laughable and marvellous." One of their best was this—a man would lie on his back, and with the soles of his bare feet roll a "thick, round log," making it dance in the air. The suite included dwarfs, hunchbacks, noteworthy cripples, and uncounted servants. In the palace menagerie were eagles, ocelots, wolves, mountain cats and all kinds of birds. When he gave audience the Emperor sat upon a low, wide throne with a high back rest, which stood upon a mat, both covered with the fur of the ocelot, the coyote, the mountain lion, or the wolf.

For breakfast the Emperor Montezuma ate no meat, but only a few peppers hot enough to make a Spaniard gasp. His favorite drink was made from cacao, which he took from a gold cup, and which he said gave him "power over women."

His heavy meal brought him "tidbits" cooked up out of chicken, turkey, pheasant, partridge, quail, duck, venison, wild pig, marsh birds, pigeons, hares, rabbits and the most tender fleshy parts of young boys. When he dined, he sat in privacy behind a golden screen put in front of him by his attendants. The soldiers found themselves becoming fond of him, none more so than the Captain General, despite treason and idolatry and a taste for stewed boy.

A system of connected lakes reaching about forty miles from north to south and almost twenty miles from east to west at the widest part lay in the central flats of the great valley of Mexico. Towns and villages dotted the shores and the approaches to the lakes. In the center of the western reach of the lake waters stood the city of Mexico on its low island. Once a town of clay, it had arisen, as the Aztecs said, from among rushes and reeds. Under the Emperor Montezuma I it was transformed during the fifteenth century into a city of stone—palaces, temples, houses, gardens. The lake where the city stood held bitter salt water where no fish could live. The lakes to the east and south were full of fish and sweet water, and sweet water was carried into the city by aqueducts that came along the causeway from the south.

Reaching the island, the city's causeways became streets, as the waters of the lake became canals. In a dense network, streets and canals laced the island. Canoes entered the city, in a lively traffic which went on between the far shores of the lake and the island. A map drawn for the Captain General and published for the first time at Nuremberg in a Latin edition of his letters to Charles V showed clusters of houses separated by canals, and the whole lapped about by the lake. To the east, basketwork weirs saved the fresh water fish from entering the brackish lake of the city.

The army was quartered in houses near the Emperor's private house in the southwest water-bound blocks of the capital. Roadways, built up and level, led to the central streets, which in turn ran to the center of the city, where the great ceremonial plaza made an open square.

This was a sight of formidable splendor for the army. Thick, crenellated walls enclosed it, with pillared gateways like classic pavilions in the centers of all four sides. Each side of the great square was about a quarter of a mile long. In its great space open to the sun stood sixteen principal buildings, of which ten were temples to the gods. These, except for one, which was cylindrical, were pyramidal in design. All were constructed of massive masonry, plastered over in a pale shell color, and each was placed in harmonious order among the others. At one side of the square stretched the long, low, official palace of the Emperor, with a pillared façade. He was again in residence there. Ball courts were placed among the buildings, and a ring where gladiators fought. The square was paved with blocks of stone. If it had splendor, it had also a vast bleakness about it, and the soldiers saw various of its details with growing horror.

Chief among the temples was one with two altars at its apex. The pyramid rose fourteen hundred steps high, with parallel flights of steps on its front, leading to the two altars above. It was large enough to hold a town of five hundred people within its heavy walls. Large chambers and halls housed the priests, and it was ornamented with "quite forty towers very high and well-worked," as the Captain General remarked. Of these, the highest was "higher than the tower of the great church at Seville." At the top, shouldering above the altars, stood smaller buildings which housed the idols who must be fed with death, on behalf of the Sun, for if the Sun were not fed with his own blood which daily he warmed in living creatures on the earth, he would die, and if he should die, so would the earth and all upon it. Sky and earth were bound in mystical union by the god which was a feathered serpent, Quetzalcoatl, whose human form the Captain General was supposed to represent, either in his own person, or that of his king beyond the sunrise. The use of lovely plumage from all sorts of birds in costume and ornament reflected the sky and its free life; the use of the serpent in sacred symbol reflected the earth and its power of death which struck all living things. Born of serpent and bird, the sculpture of the palaces and temples, marvellously wrought, showed forth every variation of feathers, claws, fangs, coils, rattles, and scales. Three sides of the principal temple pyramid in the great square of Mexico were studded in a close regular design with projecting heads of serpents, hugely enlarged, with jaws open and fangs ready, fashioned from pitted rock, and at the base of the pyramid, as if emerging from the darkest dread of earth, huge stone serpents reached outward along the ground.

Death was everywhere in the temples, for sacrifice was made not only for its own sake, but lives were offered also as punishment. Death was the penalty for anyone, for example, who without official permission dared to wear a tunic that reached below the knee, or who might trespass into a forbidden room of the palace, or who having become rich in the marketplace behaved proudly, or who while performing a ritual dance made a false step.

There was more to discover—much of it delightful—in the capital city of three hundred thousand people. It was remarkable, thought the Captain General, that in spite of the fact that though of course they were not "possessed of reason," so much of the daily life of the Mexicans "was almost the same manner of living as in Spain." He saw gardens of flowers in patios and on flat roof terraces, and in the Emperor's palace the aviary contained every kind of bird, "from eagles to the tiniest." If these were pets, they were also useful in a more direct way, for at the proper seasons their plumages were stripped from them by artisans to be used in making the wonderfully sumptuous robes of ruler, courtier and priest.

In their own quarters the soldiers discovered a greater curiosity. Seeing a freshly mortared and limed place in the wall of one of their rooms, they chipped away at it until they opened a door that had lately been sealed. Within they found treasure—jewels, bars and plates of gold, fabrics and the rest. It was good to know that this was there, but, on order of their commander, they left it there for the present, and sealed it all up again.

Seeing more of their new place, the soldiers observed Indian merchants in the large market in the northwest quarter of the city where seventy thousand people, as they guessed, came and went daily. Of first interest to them was to see how gold was used. Just as it came in grains from the mines, gold was poured into goose quills which being transparent showed how much gold each contained. The length and thickness of the quills determined value.

Elsewhere in the market, they passed along aisles where every kind of thing to buy was laid out in orderly displays. Lapidaries showed their stones, which they cut and then polished with a piece of fine cane to make them shine. Jewels of cast metals—gold, silver—showed designs of shrimps, shells, blossoms. Feather workers exhibited their stocks of "fine green feathers, chili-green feathers, those curved at the tip." There were capes to buy, ornamented in many different designs, including "those painted with bloodied faces." Food merchants sold cacao, chocolate, maize, grains, beans, amaranth seeds, gourd seeds, tortillas, tamales made with minced meat of frogs, tadpoles, rabbits, gophers—"tasty, very tasty, very well made, always tasty, savory, of pleasing odor," bread, corn meal, fruit. Craftsmen brought their creations to the market—objects of wood, metal, clay, stone. Slave sellers, who were called "bathers of slaves," hawked their wares, and among the great throng of shoppers, which contained noblemen and noblewomen, physicians, scribes, singers, and woodsmen, the soldiers encountered also those who sold damnation, like the harlot, who was described in her typical character by Aztec tradition. She was "an evil young woman or an evil old woman, besotted, drunk. . . . She consumes her inner substance—a brazen, a proud, a dissolute woman of debauched life; a fraud—gaudy, fastidious, vain, petty . . . of itching buttocks. She parades; she moves lasciviously; she is pompous. Wheresoever she seduces, howsoever she sets her heart on one, she brings him to ruin." The soldiers in their first days there learned all they could of their new city. If much was beautiful and strange, much was alien and troubling.

One day the Emperor took the Captain General and his staff to see the great pyramid where the sacrificial rooms were clotted thick with dried blood. The walls and floors gave off a stench worse than anything "in the slaughter houses of Castile." The war god was covered with gold and cut jewels and pearls stuck on with gum. His face was broad and his eyes were monstrous. About his form were coiled "great snakes made of gold and precious stones." He held a bow in one hand and arrows in another. Beside him stood a smaller idol representing his page and before him rose the fumes of copal incense and the hearts, still burning, of three men who had been given to him on that very day. The gods of the underworld and of planting and flowering were in other altars. The soldiers "could not get out of there fast enough," for the stench.

In the temple the soldiers saw a tremendous drum, so huge that its sound could be heard miles away at the lake shores. Its drumheads were made from the skins of the largest snakes of the jungles, and when struck it gave forth a sound "as dismal as an instrument from hell."

The Captain General turned to the Emperor and lightly said that he was amazed how the Emperor could not see that these idols were evil—devils, actually.

"Do something for me," said the Captain General, "let us put a cross on top of this tower, and in the room of the idols, we will put up an image of Our Lady"—the Emperor had seen it—"and you will see how afraid of it these idols will be, who have deceived you."

At once the Emperor's humor changed, and the priests with him "looked hostile."

"If I had thought you would insult my gods, I would not have shown them to you," he said angrily. "Please do not say another word to dishonor them."

The Captain General smiled and said he thought it was time for them all to leave. The Emperor agreed, but said that he must remain and make offerings to "atone for the great sin he had committed" in bringing the strangers there to speak ill of his gods. The Captain General summoned all his courtesy.

"If it is really like that, forgive me, sir."

In the temple they saw pits where serpents—including rattlesnakes, "worst of all—" and wild animals were kept to be fed on the dismembered bodies of sacrificial victims. "When the tigers and lions roared," shuddered the Spanish chronicler, "and the jackals and foxes howled, and the snakes hissed, it was horrible to hear; it seemed like hell."

It was of the first importance to have the protection of Heaven in such surroundings, and within two days of their arrival, the soldiers put up a chapel in front of their quarters to their patron Saint James of Compostela with the holy cross on top of it and there heard Mass and said their prayers.

xi.

THE CAPTIVE

FOUR DAYS AFTER THAT—November fourteenth, 1519—four captains and twelve soldiers who were in the confidence of the Captain General asked him to a private meeting in the chapel of Saint James. When he came, they spoke earnestly with him for an hour. They said,

Look at the trap they were in. The whole city was like a fortress. Just look at the bridges and causeways to see what a net held them. They said,

Remember the warnings of their Indian allies that what Montezuma meant to do was to let the soldiers enter the city and then in his own time kill them. All he had to do was to hold back their food and supplies, and raise the bridges, and he would render them helpless. If their Indian allies on the far shores should want to help them, how could they, with the lake to halt them? In the last day or two the temper of the court servants had changed. Bringing food to the soldiers, they were now insolent. Other Mexicans "seemed less willing the last two days."

The Captain General listened gravely to his captains and soldiers. They said,

If they valued their lives, for they believed death "was staring them in the face," and never mind all the treasure of Mexico until they had saved themselves, they should seize the Emperor and hold him. Holding him, they would control the highest authority in Mexico, and so be safe.

"Do not think, gentlemen," said the Captain General, "that I am asleep or that I do not share your anxiety. But how can we seize such a great king in his palace, surrounded by warriors and guards?"

The captains spoke up. One of them was Pedro de Alvarado, who "was extremely fine in body and movements, in deeds and in presence, and always seemed to be laughing," as a comrade saw him. They said,

The Emperor should be persuaded to leave his palace to pay them a visit in their quarters, and once there, he should be told he was a prisoner, and if he gave an alarm, he should be killed. If the Captain General would not do it, his officers would ask his permission to do it themselves.

He considered all they said. He reflected that Spaniards by nature were "somewhat edgy and demanding," and if any of them did anything suddenly to irritate the Emperor, he had the power to so do them "such injury" that "there would remain no recollection" of them. The Captain General made his decision. The plan would be carried out the next day. All night long the soldiers prayed that it would succeed to the glory of God.

If they needed it, they had further reason the next morning to do what they plotted. A second message came from the coast—the wounded chief magistrate and six soldiers, and a horse, had died at Vera Cruz after their return from Almería, and so had many Indian allies. At once other Indian allies there turned against the garrison—all this again on orders from the Emperor. The Captain General now had something to discuss with him—grimly, if need be.

He ordered the cross streets guarded, and taking five captains, the interpreters and the chronicler, he went to the palace.

After an exchange of pleasantries, during which the Emperor gave his visitors gifts of gold and young women, including one of his own daughters, the Captain General said,

"I have learned what has happened at Almería and about the Spaniards who were killed there"—and went on to describe it. He added that he had been told that all this was done on the orders of the Emperor, but he could not bring himself to believe it. He said he thought the Emperor should send for the chieftain who had done the treachery, which he claimed was done on Montezuma's orders, and punish him.

The Emperor's response was swift. To prove himself blameless he took his imperial carved stone seal from his wrist and gave it to an officer, ordering him to go to Almería and bring back as prisoners the guilty chieftain and all others who had murdered Spaniards.

"I am very grateful"—the Captain General thanked the Emperor for his promptness in helping to bring to account the murderers and establish the truth. Until this should be completed, "it remained only" that the Emperor should come with him and stay in the Spanish quarters "until the truth was established that he was blameless." He must not "feel pained at this." He urged him to "come quietly and without making trouble." But if the Emperor should "cry out, or make any disturbance," said the Captain General, "my captains will kill you, for I have brought them along for no other purpose."

The Emperor "was horrified." His protests and the replies of the Captain General consumed half an hour; and then, on word from Doña Marina who gently advised him to agree, he left his palace for captivity in the fortified house of the Spaniards. His litter carriers were in tears.

Later when his lords followed to ask why he was there, he replied that he "was amusing himself by spending a few days there . . . of his own free will," and sent for his women, his baths, and twenty courtiers to be with him. There he conducted the government of Mexico, while his chief nobles "hid themselves and took refuge," said the Aztec history. "They abandoned him in desperation."

In fifteen days, the messengers of the seal brought back the Indian captains who had attacked the Spaniards at Almería. They confessed and confirmed that the Emperor had ordered their action. The Captain General sent this news to the Emperor who could no longer explain it away. He deserved punishment according to Spanish law. Yet the Captain General, as the chronicler saw, "was so fond of Montezuma that he would die himself rather than see the guilt fall on Montezuma." Immediately the Indian captains were ordered to be burned to death in front of the Emperor's palace by command of the Captain General. To prevent "any difficulty" during their execution, he ordered Montezuma to be put in chains. "When these were put on he cried out with rage, and if he was frightened before, he was much more so now."

The execution was carried out without causing any public disturbance, and as soon as it was over, the Captain General went himself to remove the Emperor's shackles, and "spoke so affectionately" to him that his anger vanished. Offered his freedom now, the Emperor refused it, to prevent revolts by those of his people who wished to avenge his captivity by destroying the Spanish garrison. He told them that the war god had instructed him to remain a prisoner.

"No wonder, Lord Montezuma," said the Captain General, throwing his arms about the Emperor, "that I love you as I do myself."

When word of the execution spread through Mexico, the towns were once again awed into submission, and "once again the garrison at Vera Cruz were well served."

To keep the Emperor from pining in his captivity, the Captain General joined him in a game of little gold pellets and slabs which they tossed at a mark, while Captain de Alvarado kept score for his commander, and cheated, and was caught at it by the Emperor, which made everyone laugh, "because Pedro de Alvarado, though he was handsome and well mannered, was spoiled and talked too much." In another diversion, the Emperor, under heavy guard which included all four bronze falconets with their guncrews, was taken for a sail on the lake in one of the brigantines. Under a brilliant canopy he sailed to a sacred island to hunt, "killed all the deer, hare and rabbits he wanted to," and returned to the city to a cannon salute, which delighted him.

But the lesser kings of outer provinces were enraged to see their overlord content in captivity. One—his nephew—proposed to invade the city and destroy the strangers. His uncle, he said, was "an old hen," to submit so placidly to them. Revolts flared, but under persuasion by the Captain General the Emperor put them down, with the unruly kings in chains. The Captain General, with an air of coming to the point, was now able to turn his energies to gain peaceable possession of all the treasure of Mexico.

xii.

TREASURE AND RETREAT

THE EMPEROR was agreeable. He summoned all his subordinate lords and in the presence of the Spaniards, told them that his gods had given him orders to swear allegiance and pay tribute to the King who had sent the strangers here. He recalled again the ancient tradition of the Mexicans, and how they must one day give themselves back to their progenitor who remained where the sun rose. He reminded them that he was their overlord, and that they must obey him. He now commanded them to acknowledge their submission to the Spanish King, and to yield up tribute of their treasures.

Speaking of these things, the Emperor wept "the greatest tears," wrote the Captain General to Charles V, "and with the greatest sighs a man can give vent to." His chieftains wept with him, and even the Spaniards felt "great compassion" for him. "One soldier," said the Spanish chronicler, "cried as much as Montezuma."

But the affecting scene did not imperil the Spanish sense of legal form. With the Captain General was his royal notary, who duly recorded the Emperor's words in which he ceded sovereignty and treasure to the Spanish Crown. Promptly the Captain General sent officers to the provinces to collect tribute, and supervise the mining of gold, and found towns in the Spanish pattern. The Emperor knew—he knew all they did—that the Spaniards had opened his sealed room and had closed it again with its contents intact. He now ordered the room opened again, and gave all it contained to the Captain General—objects worth "more than six hundred thousand gold dollars" which the soldiers melted down into gold bars "three fingers wide."

Here was what they had come for, and the men in ranks

licked their chops over their expected shares. First set apart, of course, was the King's royal fifth. For himself, the Captain General reserved another fifth. Another must go, he decreed, to pay for the expedition. And then, what else: yes: the chaplains and the officers and the cavalrymen and the cross-bowmen, who had special expenses in their branches of service—these must have extra recompense. In the end, "with other trickeries," there was so little left to divide among the common soldiers that many of them refused in contempt what was offered. Those who took it went gambling with cards made by a soldier from the skins of drumheads, "very good and as well painted as the real ones." Officers ordered Mexican goldsmiths to make them great golden chains to wear across their breasts, and the Captain General commissioned a grand table service. To grumbling soldiers, he spoke "honeyed words," scoffing at the treasure so far taken—it was "but a whiff of air," compared to what was coming. All "very well expressed," it left them unconvinced but there was little they could do.

Proceeding with his program for the Mexicans the Captain General next took away their gods. He wrote to his King.

"The principal idols, in which they have the most faith and belief, I overturned from their seats and rolled them down the stairs, and I had the chapels where they kept them, cleansed, for they were full of blood from the sacrifices. And I then set up images of Our Lady and other Saints in them. This grieved Montezuma and the natives not a little."

It was a restrained statement of the effect of his orders and acts against the blood rituals of the Aztecs. If they submitted in tears to his demand for gold, they could not so simply accept the loss of their gods. Their gods, in fact, soon told them that the Spaniards must all be killed. For himself, the Emperor complied with the commands of his jailor, and even ordered his cooks not to feed him any more boy. But he could not calm away the anguished fury of his people, and the day came when he must warn the Captain General "with the greatest urgency."

Leave, he said, or be killed. There could be no doubt about his earnestness.

The sense of peril returned sharply to the Spaniards. From lords and masters they were in an hour turned into men looking desperately about for safe departure. The Captain General "sincerely thanked Montezuma for the warning," but he said he was troubled about two aspects of what had to be done.

And these were?

These were that first, he and his soldiers "had no ships in which to leave."

And the other?

The other was that when he left, he would have to take Montezuma with him "so that our great Emperor might see him."

Must this truly be?—Montezuma became "more sorrowful than ever" on hearing that he would be taken away.

Yes—and now, said the Captain General, let the Emperor command his people to withhold their attack until the Spaniards could build three ships at the coast, and to make this possible, let Mexican carpenters be sent to help the Spanish shipwrights at Vera Cruz construct the fleet. In the port there was all that was needed—iron, tackle, tow, pitch, blacksmiths and caulkers.

Urgency entered all. The carpenters were sent, the outraged public were told that their gods ordered them to keep the peace and let the strangers depart. The gods were appeased with sacrifices, though "not by the killing of men." The Emperor's page wept all day long. At Vera Cruz, "in the sand dunes," the keels were laid down in the ways, and the work was pressed, while couriers travelled between the harbor and the inland headquarters.

In the capital the soldiers "suffered great anguish" waiting for an attack to come. Their allies from Tlaxcala assured them it might come at any moment. Doña Marina heard this everywhere, too. The guard on the Emperor, their hostage and shield, was heavily increased. The soldiers never laid down their arms or armor. They slept in their steel. Their beds were made of straw on grass mats over a piece of cloth. The cavalry horses were kept saddled and bridled and armored all day long. Every man had guard duty. Hardship was the soldier's daily lot, and he could meet it with a grumble or two. But what was unbearable was uncertainty, and waiting was worse than dying. One soldier was used to wakefulness. "I can sleep only for a short time at night for I have to get up and look at the sky and the stars and walk a little in the night dew without putting on a cap or hat, and thank God this does me no harm, for it is a habit I have."

To such peaceful enjoyments were now added other concerns. What strange horrors were preparing in those square towers under the strong Mexican moonlight, and what charnel fires were readying to send up again the smoke of burning hearts? At night, in the quiet of the vast valley, the soldiers looked sharply aside at the least sound, and to listen better, they shortened their breath.

xiii.

More News from the Coast

AND THEN, SUDDENLY, just at this time of held breath and precarious future, delivery and power seemed at hand from an unexpected quarter.

The Captain General heard from the coast that first one ship, and then a great fleet, had come to Vera Cruz, which surely must be reinforcements for him in his danger. The same news came to Montezuma, who concealed his knowledge of it until the Captain General called on him and found him looking "very cheerful," and commented upon this. The Emperor then showed him pictures of the fleet painted on cloth by his Mexican messengers, and said,

"I thought you must have come to tell me the news, as now you will not have to build ships. Because you did not tell me, I was annoyed, but then I was pleased at the arrival of your brothers, for now you can all return to Castile without further words."

It was clear that each had known and withheld from the other the news of the fleet. Soon everyone knew it, and the soldiers broke into rejoicings at their delivery, and the cavalrymen dashed about on their horses, "firing off shots."

But what the soldiers did not know, which the Captain General knew by now, was that the fleet had come from Cuba to seize and punish him with death, and arrest all the others, by order of Governor Velásquez. Their joy died away when they all heard this. But if they still thought they might go home with the new fleet to escape present dangers, no matter what should happen to the Captain General, he made them a speech and once again bound them to his side with his power of the word, and with gifts of gold, and with promises for the future—though one soldier thought, as to the gold, that he was only receiving his due share of the loot.

Now they learned more of the new fleet which had come to port at Vera Cruz on April twenty-third, 1520. There were eighteen ships, twenty cannon, with much ammunition, two gunners, eighty horsemen, ninety crossbowmen, seventy musketeers—in all, with the infantry, fourteen hundred soldiers. Their arrival was proof of the fury of Governor Velásquez at the continued insubordination of the Captain General, in particular at his having sent his treasure ship direct to the King in Spain rather than to the Governor at Santiago de Cuba.

The expedition was commanded by Pánfilo de Narváez, who on landing entered into secret negotiations with Montezuma against the Captain General. Narváez at the coast received the usual golden presents and in return sent the Emperor harmful reports about the Captain General. Three soldiers of the capital garrison ran away to the new Spanish enemy and reported all the possessions the Captain General had won since arriving in Mexico, and how weak the fort was at Vera Cruz, and how the Mexican lords were ready to destroy the invaders in the capital. It was all balm to Narváez, who sent couriers to demand the surrender of the fort at the sea, and meanwhile built a gallows on a hill where, he said, he would hang the insubordinate Captain General and his followers.

But his messengers to the loyal Vera Cruz fort were trussed up in net hammocks "like sinful souls" and sent as prisoners to the Captain General, who at once set out to dazzle them, for he could use them to advantage. Ordering their release, he heavied them down with rich gifts—"for gifts break rocks"—and sent them back to preach desertion to their own comrades, who must abandon Narváez and join the real power of New Spain. This of course was the Captain General himself, who served the King, and would make them rich, while Narváez—a miser as all knew—would be driven off in defeat.

And soon enough, leaving Alvarado in command at the capital, with added guards over Montezuma, the Captain General, taking two hundred sixty-six soldiers, including drummer and fifer, marched to meet Narváez at the coast.

At the Captain General neared them, the captains from Cuba made sport of his forces, saying he commanded only "three cats," and spoke of him as "this nonentity of a little

Cortés," though one "very learned" gentleman in the expedition against the Captain General had the courage to describe him as "a good servant of the King," who should not be called a traitor. For this he was thrown in prison by Narváez. His end was superbly Spanish. Being "very noble, he died from vexation within four days."

On the march, the Captain General sent letters to Narváez offering negotiations. Narváez returned messengers with words of defiance, who were at once taken into camp as new allies of the Captain General, for he would promote them in rank and make them rich if they would return to their own army and weaken it with pledges of honor and wealth from the Captain General. It was clear that battle must be the only outcome.

Though they knew they were going into battle outnumbered five to one, and "must be victorious or die," the Captain General's men seemed as delighted to hear it as though they "were going to a wedding or a party." Their commander took them against the camp of Narváez in the rain, at night, with the password "Holy Ghost," for it was the feast day of Pentecost. Darkness was their ally—in it showed "so many fireflies that the men of Narváez thought they were the matches of muskets." The attack was a complete surprise, and by the time the camp cried out, "To arms! To arms! Cortés is coming!", it was too late.

A little after midnight the Captain General led an assault against the quarters of Narváez, which were in a tower. A sentry gave warning. Narváez was armed and waiting with two hundred men on guard and nineteen guns on the stairs leading to his lodgings. Even so, the Captain General and his suite stormed up the stairs so fast that only one gun was touched with a hot coal, and even this, "by God's will," as the Captain General told the King, "did not go off . . . Although asked many times to yield themselves to Your Highness, the men with Narváez surrendered only when we set fire to the tower." In the flame and smoke there were skirmishes, and then suddenly in other reaches of the battle the soldiers heard Pánfilo de Narváez give a cry, and knew their victory was made.

"Holy Mary," he shouted, "help me! They have killed me and put out my eye!"

The fight died off in the steaming night. The Captain General had lost only two men. The army of Narváez now belonged to him, a sovereign mercy.

"For I assure Your Majesty," he told the King, "that if God had not mysteriously intervened, and had Narváez been victorious, it would have been the greatest injury which Spaniards had done to one another for a long time past."

The Captain General went the rounds of the wounded and came upon Narváez, who said to him,

"Captain Cortés, you must consider this a great victory that you have won over me, including my capture."

The Captain General scorned to yield his victim even this satisfaction.

"I thank God and my valiant comrades for their part in it," he said, "but to defeat and capture you is one of the least important things I have done in New Spain."

When daylight came the last forces of Narváez rode in from patrols, and their captains came to kiss the hand of the Captain General. He received them like a king, seated in an armchair, wearing a great orange-colored mantle over his armor, and with his troops about him. He was cheerful—addressed with grace those who gave him submissions, and paid them compliments. He thanked his Indian allies for their help, and then ordered all eighteen of the ships of the fleet lying off the beaches to be stripped of their sails, rudders and compasses, so that no one could sail away to Cuba with news for Governor Velásquez.

But there was little time to savor new successes.

"At this moment," said the Spanish chronicler, "the news came that Mexico was in revolt and that Pedro de Alvarado was besieged in his fortress and quarters and that they had set fire to it in two places, killing seven and leaving many wounded."

The messenger said that Alvarado had ordered an attack upon Indians dancing in honor of their gods before the great pyramid temple in the city, and that the uprising had followed.

There was nothing for it but go at once to the rescue. Reviewing his forces after assigning a strong garrison to Vera Cruz, the Captain General counted seventy horsemen and five hundred infantry. And then, as he wrote to the King,

"I started in all haste with these troops for the capital."

xiv.

THE FEAST OF
UITZILOPOCHTLI

IN COMMAND at the capital during the absence of the Captain
General, Pedro de Alvarado, said the Aztec history, "wished
to marvel at and see how and in what manner" the great feast
of the god Uitzilopochtli was celebrated by the Mexicans.

The Emperor was by now serenely compliant. From his
luxurious captivity he issued orders that all preparations for
the great dance be completed, and his people obeyed. For a
year certain votaries had observed ritual fasting, and now the
women who were purified by such privation ground up the
amaranth seed and the prickly poppy with which to make
masses of dough. With this dough, then, spreading it on a
skeleton of twigs, they fashioned an image of the god, and
through many stages of refinement brought it to a clothed
and painted and jewelled likeness of Uitzilopochtli. He wore
turquoise mosaic ear plugs in the shape of serpents, and a
hummingbird headdress disguise, and a cape of cactus thorns
ornamented with eagle down. Skulls and bones were part of
his finery, and painted representations of the limbs and penes
of men. Paper scrolls, banners and weapons completed his
costume, with a shield of basketwork. Spanish soldiers in full
armament came to stare at the women who ground the seed
and fashioned his presence.

At dawn, the figure was erected and exposed in the great
temple courtyard, and from all quarters of the city thronged
the young Aztec men of prowess who were eager to enact the
feast of the god, "and exhibit proudly, and demonstrate it to
the Spaniards."

Chanting and dancing began, and "the song roared," and
when the ritual, using a great throng of priests and warriors
in dance and song, reached its fullness, Spanish foot soldiers,
armored and armed, sprang from three of the four gates in
the great wall and fell upon the celebrants. First they destroyed the ceremonial drummer, cutting off his hands with a

sword stroke, and then his head, and then thrust him through many times with lances. They then attacked the dancers, cutting and stabbing, killing many on the spot, and leaving others to run away. Many a Mexican could "only drag his entrails like something raw, as he tried to flee." Some who escaped took refuge within the temples. One who lay on the ground, if he stirred, the soldiers killed with a stroke. The army spread over the vast plaza, searching for victims.

Across the city rose a war cry from the people. Striking their mouths with their palms and shouting aloft their rage and grief, they called,

"Chieftains! Mexicans! Hurry here! Bring all battle staffs, shields, and arrows! Come! Hurry! Already chieftains lie dead, destroyed, shattered! O Mexicans, chieftains!"

The city responded. Warriors swarmed from the streets and canals to the open plaza, and there gave battle to their attackers, loosing barbed javelins, "spears, and tridents," and "darts with broad, obsidian points . . . It was as if," said the Aztecs, recalling the javelin shafts, "as if a mass of deep yellow reeds spread over the Spaniards."

The Spaniards returned gunfire and spear flights, and fought their way to their fortified houses, and there found themselves besieged. The mothers and fathers of warriors killed in the surprise attack wept aloud and burned the bodies of their sons. At sundown, the Emperor ordered a courtier to make an appeal in his name from the rooftop of his house.

"Let the Mexicans hear!" he declaimed. "We are not the equals of the Spaniards! Abandon the battle! May the strife cease!"—and the people said the Emperor spoke so only because he was the prisoner of the Spaniards. Their feeling arose against him, and him who was in times past almost a god they now called "Fool!", and a heavy Mexican guard was placed about the headquarters of Alvarado and the garrison quarters. Anyone seen trying to enter the army's houses had his brains knocked out or was stoned to death on the spot. The Mexicans worked on the canals all about the fortified houses—"the canals were dredged, widened, deepened, and made precipitous . . . dangerous and difficult. And on the roads, in various places, they erected barriers, laid walls, and placed ramparts. Passages between houses were made dangerous." For twenty-three days the siege was maintained, and then the people heard that the Captain General, with a greatly reinforced command, was hurrying from the seacoast to the city which Captain Alvarado had all but lost for him.

xv.

REVOLT

BY FORCED marches, the Captain General, with his men, caked
so thickly with the white dust of Mexico upon their unwiped
sweat that "earth flaked off" them, crossed Mexico inland
again. An ominous air hung over his way—the towns and
roads were deserted. No chieftains came out to greet him. All
that, however, he assured his new recruits from the Narváez
army, would be different at the capital, as they would see.
There he would be greeted with gold, feathers and speeches.

But to his humiliation and rage, here too all was empty
until he reached his old quarters and rejoined his garrison.

There when the Emperor came to greet him in the patio,
he coldly turned away, and Montezuma retreated to his rooms
"very sad and thoughtful."

What had caused the revolt?

The Captain General grimly questioned Captain de Alvarado, who explained, giving several reasons—perhaps too
many.

The Mexicans had attacked because they wanted to free the
Emperor; and because the gods ordered them to punish the
Spaniards for putting up the Madonna and the Cross; and because the Spaniards did not depart now that they had ships,
though they had promised to do so; and because it would be
wise to kill Alvarado and the garrison before the Captain
General should return with more soldiers; and because—.

Why had Alvarado attacked the Mexicans during their
dances?

Because several Mexicans (including a priest) told him that
when they had finished dancing they were "positively" going
to attack him.

"But they have told me," said the Captain General, "that
you gave permission for them to dance."

Yes, that was true, he had given permission, because he
wanted to "take them off guard," to attack them before they
could attack him.

"It was all wrong, and a great mistake," raged the Captain General, and added that he wished that Montezuma had escaped. "I have never heard of such a thing," he growled and strode away.

Two lords waited to tell him that the Emperor wanted him to come to him.

Tell him this, roared the Captain General: "You dog, you won't even hold a market, or order food for us all."

"Sir, sir," said four of his captains who listened, "control your anger! Remember all that Montezuma has done for us. If it weren't for him, we'd all be dead and they'd have eaten us. Yes, and remember that he has even given you his daughters!"

"Why should I pay compliments," demanded the Captain General, angrier than ever, "to a dog who negotiated in secret with Narváez, and now won't even see that we are fed?"

"Sir, it seems to us that that is exactly what you ought to do."

The Captain General turned to the Mexican lords and told them harshly to ask the Emperor to order the markets opened at once. If he did not do so, he would soon see what would happen.

The courtiers went to the Emperor and told all they had heard.

They had hardly gone when a soldier, badly wounded, came from a town across the lake to report that all along his road and everywhere in the city Mexicans were gathering fully armed for battle—as witness his two wounds.

The Captain General ordered out a captain and four hundred soldiers to investigate, and to "pacify the Indians without fighting," if possible. The detachment had come only to the middle of the street when, the Captain General wrote, "such a great multitude fell upon us from all sides that neither the roofs nor the houses could be seen for the crowd. They came on with the most frightful yells." The soldiers had to fight their way step by step back into the garrison. The storm so long expected now broke over them with furies that lasted day and night for a week.

By day the soldiers sallied forth to fight in a network of streets, canals and causeways. They put torch to the houses they had to pass, and in their turn the Mexicans burned away one whole side of the Spanish stronghold. What works the soldiers threw up by day the Mexicans destroyed by night, and by night, from the altar platforms of the pyramidal temples, came infernal sounds, amidst watch fires in the sky.

They would stuff themselves, yelled the Mexicans from their reeking platforms, with the soldiers' legs and arms, and their bodies would be thrown to the tigers, lions and snakes, so they could gorge on them, for which purpose they had been starved in their pits for two days. They showered javelins, stones and arrows over the Spanish headquarters, and they shouted their demands for the return of "their great lord Montezuma."

With every dawn the soldiers broke into the streets and always found the bridges drawn away. The Mexicans came on them in such solid crowds that the artillery did not need to aim, but only fire at random into them, and they were so many that even the most ruinous salvo made no difference.

New measures were needed. The Captain General directed the construction of three war engines with housings of wood within which twenty men with muskets, arrows, pikes, axes and iron bars could ride and be protected from attack. A night and a day passed while these were built and street fighting continued. But another measure was coming to mind, and the Captain General proposed it.

It was to ask for peace to permit him "to leave Mexico." The one who should ask it should be the Emperor Montezuma, and the Captain General sent him word by his chaplains to do this.

"What more does he want from me?" cried the Emperor in anguish. "I do not want to live, or to listen to him, because of the fate he has forced upon me." He said he did not want to see the Captain General, or hear any more of his promises and lies.

The chaplains now pleaded with him in all respect, and the Emperor replied that in any case, he could do nothing, for he was no longer the ruler of Mexico. His people had already elevated another to his place—the Lord Cuernavaca of Ixtapalapa—and had already decided not to let any Spaniard leave Mexico alive.

But in the end the Emperor consented to speak from the rooftop of the garrison. When he appeared, shielded by soldiers, the roiling crowds in the street recognized him and the commotion died away. Four of his subjects "reached a place where they were able to talk to Montezuma," and mourned his captivity, and vowed his deliverance, and told how they had all promised the gods not to cease their war until the strangers were all killed.

Their words were overwhelmed by a new shower of stones and javelins from the streets, and the soldiers assigned to shield the Emperor "neglected to do so for a moment," leaving him exposed and helpless. A stone struck his head, another his arm, and a third his leg. He fell without making his plea to his people. Soldiers bore him away to his rooms pitiably hurt. It was the twenty-fifth of June, 1520. The battle must continue.

On the next day the new war engines were launched into the streets, accompanied by four cannon, many archers, and three thousand Indian allies. They gained a bridge, but there the engines were destroyed by a cloud of great stones thrown down from the roofs, and at noon the Captain General took his people back to the garrison "with infinite sorrow."

With this success, the Mexicans crowded upon the great pyramid temple which was near the Spanish quarters. If they could hold it, they would be in a position to destroy the headquarters. Knowing this, the Captain General attacked.

His order of battle disposed the harquebusiers first. They crawled in broken formation up the steep temple steps, firing volleys as they went into the ranks of four thousand Mexicans who kept defense above. From the crest, heavy logs rolled down upon the climbing soldiers. The crossbowmen struggled upward after the harquebusiers, springing their darts. Swordsmen followed, and then the lancers.

After being thrown back three times to the base of the steps, the soldiers fought their way to the summit of the pyramid, where they would rescue the statue of Our Lady which they had left there. Leading the assault, though bearing a wound from the first day of fighting, the Captain General "showed himself to be every inch a man," said the Spanish chronicler.

"Oh, what a fight. Oh, what a battle we had! It was something to see us dripping blood and covered with wounds, and others killed, but it pleased our Lord to let us make our way to the place where we had kept the image of Our Lady."

It was gone—someone said that the Emperor had ordered her to be cared for. They fought until all the Mexican defenders, tumbled down the temple slopes "like black ants," were killed. The Spaniards set fire to the tower, and later, from his own rooftop, the Captain General called out to the

Mexican captains and told them to look about and see how they were already defeated. If they persisted, he would burn their whole city.

They replied that they had taken much damage, but they would never desist, even if twenty-five thousand Indians must die for every Spaniard. They added that they had destroyed all causeways but one, and the soldiers could escape only across water, which all knew to be impossible. If they did not kill all the soldiers, the rest would die of starvation and thirst, and all knew this too. The battle was renewed by day and by night.

On the sixth day, when they "least expected it," said the chronicler, attendants came to say that the Emperor Montezuma was dead. He had refused to eat for days, or to have his hurt attended to, and when the news of his death reached the army, the Captain General "wept for him, and all of our captains and soldiers . . . some as though he had been our father." Ordering some Mexican prisoners to bear the dead body aloft on their shoulders, the Captain General sent the Emperor back to his people, who burned his body on a pyre where flames "rose like tassels of fire."

With the next day the Captain General resolved his plans. Ever since the battles had broken out in the city, the soldiers taken over from the army of Narváez had cursed Cortés for leading them into fire, ruin and death, bitterly wondering why they had ever left their plantations in Cuba only to listen to him. The rest of his forces had little left to fight with.

"All of my company," he wrote the King, "or nearly all, were wounded so badly that they could no longer fight, and they pleaded with me to leave." And, "We could see our death in our eyes," said the chronicler. The Captain General said, "I decided to withdraw that same night." It was the night of June thirtieth, and ever afterward they referred to it as the "Sorrowful Night."

For in the escape which though it began in secret must continue as a running battle over bridge and causeway and far shore, the army lost "over one hundred and fifty men killed, and forty-five mares and horses, and more than two thousand of the Indians who aided us."

They fled by the westward causeway which passed across several small islands and then reached across the open lake until it came to shore about three miles away. As he left the city, the Captain General, worn by fury, exhaustion and grief, paused for a moment at the base of a cypress tree, leaned upon it, and wept.

The pursuit was as furious as the attacks in the city. The great part of the treasure was left behind, and in their running skirmishes, through countrysides to the south where the towns rose against them as they hurried sore and grieving, they thought of what they had won and now had lost. Finally an important Mexican commander was killed and his death abruptly ended the battle of the retreat. And then they saw the mountains of Tlaxcala to the east and rejoiced, for they knew the country, where the people were friendly.

There was good news from the coast—Vera Cruz and its garrison was safe, and the Indian allies faithful. The heat of battle cooled, and the straining hearts slowed down. Wounds began to mend. In spite of those who urged him to hurry to Vera Cruz and so be in a position to escape, the Captain General wrote to the King,

"Fortune is always on the side of the daring . . . and I determined on no account to go to the seaport. Rather, disregarding all difficulty and danger which might offer, I said that I would not abandon this country . . . I was determined to return against the enemy from all possible points, and to take the offensive against them in every way I could."

His old veterans could have expected this, for they knew him well now, and as the chronicler said, "Cortés always had lofty thoughts, and in his ambition to command and rule he wished in every way to copy Alexander of Macedon."

Twenty or thirty miles away from the capital across the lake, the Captain General recovered his energy and his imagination. At the town of Texcoco, near the center of the eastern rim of Lake Texcoco, he set up the shipyards, and there began the construction of a fleet of thirteen brigantines. In the painted records of Aztec artists, these appeared as stocky, two-masted vessels, designed like caravels in miniature, with high sterncastles, and each with a brass fieldpiece mounted straight front in the bows. The return to the capital would depend on coordinated naval and land operations. From the slopes and foothills of the volcano Ixtaccihuatl, which rose eastward of the lake, the Indian workers brought wood, and artisans with the army fashioned what they must out of their metal stores, and always to the west, across the open lake, rested the challenge and the prize.

Ten months after the retreat, having beaten down unrest

in the lesser kingdoms of the mountains and valleys about
the lake system, even to branding rebellious natives in the
cheek, the Captain General was again moving against the
city of Mexico. He came now by land and water.

xvi.

RETURN TO BATTLE

THE FLEET was manned by a total of three hundred crossbowmen, harquebusiers, artillerymen—for all the cannon
were on board—and oarsmen. To reenter by causeway, when
the road should be cleared, he had almost a hundred
cavalry and more than six hundred foot soldiery. He ordered
the land forces into two divisions. All were heavily armored,
body and soul. For body there were helmets, gorgets, greaves,
with quilted cotton padding, and shields. For soul, there was
that faith which gave the familiar act of combat a protection
under glory. A popular war song in the metre of a Christmas
carol spoke for the Spanish soldier in both his need and his
belief:

> Into battle,
> Knighted soldiers in your flower!
> Holy angels in this hour
> Are on earth to give you power!
> Into battle!

> From heaven, flying near
> In their flashing armor clad,
> They call on man and God
> To help our people here!

> Into battle,
> Noble soldiers in your flower!
> Holy angels in this hour
> Are on earth to give you power!
> Into battle!

The Captain General first swept the lake shores, establishing garrisons in the towns from which the causeways

reached to the great city in the center of the lakes. Meeting in skirmish the first sallies of the Mexicans who came forth in canoes each manned by forty warriors, he defeated them. It was clear, as he wrote the King, that "the brigantines held the key to the whole war." He now sent columns marching on the causeways toward the city, guarded by the brigantines which paralleled their course by water.

Near the city they met the Mexicans, who knew well enough that their stronghold was now in a state of siege. They broke the causeways at the city entrances, and if the Captain General landed detachments in the streets he had to order his men to withdraw by nightfall, after burning what they could. Thereafter, he brought battle daily to the gates of the city, and the garrisons of the shore towns fought off continuous attack. The twelve brigantines—one had been laid up as too small to be useful—met swarms of canoes in repeatedly renewed combat. The bow cannon blew terrible destruction upon the canoe fleets. It was late in the month of May and in the clear golden air smoke signals between shore and city united the defenders.

Gradually the Captain General cut off the city from its allies on shore, who tried to supply it by night with food brought in canoes. "There was never a day," said the chronicler, "when the brigantines didn't bring in some captured canoes filled with food, with many Indians hanged from the yardarms." At last, wrote the Captain General, "as we had the enemy completely surrounded and had many friendly warriors, I decided to penetrate into the city as far as possible by causeway, while the brigantines covered our rear on both sides."

With greater numbers than before, he led the penetration and now reached the great market square, which was larger than that of Salamanca. In the main square, once again the soldiers stood on the towers of the great charred temple. In the streets soldiers killed Mexicans with lances, and held the defenders back. Having come so far into the city, the Captain General expected the Mexicans to ask for peace at any moment. But no offer came, and he "inferred two things: first that we should recover little or none of the treasures they had taken from us"—which he had first taken from them —"and the other, that they gave occasion and forced us to destroy them totally." He gave the command to set fires in the square and then through skirmishes retired for the night.

In the following days he continued to probe into the city, but with no evident advance in his position, for he had to fall back at night upon his base camps. At last his captains proposed in council that he lead them in full force to the great market square and there establish a fortified camp and remain, fighting the city from within rather than from without. He was doubtful, he said, whether all his troops would be in favor of the move, with its terrible dangers. His captains pressed him, and in the end he agreed with their strategy. It led swiftly to a disaster.

Attacking the city from the two causeway entrances, south and west, the soldiers met heavy resistance, and the greater of the divisions, under the Captain General, entered a trap. The defenders had bridged a break in the southern causeway with a narrow foot bridge, so loosely made that in places it sagged into the water. The soldiers swarmed across this, and then, instead of pausing to fill in the gap as the Captain General had commanded in general orders, they pressed ahead in the street. There they were overwhelmed with numbers in a wild assault and forced back. The bridge could not take them all in their rush to escape. Spaniards and Indians fell together into the water and the Mexican canoes swept in from the lake on both sides to kill many Spaniards and take many others alive.

"Stop! Stop!" roared the Captain General when he came in his turn to the "wretched bridge," as he called it. But he was not heard. Heedless of himself as he fought, he was taken and held by five Mexican captains as the greatest prize of the battle. He would have been carried off if Cristóbal de Oléa, "a very brave soldier from Old Castile," had not sprung to his aid. Oléa killed four of the Mexicans before he was killed himself. Another soldier helped to free his commander, and others came, and took him "by the arms and pulled him from the mud and water," and finding a horse in the rampaging retreat mounted him on it and sent him safely to the rear. He was wounded in the leg.

On the western causeway the division under Captain Pedro de Alvarado also met defeat at the hands of warriors wearing "beautiful feathered headdresses" and carrying banners. They threw before the soldiers the severed heads of five of their comrades who had been killed in the Captain General's division, and later he was shown by the defenders the heads of four taken from Alvarado's force. Fighting their way back to their camps along the two causeways, the soldiers counted their losses of over seventy soldiers and a thousand Indian allies.

As for soldiers captured, the army could see and hear what befell their lost comrades, who were offered day and night to the blood-hungry gods of the pyramid. Those lost alive numbered so many that it took ten days for the Mexicans to sacrifice them all, beginning with nightfall upon the army's defeat.

The soldiers saw great fires on the pyramid which threw light on the blood rituals. They heard the tremendous snake-skin drum thundering out over the lake, that "cursed drum," with the "most accursed sound . . . like an instrument of demons." With it sounded horn calls from conch shell trumpets, and the shriek of whistles, and the rasp of rattles. They could see priests jerking their way up the temple risers carrying the bodies of captured soldiers, which shone naked and pale amidst the darker people.

Once on the platform before the sanctuary of the idols the naked soldiers were adorned with feather headdresses and given plumed fans to hold and made to dance against the sky in firelight before the waiting gods. When they had danced enough they were taken one by one and thrown on their backs across the narrow stone tables of sacrifice. The soldiers in the distance watched the priest lift his obsidian knife curved like an eagle beak and then saw him open the breast of the soldier so far away from help and pull out his beating heart and offer it to the gods. His body was then kicked down the high steps where "Indian butchers who were waiting below cut off the arms and feet and flayed the skin off" his face. The tender parts were kept to be eaten. The rest was thrown to the animal pit. The flayed face with its beard still on was later dressed "like a glove" and kept for ceremonies. The fires glared and the deathly drums and trumpets sounded until, said the Captain General, "it seemed the very world was sinking." Soldiers watching from their bivouacs on the causeways turned to each other and said,

"Thank God they are not carrying me off today to be sacrificed!"

One said,

"They had already seized me twice to take me to be sacrificed, and it pleased God that I escaped from them, but ever since then I feared death more than ever. Before going into battle a kind of terror gripped me. But then when I went into battle, commending myself to God and His Blessed Mother, the fear left me."

He said his battle prayers soon again, for "it was necessary to show more valor than ever," declared the Captain General.

xvii.

THE CONQUEST

BUT FIRST THE wounded must begin to recover, including the Captain General. His armies were sharply reduced—all his Indian allies except forty had vanished without taking leave. They had heard the defenders proclaim how the gods would cause the complete annihilation of the invaders within a week. Night after night the soldiers were attacked in their camps while the sacrifices continued and the Mexicans shouted that the Spaniards were so evil that even their flesh was corrupt, "bitter as gall," so bitter they could not swallow it. Keeping up a "cheerful" aspect, the Captain General took thought of his problems, one of which was how to avoid wrecking the entire city if he should resume the battle. The city, he thought, was "the most beautiful thing in the world." He sent messengers to propose peace talks, but if the new emperor, Cuauhtémoc—the third after Montezuma—would consider peace, his priests refused. The war must continue.

But the pause of more than a week worked for the soldiers, for their Indian allies presently returned, seeing that the threat of the gods was an empty one. Once again commander of a huge force—in the end it numbered a hundred and fifty thousand—the Captain General renewed his action, and the battles covering ninety-three days began to show an end.

For many days he saw his men repair the causeways. When they could safely pass along them, he led them again into the edges of the city. Now he went slowly, demolishing every house he came to, and pouring the rubble of "adobes and roof beams; door lintels, pillars, and round logs; bundles of reeds" into the "water streets" to make solid roads. Fire brought down houses and forced the people of the city to go deeper into their streets to take refuge in houses already crowded. The siege was tightened and the people began to die off in great numbers. Again the soldiers reached the great square and took the pyramid. From its towers the Captain General showed himself daily to the Mexicans.

"I knew," he stated, "that they would be much vexed to see me mounted on the tower."

After a week of this he planned a great ambush by which he and his horsemen hidden beyond the square drew the Mexicans across the square into the side street. There with their battle cry of "Lord Saint James!" the soldiers fell upon the Mexicans and killed "more than five hundred, all the bravest and most valiant of their principal men." It was a blow that sharply weakened resistance within the city.

And now there was a feeling of fortune in the army, for even as they were running out of powder in all their ammunition dumps, a ship arrived at the seaport with stores which replenished the soldiers' guns. It was the guns and the horses that swept the streets daily of their occupants. It was the blockade maintained by the brigantines that brought starvation to the city. At night the soldiers would come upon Mexicans picking among the ruins to find herbs and roots to eat, and in the morning would see what hunger was when they found scraps of gnawed bark taken from patio trees.

"All the common folk," said the Aztec history, "suffered torments of famine. Many died of hunger." There was no longer fresh water to drink, and drinking the brackish water of the surrounding lake, "people therefore suffered from a blood flux," of which many died. "And all was eaten," said the history, "—lizards and swallows; and maize-straw; and salt-grass." The starving people ate flowers, and animal hides, toasted, baked or burned, and even mud bricks. "Quite calmly," said the Mexicans, "the enemy hemmed us in and contained us."

A day came when the Mexicans had no weapons to use, and another when they were too enfeebled to throw stones. Even so, talk of peace brought only replies asking to die. The dead in the streets were so many that the Captain General said the people had nowhere to stand "save upon the bodies of their own dead." He gave orders to kill no more, but the Indian allies could not be restrained in their lust for blood and plunder, and when they swept into massacre, the suffering and cries of the dying women and children were such that, said the Captain General, "there was none whose heart did not break."

In a gesture which must surely give new strength to themselves and bring terror to their besiegers, the Mexicans chose one of their greatest nobles to be clothed in a wonderful guise—that of the quetzal feather owl—a costume of ceremony which for his own people made him "indeed terrifying," and "truly wonderful." They sent him to the rooftops to be seen by all, and they said the effect on the Spaniards was so fearsome it was "as though a mountain had burst." But the soldiers forced him from the roof, and night fell on stillness. Late at night the Mexicans saw in the sky a "large coal of fire . . . like a coppery wind . . . cracking, snapping, and exploding loudly. It was an omen. Watching, none of the people shouted; none spoke aloud."

When finally the Captain General had taken "over seven-eighths of the city," with all the surviving people crowded in the last houses of a district edged by the lake, he had come through the networks of water streets and little islands and separate house clusters every one of which was a separate obstacle to be fought down. Now he attacked from the streets while the brigantines bombarded from the water. It was the last move of the war.

From the houses, canoes put out in a try at escape. A brigantine swept down upon one of them and captured it as a yellow evening drew over the water. In the canoe was the Emperor Cuauhtémoc. He was taken and brought before the Captain General, and seeing a dagger at his belt, asked that it be used to kill him.

"This lord having been made prisoner," Cortés could tell the King, "the war immediately ceased."

Released by victory, the soldiers looted for gold. Looking for it everywhere, they took hold of people, and ripped away gold objects hidden in the bosoms and skirts of the women, and in the mouths and the breech clouts of the men. Young, beautiful women—"those of light bodies, the fair-skinned ones"—were set aside for uses in love, and some women, to escape this fate, put mud over their faces and rags on their bodies. Strong young men were held, and boys, to become servants and pages, and some were branded with hot iron or initialled with paint in ownership.

When night darkened over the charnel city on August thirteenth, 1521—reckoning by their calendar, the Mexicans

noted that their defeat was made final in the year count of
Three House, on the day of One Serpent—the strife of arms
was silenced and the blood fires were cold. In the waters of
the lake stirred the dead in an illusion of life under breeze
and wave. Death rose from the streets on drafts of sickening
air, until the conquerers "pressed white linen cloths against
their noses as they passed by." Rain fell during the night.

III

OTHER NEW WORLDS

I am the man who brought Your
Majesty more kingdoms than your
father left you towns.

—*Hernando Cortés.*

i.

Faith and Law

NOW THAT THE conquest was completed, what earthly power other than main force had helped the Captain General to achieve it? It was the power he derived from moral certainty vested in the forms of law.

Among the Captain General's most important lieutenants was an officer who observed the acts of conquest as a legal witness and recorder. He was the notary, who represented that portion of the King's power which rested in the law. Battle, conquest and annexation meant nothing unless they were first rooted in proper legal procedure.

Before hostilities, and upon a command from the Captain General, the royal notary would produce a document called the Requirement of 1513 from which he would formally read aloud, in Spanish, to gazing Indians who understood no word of it, those conditions upon which alone the Spanish soldiers could legally offer battle.

The Requirement opened with a brief sketch of the history of the world. It then moved on to a discussion of the papacy, out of which it derived the proper basis for Spanish claims to lands of the New World; for in 1493 Pope Alexander VI had assigned ownership of any lands discovered in the Western hemisphere to Spain and Portugal.

The ritual, abstract to the Indian ear, continued with a demand that the Indians yield themselves to the Spanish Crown and accept the preaching of Christianity. If, legally warned, they should agree, then no hostilities would follow. If, however, hearing all that the royal notary had scrupulously read to them, they should resist, then "with fire and sword" the newcomers would impose their will.

"We shall take you," intoned the royal notary before an army of mystified Indians on a beach where emerald combers broke over coral reefs to die away on white sand, or at the edge of a jungle, or before a town whose roofs were outlined with warriors, "we shall take you and your wives and children, and shall make slaves of them, and as such shall sell and dispose of them, as their Highnesses may command; and we shall take away your goods, and shall do all the harm and damage that we can, as to vassals that do not obey."

Form and justice thus satisfied, the Spaniards waited for submission. If it did not come, commands rang out, fire was put to powder, attack began on the one hand; and on the other, arrows flew in defense. Convinced that their cause was lawful and just the conquering soldiers and their Captain General fought their way to victory in the name of Christ and King. If outrage was often an instrument of conquest, then it was of a kind usual to the times and the measures of war. The virtue of the Spanish cause claimed all, for it was rooted in an authority which in turn drew its analogy from the Divine.

Jesus Christ instituted the papacy in the person of St. Peter and his successors, through whom the Catholic kings of Spain renewed the authority of the crown with the death of each king and the coronation of each heir to the throne. It was an authority unquestioned because to any Christian it was unquestionable; and the conquering lords of Spain and all their followers were Christian. The Captain General, and all who commanded Spanish expeditions in the field, believed in their rights as conquerors and acted under these with a powerful sense of obligation to themselves, their King, and the pontiff. Not to have believed so, and to have acted accordingly, would have seemed irresponsible and must have led to disgrace and demotion and worse.

Power carried with it obligations beyond the satisfaction of him who wielded it. The King was the source of power, and all who served in positions of authority under him did so in his name; but the King himself was responsible to those whom he governed. The parliament of Valladolid in the time of the Captain General declared that "the King is the paid agent of his vassals." At its best, the Spanish government recognized that all the vassals of the Crown were equal before justice and the law. At its worst, the Spanish government used justice and the law to impose vassalage where it did not come voluntarily.

Along with civil submission, the Indians were expected to offer allegiance to the faith of their conquerors. Failing to do so, they might be submitted to conversion by force, as a matter of duty on the part of the Christians—though a commander was more than once advised by his chaplains not to accomplish the salvation of souls by the aid of pain and terror. But the conquerors, wholly believing they brought the greatest of gifts to creatures of God who yet did not know Him, imposed their faith as they imposed their will—in acts of war. The Lord Admiral Christopher Columbus, finding the earthly paradise, "always left a cross set up," wherever he went, and in his rosters of expeditioners was careful to include only those who could qualify for the westward expedition, for, as he wrote, "this was the alpha and omega of the enterprise, that it should be for the increase and glory of the Christian religion and that no one should come to these parts who was not a good Christian."

Faith and law were both, then, extended by the power of Spanish arms; and of these the weapon most expressive of the style of Spain was the sword made of Toledo steel. The blade was the most famous in the world. Its creation was attempted only under certain ideal conditions and every step was marked by ritual blessings.

The iron core of the blade was called its soul, to which veneers of steel were welded in white-hot coals. The work was done only on moonless nights, the better to see the true weld of the red-hot metal, and only on nights when the warm south wind blew, the better to let the steel retain its heat while passed through the air to be plunged into a vat of clear cool water from the Tagus River. "Blessed be the hour in which Christ was born!" sang the apprentice who helped the master, and for just so long as it took to sing this blessing, the blade was immersed the first time. Heated again, it was repeatedly tempered in the water, while the ritual chant provided the proper timing for each immersion—"Holy Mary, who bore Him!" and "Hot is the iron!" and "Good will be this tempering!" and finally, "If it is God's will." In one last firing the blade was brought just to a dull glow, and then while the master held it with tongs, the boy smeared the blade with whole fat from the kidney of a he-goat or a ram. Set in a rack to cool through hours of air, the blade darkened. In daytime it was sharpened and polished, and then if it was to bear a motto, it went to the engraver's bench, where letters were chiselled on the flat bevel to read, perhaps, "For my King" on one, "For my Law," on the other. The basket hilt was then affixed, and the master sword maker sent to the city hall for his metal die and with it punched his device into the blade at its thickest part near the guard. Born of skill and piety, and wielded with style and courage, the Toledo blade was both symbol and weapon in the conquest and government of the captaincy general of New Spain.

ii.

FABLED WORLD

IN THE RIGID primness of their society and its beliefs the Spaniards had a clear point of view from which to stare at the people and places they discovered. All that was different, to the degree of the difference, was marvellous, and in first impressions of the Novo Mondo—a phrase which once held pristine wonder—the marvels seemed those of Paradise. Columbus found his most gentle of people, and heard the chirping of crickets that went on all night, "at which all were delighted," and took pleasure in seeing wild birds living tame in Indian homes, and exclaimed over dogs that never barked.

But beyond immediate vision, other marvels were heard of, and the conquerors nodded in recognition of much that learned historians of the medieval European world had already described. The fountain of youth would surely be found in the New World. El Dorado, the Golden Man, lived there. There were seven enchanted cities in the New World, founded by seven Portuguese bishops who had fled before an Arab invasion of Iberia in the eighth century. St. Ursula and her eleven thousand virgins may well have ended their voyage in the Novo Mondo. There was an island inhabited only by women who were more warlike than men. Giants were known, and pygmies, dragons, griffins, sirens of the sea, trumpet-blowing apes, and every sort of wild man. There was a race of one-eyed men. There was another with the snouts of dogs who when they captured a man cut off his head, castrated him, and drank his blood.

Even after taking America, the conquerors for a time saw her through the eyes of the Old World rumor. In Peru there was a monkey covered with vari-colored feathers and reddish fur which "when it felt like it" could sing like a nightingale or a lark. Natives lived sometimes as long as a hundred and fifty years. Certain natives were blue and had cubic heads. A unicorn was seen in Florida. The Devil lived on a certain island of the West Indies. "America as fantasy" * held power over the ideas of the conquerors as they voyaged and landed and conquered. In turn, their news of America as they found it had limitless effect on the ideas coming to light in the European renaissance.

How swiftly the outline and substance of the Novo Mondo changed and grew. It must seem that every ship from the far Indies brought something new for the map. In 1498, the edge of South America was touched at Venezuela by the Lord Admiral Columbus, and two years later Brazil was coasted though not exploited by the Portuguese Pedro Alvarez Cabrál. A map of 1506 showed a "Mondo Novo" which comprehended much of South America. In 1513 Vasco Nuñez de Balboa crossed the Isthmus of Panama to see the Pacific Ocean. Among his soldiers was a young adventurer who had begun life as a swineherd in Estremadura, Francisco Pizarro. With other colonists of Panama he heard rumors of great riches and wonders in the empire of the Incas along the west coast of the new continent of South America. There, perhaps, awaited glories and rewards like those achieved by 1521, in the North, in New Spain, by the Captain General Hernando Cortés, who was at work building the first and the greatest Spanish capital of the New World.

iii.

MAKING A KINGDOM

THE PYRAMIDS of the Great Square in the ruined Aztec city were pulled down, and in place of the temple of the Sun, the outline of a cathedral church was laid with the captured stones of Mexico. Where Montezuma's house stood the Captain General began to build for himself a palace more magnificent, as befitted him who having conquered intended him-

* This lovely and provocative phrase is taken from Lewis Hanke's book, *Aristotle and the American Indian*.

self to retain the city and the kingdom in trust for the King of Spain. It was built of cedar and limestone, with a moat at each end, and three patios which united four large wings. Rising on Aztec ruins, presently Mexico would be called "the noblest city in all India."

But the tasks of settling what he had taken were soon complicated by threats from elsewhere. News of danger seemed to come most often from Vera Cruz, and once again the Captain General had word of the landing there of a new governor, with a new royal commission, sent to displace him. This was Cristóbal de Tapia, with papers drawn over the name of the King. But once again the hand of Velásquez of Cuba could be felt behind the intrigue, and the Captain General met it with every air of reasonable interest, courteous argument and smiling inflexibility, until Tapia became uncertain.

His royal charter had told him to proceed also against Pánfilo de Narváez, as though Narváez were in a position of command. Narváez sought him out and in his voice that sounded as though it came from a cave, weakened further the purpose of the new governor, saying,

"I think, Lord Cristóbal de Tapia, that you'll do no better than I have done"—for Narváez was still a prisoner-at-large of Cortés. "See what I have come to, with my great fleet. Look to yourself and lose no time. The good luck of Cortés has not yet run out." Narváez's one eye surely burned with conviction as he advised the invader how to deal with Cortés. "Try to settle with him for gold, go to Castile, and report all this to His Majesty. . . ."

A deal was arranged. Adherents of Cortés brought from Tapia "a few Negroes for a great sum!" He sailed away never to give serious trouble again, however much he tried to do so in Madrid.

Yet the possibility of more such trouble hung over the Captain General, if not in fact, then in mind; for despite all his victorious dispatches to the King, his embassies with marvels of gold and feathers and jewels, his mighty labors to settle a new kingdom for Spain, he had never received what he so greatly wanted—a royal appointment as ruler of the lands he had conquered. Until this should come to him, he must hold his command by force, and by improvised legalisms, and by the power of his gusty charm.

At last, in December 1522, a ship of Spain brought him two letters from Charles V, King of Spain and Holy Roman Emperor. One officially appointed him governor, captain general and chief justice of New Spain; the other personally thanked him for his great services to the Crown. He had come into his own.

But royal caution was at work also, for the King sent to New Spain various officers of his own to administer certain departments of the colonial government, and certain guiding policies were laid down in Madrid, almost as though to limit the power granted to the Captain General, and to remind him where power came from. He received his new assistants affably. As for the instructions they brought, of course he would obey them, but he indicated that local conditions must be considered also, and he wrote to the King that "Things examined and seen from afar cannot be fittingly handled."

For example, he said, referring to the royal order that the colonists mingle freely with the natives the sooner to civilize them, it would be wiser to prevent such mingling. "Most of the Spaniards who come over," he declared, "are of low condition and manner, and vicious with various vices and sins, and if they were to be free to move about in Indian towns, they would sooner convert them to their vices than attract them to virtue."

At the end of the year he sent an embassy to Madrid, to lay before the King the evidence of the second conquest of Mexico—a fortune in raw gold, lovely objects fashioned of gold, silver, jewels and feathers, and the charters of new Spanish towns founded in the wilderness. His messengers carried letters and petitions from colonists—one from the soldiers of the Captain General asked the King "not to send lawyers over, for on entering the land they would upset it all with their books and there would be lawsuits and discussions." On their way to Spain, the ambassadors were beset by pirates and their treasure fell into French hands and was conveyed to Francis I, in Paris. As the grand enemy of Charles V, Francis took pleasure in displaying the booty, which became the marvel of Europe. Indeed, the first word of it reached Madrid from France.

Meanwhile, Cortés worked to extend the New World kingdom. In December 1522 he sent Alvarado to conquer and colonize Guatemala, and in the following month, Cristóbal de Olid to Honduras on a similar mission. The two conquerors were to approach each other from north and south, searching for straits which surely, thought the Captain General, must lead one ocean into another across the great isthmus.

Presently trouble looked again, now on the northern coast in the vicinity of the Pánuco River, where already the Captain General had founded the Spanish city of Santiestevan. Francisco de Garay, Governor of Jamaica, held a royal charter under which he claimed all lands from the River of Palms (the Rio Grande) to the Pánuco. In 1523 he now came to colonize his grant and make his claim real. With sixteen ships, seven hundred and fifty troops mustering two hundred guns, three hundred crossbows and some artillery, he seemed in a position to hold his lands. In a great sweep down the Gulf coast he marched his army by land while his fleet kept pace offshore.

His movements were known to the Captain General who went to defeat him by force of arms. But—Narváez was right—luck was still with Cortés. In the jungle on his northward march he was overtaken by couriers bringing a new royal charter giving him legal claims to the Pánuco, which superseded the charter of Garay, who could only bow to the King's instrument. Instead of making his boast good in battle, Governor de Garay went tamely to Mexico to be retained, like Narváez, as a guarded guest of the Captain General. His troops deserted to the army of New Spain, his ships were booty, and he was left only with the consolations of his fellow-prisoner.

"I hear," said Narváez sourly, "that you warned your soldiers to 'see that we are not caught napping, as they caught Narváez.'" He pointed to his dead eye and began bitterly to brag. "Well, Don Francisco de Garay, they put out this eye, and burned and stole everything I owned, and killed my lieutenant and many of my men, before they could beat me. But you have to know that there was never in the world"—he brought up again his own explanation of his defeat, which excused him—"a luckier man than Cortés, as fortunate in his enterprises as Octavian; in victories, like Julius Caesar; and in battle more active and brave than Hannibal."

If they were prisoners, they were also courtiers and had the ear of their lord. One day Garay urged the Captain General to free Narváez and let him return to Cuba to his wife, who had money, and his estates and his Indians. Narváez had been held for four years. It seemed long enough. Surely he was now harmless, and beyond that, he was a bore—by

turns bridling with dismal pride and humbling himself before
his captor. He had once said to the Captain General,

"Now, my lord captain, I really think that to defeat me,
even if I had had larger forces, was the least of your deeds.
But I have seen so many lands and cities which your lordship has conquered and brought to serve God and the Emperor, that your lordship may well consider yourself greater
than the most illustrious men in the universe."

The Captain General refused to be flattered by such a man.

"We are not big enough," he said wryly, "to have done
all we have done; but the mercy of God has always helped
us and the good fortune of our Emperor."

He now agreed to free Narváez, gave him two thousand
pesos in gold as a farewell, and heard his promises "that he
would always be his servant." As soon as possible, Narváez
was in Spain, doing all in his power to ruin Cortés with
gossip and accusation. He found many an ear to listen at
the Madrid court. If many there regarded Cortés as a great
servant of the Crown, many others helped to enlarge with
whispers his reputation as a potentially dangerous rival of
the monarch himself in the colonial empire.

Narváez pressed claims of his own upon the King. Still
seeing himself as a great commander, and longing for lordship, he asked for the lands once chartered to Garay. If he
did not receive exactly what he asked for, he was eventually
given even more, with consequences which, through no virtue of his, would lead through mystery and heroism to the
discovery and colonization of a new kingdom in the vast
new continent.

iv.

Broken Trust

A FEW MONTHS after releasing Narváez and so setting in
train a fantastic chain of events which would involve him
at their end years later, the Captain General, in May, 1524,
moved out of his capital at the head of a splendid procession to welcome a band of new arrivals who had recently

landed at Vera Cruz. He took with him his mounted troops in full dress, and also the ceremonially robed lords of the conquered Aztec nation, headed by the ex-Emperor Cuauhtémoc. By his own example he was preparing the most impressive possible welcome for the new arrivals.

They had come at his request. Their presence would complete the conquest in the double image of the Spanish world —the image of Christ and King. They were twelve Franciscan friars and they were walking barefoot from the seaport followed by a great throng of natives who marvelled at their simplicity. "Poor ones!" cried the Indians, regarding the threadbare monks who seemed to have no notion of what other Spaniards valued so highly—gold, luxury, and weapons, servants, and style. "Poor ones!" they said in pity, for they thought the newcomers must be gently crazy. In every town on their march, by command of the Captain General, the new Spanish church bells rang out, and the Indians greeted the twelve Franciscan apostles with lighted candles and knelt to kiss their hands and robes and rose to follow them in the long walk to the capital.

There at the outskirts the Captain General met them. He dismounted, went forward and knelt down to kiss the hand of Fray Martín de Valencia. The priest took his hand away and the Captain General instead kissed his robe. Marvelling at this devotion, the Aztec lords did likewise, and from this simple beginning which combined splendor and humility, the Captain General laid the foundations of the Church in his kingdom, and the transit of Spain was completed.

Four months later he was on his way to the most difficult of all his campaigns. Marching through Yucatán to Honduras, he went to punish disloyalty on the part of Cristóbal de Olid. To do so he was obliged to leave his powers in the hands of others in Mexico. It was a dangerous thing to do—and possibly unnecessary, for an expedition against Olid could have been commanded by any loyal subordinate. The Captain General had always done everything himself, and now he must try again.

The physical obstacles were appalling—jungle and river. Where there was a footing, the tropical thickets had to be cut away step by step, and where the jungle ended, a river halted him. In one passage of ninety miles, he had to order the building of fifty bridges, some of them marvels of engineering wit and skill. His chronicler was still with him, and long afterward wrote, "Nowadays there is a saying, 'Here are the bridges of Cortés,' as if one said 'the Pillars of Hercules.' " Even as he hacked his way southward on the great isthmus, he was planning to extend the empire to the north, for he wrote to the King that he had already had "a goodly number of people ready to go to settle" at the River of Palms. He understood that "it was good land" and that there was a seaport. Even while making good the physical reality of one vision, he was projecting another.

But behind his back, his trust was broken. Word reached him in the jungles that the officers whom he had left in charge in Mexico had seized and shared the governorship which was his royal charter. They had put out the story that he was dead, along with his army in the field. His possessions, his palace, were confiscated. When a soldier's wife, keeping faith in spirit with her absent husband, refused to believe the stories, she was whipped at the stake as a witch. A funeral mass was sung for the Captain General in his Mexico church. The last word of news from Mexico told him that by royal charter the River of Palms and all lands eastward to Florida were granted not to him, but, of all people, to the gloomy, one-eyed wretch Pánfilo de Narváez, to whom he had shown magnanimity, and who was now styled Grand Constable of the new lands which awaited him.

"Under the greatest agitation" he took to his tent and remained alone for a day. When he emerged, he told his comrades of the disasters at home, and announced that he would go at once, and in secret, to Mexico to recover his empire.

He managed well, for his return, nearly two years after he had left, confounded his enemies and brought him a popular triumph. He quickly restored his government. Vera Cruz was relocated again, now in the estuary of the Rio Antigua about twelve miles north of San Juan de Ulúa, which was still in use as an anchorage. It seemed that the old times were come again, with all power drawn into his hands.

But this was not to be. A tide had turned. The gossips in Madrid, the King's far distance from the Novo Mondo, the tendency of government to perpetuate its forms—many forces now worked against the Captain General. His appointment as chief justice was rescinded and one Luís Ponce de León was sent from Madrid to assume the powers of the office. His first duty was to conduct a legal inquiry into the actions of the Captain General in the conquest. The chief justice died early in the proceedings, and his successor died soon after assuming office. The third chief justice survived, and subjected the Captain General to a series of affronts which he bore with dignity, out of respect for the Crown which had sent this officer to perform a duty.

At Coyoacan, where the southern causeway from the city touched the lake shore, the Captain General maintained a country place. His palace there was a great square of one story, enclosing a patio, with a massive double entrance to admit carriages and horsemen. Heraldry decorated the doorway, and the outer walls were topped by a scalloped line whose repeated points supported grey limestone caps shaped like slender pyramids. At last, when the chief justice ordered him to leave the capital and live in exile, the Captain General rode off to the palace at Coyoacan loftily declaring, "I thank God for being exiled from the lands and cities which I won, by individuals who are unworthy of the posts they occupy."

But he owed it to himself to be heard by higher authority, and on March seventeenth, 1528, he sailed for Cuba, and on for Spain, where, he said, "a strict inquiry should be held, so that I may complain of the disfavours which His Majesty had been pleased to order that I should undergo . . . for I wish His Majesty to know my services and loyalty more than to possess all the States and treasures of the world."

A month later, the Grand Constable, Pánfilo de Narváez, commanding four hundred men, eighty-two horses, four ships and a brigantine, ran before a wild southerly gale into harbor on the west coast of Florida—"a place of flowers"—with plans to explore and conquer the great crescent of the Gulf as far westward as the Rio Grande.

v.

ANOTHER MEXICO, ANOTHER PERU

MADRID WAS like a nerve-center for the New World. There expeditions were conceived and chartered, and there commanders from oversea returned to defend their acts, or to seek more power, or to salvage their futures, which were often precarious. Even their great forerunner, the Lord Admiral Christopher Columbus, despite his gift of a hemisphere to his sovereigns, did not escape disgrace. During his third voyage he was arrested by a royal officer newly appointed in his place, and sent to Spain in chains. In due course, he was released by the Crown and his position restored. He undertook his fourth and final voyage, during which he sighted South America, and gave first knowledge of another new continent to his time. Until his death in 1506, said his son, he kept his shackles on his bedroom wall as a trophy of that honor which no one, sovereign or vassal, could take from him.

The Captain General arrived from Mexico with a staff of Spanish officers and a company of noble Mexicans. The Mexicans were dressed in their robes of red, yellow and green parrot feathers and as they moved they softly chimed with ornamental golden plaques studded with domed jewels. Like a monarch he travelled with a menagerie of human oddments and animal fantastics—albinos of both sexes; tigers and tropical birds. His suite included several of those native entertainers who could juggle logs with dazzling movements of their feet. His treasure displayed immense emeralds carved by Mexicans, bars of gold and vessels of gold, fabrics and cloaks of wonderful design, and always the fiery plumes of Aztec ceremonial dress. He brought specimens of exotic plants and an extract of liquidambar, the sweet gum of incense and balsam.

If New Spain was first an act of the imagination, it was now a reality made of amazing facts. Seeing the grandsons of Aztec kings walking about the royal halls in floating plumed cloaks the Spanish courtiers were already used to them, for the reports written by the Captain General to the Emperor had been published under royal approval and made talk everywhere.

Another overlord of the new world was in Spain while the Captain General was there in 1528. This was the explorer of Peru, Francisco Pizarro, who came to petition the Crown for permission and new official powers under which to conquer and colonize Peru. He too had brought his specimens of a new land—the usual natives and cloths and hampers full of gold and silver, raw and fabricated, but with the addition of three llamas. New Spain, the first great conquest, was his example of plausibility, as it remained for all other conquerors who promised the Crown to bring it riches in

exchange for powers and titles. Pizarro wore a black cloak,
a white hat and white shoes, and presently was able to add
the chain and medallion of the Order of St. James, for the
Emperor was pleased to grant what he asked, including
a heraldic charge which bore the black eagle and two pillars
of the royal arms, and an Indian town, and a Spanish ship
riding a New World ocean, and a llama to mean Peru—a
land which was now his to conquer and govern. Government
was made up of many offices. Pizarro took for his own all
offices and titles but that of bishop, and presently returned
to the New World where swineherds became lords.

Though he had arrived in the spring of 1528, it was autumn before the Captain General was brought to the Emperor.
He came with one hope uppermost—that he would be reappointed as Governor of the land he had conquered, and
that the investigations against him would be discredited in
Madrid and Mexico.

But there was a feeling that the great question of his
authority was now avoided. Royal delay seemed a device of
policy. Meanwhile, the Emperor showered him with lesser
official honors and personal attentions. He was by royal direction seated near to the monarch at Mass. The knighthood
of St. James was given to him. His military office as Captain
General of New Spain was renewed and confirmed. When
he fell ill in Toledo, the Emperor himself came to visit him,
to the dumfoundation of the court. He was given property in
the city of Mexico. Most astonishing of all, he was en-
nobled with the rank of marquess—all but a duke or a
prince—and given the title of Lord Marquess of the Valley of
Oaxaca, with twenty-three thousand vassals dependent upon
him and subject to him in the vast domain of his grant.

But the great prize was not forthcoming—the overlord-
ship of his colonial country. No reasons were given, and
rumor could only gnaw away at whatever they might be.
No gossip was too ugly to be heard—he was even accused
of murdering his wife, who had crossed from Cuba to
live with him in Mexico after the conquest. The death of
anyone in odd circumstances was certain to be laid at his
door. Had he presented himself to the Emperor in grandeur
too close to the royal manner? Power, grace, intelligence
and style—perhaps he showed too much of all these.

His bitterness was great at the Emperor's refusal to give
what he asked, and his response was proud. He declined
to accept certain of the official royal favors, having been

denied the one he wanted most of all. Charles was patient, urged him to reconsider, and declared that in time he would do better about rewarding him. His genius was for exploration and conquest—let him now take a new charter for further entry into the unknown.

It was a charter to explore the South Sea, by which the geographers of the time always meant the Pacific Ocean. There, anyhow, he would officially be governor and captain general of any new lands he might find. Who knew? These might even be greater than New Spain, with cities and treasures even more opulent than those of Mexico.

It was the best he could get on this visit to Spain, which brought him comfort in only one condition of life—he was married again, now to a young, beautiful, highborn lady who captivated him. Bestowing on her five of his most superb Aztec jewels—emeralds of great size carved in the likenesses of a fish, a trumpet, a cup, a rose, and a bell with a pearl for a clapper—he returned to Mexico in a spring sailing of 1530 as Lord Marquess of the Valley, but with no real power left to him except that which a nobleman might exert over the people on his estates.

He was still not welcome in the colonial capital. If he had returned with marks of royal favor, he was not yet free of the royal commission set up to investigate his conquest. The commission president, Nuño de Guzmán, was resolved to discredit him. Guzmán held a royal charter to the governorship of lands to the northwest of the capital, where with every cruelty he conducted to his great profit a thriving business in Indian slaves. Destiny gave the Lord Marquess no rivals worthy of him. They were either scoundrels or weaklings.

There was mysterious news of one of these rivals by the time the Lord Marquess returned to Mexico—Pánfilo de Narváez. The ships of his expedition had recently docked at Vera Cruz bringing partial news of his enterprise. It seemed that Narváez, coming to Florida two years ago in the gale, had actually missed his destination, which was the mouth of the Rio Grande—or River of Palms—far to the westward. In a familiar tactic of Spanish commanders he resolved to divide his forces, with the soldiery moving overland along the Gulf shore, while the fleet—three ships and a brigantine —sailed along in the Gulf opposite his course. The two elements were to meet at the River of Palms, and support each other from land and sea until then.

Some officers of the expedition opposed this plan, and one of the ten married women in the fleet even said to Narváez that he should not take the troops on the land march, for she was certain that few or none would ever return.

He shrugged. It was true that since they were going into strange lands to conquer unknown people, some soldiers would die in battle. But for those who lived, it would all be a fine thing, for they would become very rich.—Where, in any case, had she come by such an idea?

The sibyl replied that she had learned what would happen from a Moorish woman of Hornachos in Castile who had told her all this before they had left Spain. The soldier's wife said she had given her own warning even then.

Her ominous words were ignored. Making ready to sail, certain people who boarded the ships heard her say to the other wives that they might as well forget their husbands, if they went ahead and marched off into danger, and each of them might as well begin looking around for a new husband, as she for one meant to do. It seemed that she and others of the women either did this, or "became the concubines of those who remained in the ships."

Under Narváez the troops moved inland, and the ships, as ordered, sailed for the harbor of the River of Palms. They never found it. They never again saw their commander, though they returned to their starting point in Florida, and sailed back and forth along the Gulf coast for almost a year looking for him. At last they gave up and went on to Vera Cruz, where no one at all had any news of Pánfilo de Narváez. Nobody knew what had become of him, and his four hundred men and eighty horses—more than the Lord Marquess had with him when he took New Spain.

Still denied a place, great or small, in the life of the city of Mexico, where all that there was of society as his countrymen knew it was originally his creation, the Lord Marquess busied himself with large projects in the country to the south.

At Cuernavaca, a beautiful town two or three days' ride across mountains from the capital, he built an oddly ungraceful palace of small stones set in mortar with a central entrance under arches. On a hill facing him across the cup of the town rose the new Spanish church.

In his lands he cultivated silk, grapes and wood, and at Vista Hermosa, again to the south by a ride of some hours from Cuernavaca, he built the processing rooms and dwelling quarters of his sugar plantation. The central buildings were put together of massive blocks of stone, superbly cut and matched, with four aisles in rows of magnificent intersecting vaults, where the cane and its products were stored. Underground tunnels connected the buildings, and led to egress beyond the walls, possibly for emergency purposes. There were great halls for cooking and dining and meeting, all built as thickly as a fortress and as grandly as a palace. On the second story the sleeping rooms opened upon a long wide corridor with a high barrel vault unbroken for the whole length of the wing. In refuge from the hot glare of the south, the hacienda bestowed cool shade as deep as that of a great cave. In its style—splendid vaults, devious tunnels, noble halls and the grace of arches all considered—Vista Hermosa seemed like a self-portrait of its restless master.

With all his ventures, he did not neglect his new charter as explorer of the north, and in the next few years he dispatched two expeditions to explore the South Sea, which might hold the secret to the revival of his fortunes. The enterprises ended in failure and finally in 1535 he himself led forth another. It took him to the tip of Lower California, where bleakness, hardship and disaster would have thrown the company back except for the brilliant play of the Lord Marquess's old powers of improvisation and courage.

His purpose was not either fantastic or absurd. He had made one of the richest finds in the history of exploration only a few years ago—it seemed sensible to think that another could come into view at any time in lands unknown before to Europeans. He clung to his foothold in the new peninsula through months of privation. Finally a ship came to summon him home to Mexico with messages from his wife, and another from the man, newly arrived, who had received from the crown the post of Viceroy of New Spain.

Conquerors, then, inevitably gave way to administrators.

All hope was gone that the Lord Marquess would ever again rule in the city of Mexico. He returned as ordered, and was kindly received by the Emperor's deputy, the Viceroy. Antonio de Mendoza. The public rejoiced to see the Lord Marquess again, as he took up his residence in the capital with all his old splendor, and vied with the Viceroy—who was said to be "attended by one hundred twenty Indians daily" for whose services he paid nothing—in exchanging magnificent courtesies.

But as there was more to the life of an active man than banquets with gold and silver plate and feathered servants, all his response to the challenge of the unknown rose with its old energy when on July 24, 1536, four emaciated travellers appeared in the city of Mexico with news out of the blind country north of New Spain. They were taken first to the Viceroy to tell their tale, but in due course, the Lord Marquess heard what their leader had to say.

He was Alvar Núñez Cabeza de Vaca, who, with his three companions, were the only survivors of the enterprise launched seven years before under the command of Pánfilo de Narváez. Once again the map of the Novo Mondo cleared in the mind's eye with a new and farther light, and again the possibility of another Mexico, another Peru, arose in mind. The Lord Marquess was determined to undertake the discovery and settlement of the new kingdom to the north. The Viceroy was equally determined to control any such enterprise himself, in the interest of the Crown.

Meanwhile, all Mexico listened to what Núñez Cabeza de Vaca had to tell.

vi.

THE CASTAWAYS

LONG LATER, when he published his "relation" of his adventures, he said in a letter to the King, "Rather than to exaggerate, I have under-stated all things." It was a style in his own manner, for he was a trifle wry in his judgments, clear and circumstantial in his narrative passages, and in his conclusions quite selfless, ascribing his triumph of survival to the power and the mercy of God. Certainly he made it plain that nobody owed anything to the Grand Constable Governor Pánfilo de Narváez, who could be relied upon in any situation to make the wrong decision. Even though many of the command were opposed to the plan of Narváez to divide the forces between land and sea, in his obstinacy he persisted. Now the world could hear what had become of those who had followed him inland in Florida, and after.

Soon after landing in Florida, reported Núñez Cabeza de Vaca, who was the treasurer and high sheriff of the expedition, they had come to a curious find—many chests of wood like those used for goods in Castile. In each was a dead man covered with painted deerskins. With the cases they found scraps of wool and linen, and sprays of feathers which looked "like those of New Spain." Yes, and "there were also traces of gold."

Where, asked the Spaniards in sign language, did these things come from?

There, replied the Indians, gesturing, far away, was a place called Apalachen. It had much gold and an "abundance of everything we desired," said the treasurer. The Grand Constable had seen Mexico. He knew what Apalachen could be like. It could only be approached on foot. Ordering the bodies in the boxes to be burned, on the advice of his chaplain, he organized his march.

To each overland soldier the Grand Constable issued two pounds of biscuit and half a pound of bacon. The marching party consisted of two friars, three hundred soldiers, and officers. For two weeks they marched without seeing "an Indian, a village or a house," and the land gave them nothing to eat except palmitos. At last they came to a river and saw on the opposite bank two hundred Indians.

"They so insulted us with their gestures," said the treasurer, "that we were forced to break with them."

They seized a half dozen natives who under prodding led the way to their houses. There the soldiers found corn and thanked God for it. The march seemed useless, and the treasurer and those who shared his view asked the Grand Constable to abandon it and seek "the sea and a port."

These were remote, replied the Grand Constable.

The treasurer insisted.

Very well, replied his commander, take forty foot soldiers and "find a harbor."

The treasurer tried, but found only a bay that was knee-deep where no ships could lie. He returned to the main body and the march for Apalachen continued. They met a chief who was preceded by a company of musicians playing on reed flutes. He rode on the back of another Indian and wore a painted deerskin and knew the Apalachens and offered to fight against them. In his village the next night a soldier was "shot at" and at daybreak the army left. Passing through "a very difficult country that was wonderful to look upon," they made their way slowly through "vast forests with astonishingly high trees." A day or so later, they "gave thanks to God," for there ahead of them they could see Apalachen.

"We believed," said the treasurer, "what had been told us of this land, and that there would be an end to our great hardships. . . . Having come to where we had been informed there was much food and gold, we already felt recovered in part from our sufferings and fatigue."

The army took the town by surprise, with only a brief skirmish. Eagerly the Grand Constable and his followers examined it. Their spirits fell. Apalachen consisted of forty thatched huts inhabited by women dressed in scraps of cloth and deerskin and men dressed in nothing at all. At a distance the men looked like giants. The wealth of Apalachen consisted of corn, stored in jars or growing in fields. There was no gold.

But surely, then, greater and richer towns lay beyond?

No, said the Indians, Apalachen was the largest town anywhere. There was another town, to the south, called Aute, which had corn, pumpkins, beans, and fish, as it was near the sea. After twenty-five days at Apalachen the army moved on for Aute, harassed by hunger and attacks by Indian archers, whose bowmanship was marvellous. In nine days the soldiers came to Aute and found it abandoned, its huts burned, but its harvest of corn, pumpkins and beans intact. The army rested for two days, and then, said the treasurer,

"The Governor begged me to go and look for the sea."

He obeyed, and by evening the following day he came to a shore where "oysters were abundant, and we rejoiced." But it was only a marshy inlet miles from the sea, and the coast in both directions was marked by creeks and bays "so far inland that it was difficult to examine them." No fleet could come there.

Reporting back to Aute, the treasurer found the Grand Constable and many others ill in epidemic numbers. Still, in spite of Indian attacks, they would do better to move to the oyster marshes. They followed the treasurer there in great distress.

"There were not enough horses to carry the sick," he said, "who increased in numbers day by day, and we knew of no cure for them."

All was "piteous and painful," but worse was to come, for there was treachery among the horsemen, who were planning to ride away to save themselves, leaving the sick and the slow behind. The plot was given away by "persons of gentle condition," and in the end, the traitors "decided to remain, so that whatever might happen to one should be the lot of all."

And now "it was clear," said the treasurer, "that we could leave this terrible land only by dying."

They reviewed all means of escape, and in the end resolved upon the only one which seemed logical. This was to build boats in which to go. But with what builders, and with what materials? The scheme "appeared impossible to everyone." No one in the army knew how to build a boat, and there were no "tools, iron, forge, tow, resin, rigging, or many other necessary things." Worst of all, "there was nothing to eat, while building, for those who should work." The idea seemed hopeless.

But after sleeping on it, the army began to think of ways to kindle the fire to make the tools to drive the nails to build the ships to sail away.

One man came forward and said he could make pipes out of wood and contrive bellows out of deerskins. Others found that "nails, saws, axes, and other tools should be made from the stirrups, spurs, crossbows" and other iron implements in the army. A Greek named Theodoro made resin from pitch pine. If the boats could not be caulked with tow, their planks could be sealed with pulped and twisted palmito. Ropes for rigging were made from the tails and manes of horses. Soldiers gave their shirts to make sails. Somebody carved oars out of cedar branches. In the bare sandy country it was "only by very great search" that the soldiers found stone for ballast and anchors. To fit the boats with containers for fresh water, they took whole the skins of horse legs and tanned them to make bottles.

A horse was killed every third day to provide food for the boatbuilders and the sick. Now and then a squad went out to gather corn and another "to collect shellfish in the coves and creeks." They had to fight for food. Indians killed ten soldiers "in sight of the camp without our being able to help," said the treasurer. Later he saw the corpses "pierced from side to side with arrows," against which even the good armor of the soldiers gave no protection. While the boats were taking form, forty men died of the epidemic and of hunger.

The builders worked so hard that in sixteen days, by September twentieth, 1528, they had completed five boats, each thirty-three feet long. Two days later the Grand Constable, taking command of one of the boats, and assigning a detachment to go with him, divided the rest of the army among the other four boats. Each boat carried from forty-seven to forty-nine men. The treasurer was given command of the fifth boat. They took along what possessions and supplies they could, and when all were loaded, the boats rode so low that only a hand's breadth of the hulls remained above water. The boats were so crowded that the men could hardly move. No one of the company knew anything of navigation.

"Desperation drove us to hazard our lives in this way," remarked the treasurer.

On September twenty-second they went by oar and sail toward the open Gulf, and then headed westward to look for the River of Palms. The treasurer had nothing but hazard and calamity to report of the voyage. Thirst was their great enemy, for the horse-skin water bags soon rotted and let water out. When they put inshore to find creeks or rivers with fresh water, the sounding was shallow, and they risked damaging the boats aground.

They met Indian fishermen who let them alone and other Indians who drove them off. A great storm held them once for six days on a waterless island and in the end they decided to sail on into high waves rather than await death by thirst. Some men drank salt water and of these some went mad and others died. Waves nearly swamped the boats day and night and sick men kept bailing, while stronger men rowed. Once when they landed among Indians who seemed friendly they were suddenly attacked at night by their hosts, and both the Grand Constable and the treasurer were wounded in the face. By dawn they had fought off the Indians and they sailed on in bitter cold, staying in close formation. At another stop they lost two of their company who went ashore with Indians to find supplies and did not return.

A few days later they found a great issue of fresh water running from a vast river—the Mississippi—out into the Gulf and they drank but could not land because of the strong current made by the river against the sea. Now the north wind blew and drove the boats away from shore. It took them three days to come near land again but as night fell they decided to wait for daylight to go inshore. Under darkness the boats lost contact, and it was not until evening that the treasurer sighted two boats, and drawing near, recognized one as the Grand Constable's. The Grand Constable asked him what he thought they should do.

The treasurer replied that they ought to join the other boat which was in sight and not lose her, and that the three boats must keep together.

This could not be done, said the Grand Constable, because that other boat was standing far out to sea, and he wanted to come to shore. He said that the treasurer, if he wished to follow him, should tell his men to fall to their oars and row, "for it was only by strength of arm that the land could be gained."

Until sunset, then, they rowed. But the men were sick and weak, and the Grand Constable had the strongest soldiers in his boat. The treasurer was unable to keep pace with him. He hailed him.

"I asked him to pass me a rope so that I could keep up with him."

The Grand Constable refused, "saying that he himself would have all he could do to reach the land that night."

The treasurer said to him, that since "he saw we did not have the strength to follow him, he must tell me what he wished me to do."

The Grand Constable Governor Pánfilo de Narváez had come to the end of responsibility and honor.

"He answered," said Núñez Cabeza de Vaca, "that it was no longer a time for one to command another, but that each should do what he thought best to save his own life, and this was what he intended to do. Saying this, he left with his boat."

The treasurer never saw him again. With his boatmen, he disappeared forever into the unknown.

The treasurer turned about and joined the other boat at sea, which waited for him. Four days later, in a storm, he lost the other boat, and was alone with his own crew in the heavy seas and deep cold of full winter. Out of the whole company in his boat only five were "on their feet," and at night only the treasurer and one other soldier were able to manage the steering oar. Despair was close.

"All the people in my boat," observed the treasurer, "had collapsed one on another, so near to death that there were few in a state of sensibility."

In this condition they were all jarred into life again one morning before dawn when a huge wave lifted the boat and

drove it deep into the sand of an offshore island. The day
was November sixth, 1528. The sick and starving soldiers
crawled ashore on their hands and knees. The stronger ones
made a fire, roasted some corn, found rainwater, and saw
their companions slowly revive.

In daylight, Indians appeared—over a hundred of them.

"If they were not large, our fear made giants of them," remembered the treasurer.

But the Indians were friendly, and soon the last Spanish
trinkets were exchanged for fish, roots, water and other provisions. When the Indians left, the soldiers felt equal to sailing on. Throwing off their clothes they waded to the boat to
dislodge it from the grip of the sand and when she was
launched threw themselves and their bundled clothes aboard
and worked their way slowly away from shore through high-
rolling surf. Their hands were stiff with cold as they rowed,
and they had not yet had time to dress when a great wave
swamped the boat. The next wave capsized her. The Spaniards
were thrown half-drowned on the beach, "naked as the day
they were born, with the loss of all they had." Exposed to
view, their bodies "were so emaciated that the bones could
be counted," and they "looked like the perfect figures of
death." At sunset the Indians returned, and at the suffering of
the soldiers, sat down among them and "howling like brutes"
yielded themselves up to sympathetic lamentations, which,
said the treasurer, gave to him as to his companions "an increase of feeling and a livelier sense of our calamity."

vii.

PRISONERS OF SPACE

HOW GREAT their calamity was, they did not yet know. It was
unfolded to them daily during the hopeless passing of seven
years. The castaways were prisoners of ignorance and space.
(It was evidently Galveston Island where they had been
stranded and it was the mainland of Texas where they went
next.) If the Indians were friendly at first, they soon used
the soldiers as slaves. Another boatload of men from the

expedition presently appeared, and Spaniards rejoiced at being united again. The two boatloads made up a company of eighty men. But it was not long before hunger and desperation took their toll, and the treasurer remembered how some men of the second boat actually came to the point of eating the flesh of dead comrades. Soon the eighty were reduced to fifteen, and in the end, only four were left. In addition to the treasurer, who identified himself as a grandson of the conqueror of the Canary Islands, they were Alonzo Castillo Maldonado, son of a doctor of Salamanca; Andres Dorantes of Béjar; and an Arabian Negro, native of Acamor, in Morocco, about thirty years old, who was called Estevanico.

After a year on the island, they passed five years on the mainland, living the life of the coastal Indians, wandering at the change of seasons in search of seasonal food—berries, prickly pear, walnuts, in the vast plain which was veined with rivers that flowed to the Gulf, and fish, in weirs along the shore. They were tormented by heat and mosquitoes in the summer, and by piercing cold in winter. They lived naked, becoming creatures of that land to such a degree that they shed their skins twice a year "like serpents." Separated from each other, and made to travel as bearers by the Indians, the four survivors were lacerated by the thorny brush of the Gulf coast until they bled. They could only think of the thorns which Christ had endured and suffer in His name. Escape was always in mind, and when they could meet, the treasurer and his comrades made plans. But it was not until September first, 1534, after several unsuccessful attempts, that deliverance came. It was during the prickly pear season, when the Indian villages were on the move. The four survivors ran away from their masters and met again in the village of other Indians who received them kindly.

Now began new careers for the Spaniards, for they were believed by these Indians to be gifted with the powers of doctors who could cure.

"The night we arrived," stated the treasurer, "some Indians came to Castillo and told him they had great pain in the head, and begged him to cure them."

Castillo had qualms. He knew he was only a man and as such full of sin, and he was afraid that if he used the only power he knew, which was that of prayer, his unworthiness would tell, and make any cure impossible. But he made the sign of the cross over the suffering Indians and "commended them to God." They were cured instantly, and they rejoiced, bringing food—the first venison the soldiers had seen —and danced and sang for three days.

When the village moved on, word of the cures went over the country, and people came from far to plead with the new doctors to be cured. In the end, not only Castillo, the doctor's son, but the treasurer and Dorantes and Estevanico also practiced the medicine of prayer and incantation, with amazing results. The treasurer once seemed to raise a man from the dead, causing "great wonder and fear." All whom they treated declared that they recovered. For eight months the Spaniards roved, working their wonders, and were given all in return that the meagre country would afford. It was little enough, and they barely subsisted.

But in constant movement lay their hope of release from the endless land, and as they moved generally westward, they asked always what lay beyond, and one day they saw mountains for the first time, and went toward them, hearing that there was more food to be had there. As many as three or four thousand Indians travelled with them, unwilling to part from men with sacred powers. They were now not only doctors—they were priests, with priestly duties, which weighed heavily.

"As we had to breathe upon and sanctify the food and drink for each, and grant permission to do the many things they would come to ask, it may be seen how great was the annoyance," noted the treasurer. For their godlike powers, he and his companions were called "children of the sun."

When they came to the mountains they found people with news of lands to the north. On being asked to take the travellers there they refused, saying those were enemy lands where they could not go. When they persisted in their refusal, the treasurer withdrew from them. He slept alone in the woods to show his displeasure. They became fearful and begged him to return, promising to conduct him to the north, though they would die along the way. He thought to use their wholesome fright to his future advantage, and then a most curious thing happened—many Indians fell ill, and eight died. It seemed like punishment to the people. They begged him not to will further death among them, which of course, he said, he had not done, but he "prayed to God our Lord to relieve them; and from that time the sick began to get better."

The way north was followed, then, and it was not long before the Spaniards came among a new order of Indians, who lived in houses instead of weedy huts, and who hunted great cows on the plains, and who lived in settled towns and grew food—beans, pumpkins and squash—instead of roving in search of berries in season. Parting company with the Indians of the plains (east of the Pecos), the treasurer and his comrades followed directions of the house Indians to the north and then to the west. The farther they went, the more bountiful became the stores of the people in their towns. They saw chains of "very great mountains," and passed across a great river out of the north—the Rio Grande—and as they advanced, they began to feel like the "happiest creatures on earth," for the town Indians loaded them with more food than they had seen in seven years. And there were other gifts which might hold promise of another Mexico with all its riches. These they saw, and associated with reports of great house towns to the north on the great river—cotton shawls "better than those of New Spain," and "fine turquoises," and "five emeralds made into arrowheads."

"And so," reported the treasurer, "we travelled all across the country until we came out at the South Sea." This land produced beads made of coral, and further, it yielded up hope; for if Spaniards were sailing their ships on that ocean, the castaways might find them. The blind misery of seven years seemed about to yield to justice.

One day Castillo saw an Indian who wore a curious object around his neck—it was the "buckle of a sword belt, and stitched to it the nail of a horseshoe."

What are these? asked the Spaniards.

They came from heaven, answered the Indian.

Who brought them here?

Men who wore beards like all of you, declared the Indians, came from heaven to this river, with horses, spears and swords. They speared two Indians.

"With the utmost indifference we could feign," said the treasurer, "we asked them what had become of those men."

It seemed that the men had gone on the sea, and "that afterward they were seen on the surface going toward the sunset."

The Spaniards had almost given up hope of ever hearing of Christians again. Now they "gave many thanks to God," and pressed on their way, finding as they went many more rumors of Christians who had been in the country. But much of the news was shameful and saddening and the treasurer reported it bitterly.

For as they advanced, they came upon whole districts

which were deserted, though they were "fertile and beautiful"
with flowing water. The towns were burned and empty. The
people had fled to the mountains where they grew thin eating
the bark of trees and what they could scratch out of the
rocks.

Why was this? asked the Spaniards.

Fear of slavery, replied the Indians, telling how Christians
had come, destroying the land, burning houses, and taking
away in chains all the women and boys and half the men. The
rest who escaped could only hide in the uplands, keeping a
lookout against the raiders.

The treasurer and his companions won the trust of these
Indians, who led him to the mountains where they found
"many people collected there out of fear of the Christians."
From their stores they gave him "more than two thousand
backloads of maize," which he distributed to the hungry
people who had brought him there, and then taking all the
people with him he resumed his march.

Within a few hours he came upon the trail of a Spanish
raiding party. Indian scouts watching from cover had seen
during the previous night how the Christians "were carrying
away many people." Their trail seemed to indicate that
they were heading eastward. They were mounted, as the
treasurer saw by "the stakes to which horses had been tied"
in the raiders' campgrounds.

Evidence of Christians nearby lifted the hearts of the
wandering Spaniards, while at the same time it frightened the
Indians, many of whom ran away to give warning over the
countryside. Others would have followed, but the treasurer
calmed them, promising them protection from the Christians
whom he must find. One of his party must go looking for the
mounted Spanish troops, "who were moving about the country." He asked Castillo and Dorantes if either of them would
go. They refused, "excusing themselves because of weariness
and exhaustion." Both were "younger and more athletic" than
the treasurer, but in the end, it was he who, with the Negro
Estevanico and eleven Indians, went in search of the Christians who could rescue them all.

He walked for thirty miles, passing through three villages
where the Christians had camped, and on the second day he
overtook "four of them." They were mounted.

He spoke to them. They turned in wonder to see him where
he stood with his Negro and eleven Indians.

He knew how strange he looked.

"Confounded," the Christians neither called out to him nor came closer, but stared at him in silence for "a length of time."

He ordered them to conduct him to their captain.

They did so.

He heard the sound of his own language, he met again human intelligence as he defined it, for the first time in seven years. He said to Captain Diego de Alcaraz,

"Give me a certificate of the year, month, and day I arrived there, and of the manner of my coming."

He reckoned that he and his companions had journeyed six thousand miles on land and water since the collapse of the Grand Constable's expedition. He had crossed "from sea to sea," and learned "that on the coast of the South Sea" there were pearls, and that near there were "the best and all the most opulent countries." It was the very kind of news Spaniards hoped to hear and must tell each other.

IV

TO THE NORTH

Everything else rests on the
powerful Lord of all things,
Almighty God, Who knows how
and when these lands will be
discovered and for whom He has
guarded this good fortune.

—*Pedro Castañeda de Náxera.*

i.

CÍBOLA IN FANCY

OUT OF THE REPORTS of Núñez Cabeza de Vaca and his companions came new plans for northward movement.

The Lord Marquess saw the treasurer privately to pick his brains, intending to launch the northern expedition himself. His charter of 1528 granted him any new discoveries he might make in the South Sea, and it was near the South Sea where the treasurer had come back to civilization.

But the Viceroy, on the other hand, believed that it was his own privilege and responsibility to exploit the new lands, and he acted firmly to exclude the Lord Marquess from playing any part in their conquest for the Crown. The Crown had already made it plain that the Lord Marquess was to be regarded as an officer who, though not actually in disgrace, was in retirement, and was to be kept there.

The Viceroy now asked the treasurer to guide an expedition back to the northern lands, but weary and eager to return to Spain the treasurer refused. His companions also excused themselves from the assignment, but in the end the Viceroy acquired title to the Negro slave Estevanico who had seen everything his masters had seen. With him as guide, another reliable witness could go to the north, see what he could see, and return to report. If what he saw should enlarge the news brought by the seven-year wanderers, then a penetration in force could be arranged. The Viceroy soon found his witness.

He was a Franciscan friar—a Frenchman from the Duchy of Savoy—named Marcus of Nice who was in the capital as guest of the Bishop of Mexico. A holy man, he was also venturesome and intelligent. Travelling on foot, dressed in his robe of grey zaragoza cloth, and accompanied by Estevanico and a party of Indians who knew the first steps to take toward the unknown north, he set out from the frontier province of New Galicia on March 7, 1539. Estevanico was gallantly dressed in bright colors, with jingle bells at wrist and ankle, and carried a gourd rattle which he and his fellow castaways had picked up long ago out of a river they had passed on the plains. With him, like a hunting lord, he took two greyhounds. He was commanded by the Viceroy to obey Friar Marcus in all matters.

"You must always try," ordered the Viceroy in his instructions to Friar Marcus, "to travel as safely as possible," and to observe all conditions of the people whom he would meet, noting their number, "whether they are few or many, and whether they are scattered or living together. Note also the fertility and climate of the land; the trees, plants, and domestic and wild animals there may be; the character of the country, whether it is broken or flat; the rivers, whether they are large or small; the stones and metals which they are; and of all things that can be sent or brought, bring or send samples of them in order that His Majesty may be informed of everything."

If he should reach the coast of the South Sea he must leave evidence of his passing.

". . . Leave letters buried at the headlands, at the foot of some tree outstanding for its size, telling of what you think should be known. Mark the tree with a cross where the letters are left, so that they may be found. Likewise, at the mouths of rivers and suitable harbors, on prominent trees near the water, make the same sign, a cross, and leave letters."

And why?

"Thus," wrote the Viceroy, "if I send ships they will be advised to look for this sign."

For the rest, Friar Marcus must send messages back by Indian runner when he could, look out for proper sites for establishment of monasteries, and in his reporting, observe with "the utmost secrecy so that appropriate steps may be taken without disturbing anything"—which might have been a reference both to the Lord Marquess and Indians who might be conquered later. In any case, the friar was to explain to all natives that there was "only one God in heaven, and the Emperor on earth to rule and govern it, whose subjects they must all become, and whom they must serve." How far he must go, what he would find, nobody knew.

But in the eyes of the Lord Marquess he was plainly the agent of a rival, and it was again a time for action, in the name of pride and perhaps glory. The Lord Marquess had written two years before to the Emperor, "So long as I live

I shall not cease to pursue my purpose," which now took the form of discovering the north for himself, under his famous charter. He had been building ships at Acapulco, and now in the summer of 1539, five months after the departure of Friar Marcus, and before his return, the Lord Marquess sent his ships north by sea under the command of Juan de Ulloa, determined to discover an all-water route to the northern kingdom and claim it for his own before Friar Marcus could return to deliver knowledge of those lands to the Viceroy, who could then claim title to them.

The dazzling personal powers of his earlier years now gave way in the Lord Marquess to the devious and the desperate; and in his rage he resorted to the tactics of lesser men. He set abroad efforts to disgrace the Viceroy by rumor and remark—a process by which he himself had suffered. They did not succeed—the Crown's power was firmly vested in the Viceroy, and in early September, it was further strengthened in the affair of the northern kingdom.

For on the second of the month, Friar Marcus of Nice was back in the capital, reporting to Viceroy Mendoza what he had seen and heard. In some ways his report was disappointing, in others highly promising. The will to find a great kingdom was so strong that even an honest man might mistake fable for truth, and bring home the same confusions he had gone away with.

What was it about the seven bishops who had fled Portugal centuries ago? Everyone had heard how they must have founded seven cities in the New World. Somewhere in the northern lands, now, Indians declared that there were seven rich cities, together called Cíbola, and everyone from the Viceroy and his emissary Friar Marcus to men-at-arms gossiping in their guard rooms wondered if these could be the cities of the persecuted bishops. Where so little was known, legend was as powerful as fact.

But Friar Marcus brought much new information with him, and the Spanish colonists passed it around, enlarging it as it was repeated. In any case, he gave in writing, duly notarized, a clear statement of his journey.

As he left the frontier, which was loosely defined, some Indians came to see him from a northwestern province which the Lord Marquess had visited. If the province was part of the mainland, then it might be part of the northern kingdom; and if the Lord Marquess had been there, he might already have a claim to the kingdom under his royal charter. If on the other hand the province were an island, its limits would contain any claim to new land. Friar Marcus quizzed the Indians who came to see him.

"From them," he said, "I assured myself that it is an island, and not the mainland, as some claim"—a report which held reassurance for the Viceroy.

Once beyond the frontier, crossing desert land, through many days of walking, he met other Indians who had never seen Christians. They were full of news about towns to the north and east, beyond the mountains, where people lived in an open valley and wore cotton. He showed them specimens of metals he had brought along, and they took up those of gold and assured him that in the towns they spoke of the people had pots and jars made of the same and wore golden jewels in their ears and noses and even had little blades of gold with which they swept the sweat off their bodies.

Turning his course toward these rumored towns, he arranged to send out a light scouting party in advance of his own slower progress. Estevanico was put in charge of several Indians. He was to go ahead and look out for the towns, and if he should hear of populated places with wealth— "something really important," as Friar Marcus put it—he was to come right back, or send Indian messengers with a sign according to a code. If the news told of "something moderate," the sign was to be a white cross as wide as a hand with spread fingers; of "greater importance," then a cross two spans wide; and of "something greater and better than New Spain," then he was to send a large cross.

The Arabian Negro left "on Passion Sunday, after dinner," and had not been gone four days when his first cross arrived by messenger out of the blind country to the north. It was a huge cross—the "height of a man," and as such it must mean that a greater land than New Spain lay ahead. The messenger said that thirty days farther on lay "the greatest thing in the world." There were seven large cities, all ruled by one man. The first of these that would be seen was called Cíbola. The houses were large, built of stone and lime, "all joined in an orderly manner." The ruler's house was four stories high. Stone and lime—they sounded like the city Cortés had found on the lake islands of Mexico. But more —they had doorways richly paved with turquoise "of which there is a great abundance." The inhabitants were well dressed. Still farther inland were more such cities, each more wonderful than the first seven. Friar Marcus thanked

God and pushed ahead following the trail of Estevanico.

Another cross arrived, quite as large as the first one, with a message to hurry. Within a few days Friar Marcus himself met the people who had told Estevanico about Cíbola. They had more news of three great kingdoms ahead, and they gave the friar some beautifully tanned and worked cattle hides which they said came from Cíbola. On the next day he found a large cross left by Estevanico "as proof that the information about the good country was always increasing," and another message calling upon him to hurry, hurry, saying that he would await him at the edge of the next desert. Friar Marcus erected two crosses and then performed the formal act of annexation, as "it seemed proper to institute acts of possession from here on."

For the next five days he passed through many settlements where all he heard confirmed the splendid news sent by Estevanico. In one of these the people showed him with dirt and ashes mixed into mortar how they set stones and raised houses with receding terraces. He asked,

Do you have wings to ascend to these terraces?

They laughed and drew a picture of a ladder for him. They did it, he said, "as clearly as I might do for myself."

Here too he heard of a city where woolen cloth was to be had, and he learned that the seacoast turned west abruptly. He went to determine this, determined it, and resumed his march toward Cíbola, which now lay only a few days away.

He presently received evidence of a marvel such as any philosopher in his library in Europe would have recognized —a species of unicorn. For the Indians brought him a hide half again as large as that of a great cow, and said it came from a creature who had only one horn "in the front, and that this horn is curved toward its breast, and then turns in a straight point." The beast was strong enough to tear apart anything it struck. There were "thousands" of them in the farther country. The hide looked like buckskin, and the hair on it was "as long as a finger is thick."

Again he received word from Estevanico, who was "very elated" with "proof" that his discoveries would be rich and wonderful. He sent word that everything the Indians had described to him proved, as he went on his way, to be exactly as told to him. He said "he had never caught the Indians in a lie." Friar Marcus could say the same. They were still several days' journey apart, but soon they must meet, for Estevanico would wait for his superior at the first great city.

Friar Marcus with his Indian escort pressed on over the deserts in the fortnight after Easter.

And then one day "on the road to Cíbola" a messenger arrived "very grieved, his face and body covered with sweat." He had dreadful news, and what he must tell he had seen for himself. Estevanico was dead at Cíbola, and this is what had happened.

Whenever he came to a town, Estevanico sent ahead as a mark of his authority that gourd rattle he always carried. It was a sacred object of some sort once belonging to Indians far away on the plains. It was ornamental with two feathers, one red, one white, and from it hung several strings of little bells. One day's travel away from Cíbola, Estevanico sent the gourd into the town by Indian messengers. An official of the town took the gourd, and when he saw the jingle bells, he "at once hurled the gourd to the ground with much wrath," saying that by this gourd he knew "what sort of people" asked to come here. He ordered Estevanico's messengers to leave Cíbola at once, and sent word to the strangers waiting a day's distance away in the desert that if they tried to enter Cíbola he would "kill them all."

They went back and told Estevanico what had happened at Cíbola. He said,

It was of no importance. When people showed anger, they always ended by receiving him all the better.

He went to Cíbola. There he was arrested, all his turquoises and other trading effects were taken from him, and he was detained in a large house somewhat removed from the town, along with his Indians, who now, with all those added to his company along the way, numbered more than three hundred men, and many women. They were all kept without food or water that night.

By morning they were thirsty, and "this Indian" who brought the news to Friar Marcus left the house to go to the little river that ran near the town. When he had drunk his fill, he rose up from the river and he saw Estevanico running away from the house, and "people from the city pursuing him." His Indians ran away with him, and soon were overtaken, and many were killed. After seeing all this, the Indian by the river ran upstream until he found a place to cross and take to the desert trail which brought him back to Friar Marcus with his terrible report.

Listening to him, Friar Marcus thought,

I am lost.

He feared not so much to lose his life as to lose the power to "return and report on the greatness of the country, where God our Lord can be so well served, His holy faith exalted, and the royal patrimony of His Majesty increased."

The Indians with him wept to hear the news for their own people who had been killed at Cíbola. Friar Marcus gave away to them "all the clothing and articles of trade" which he carried, heartened them, and led them forward again. A day's journey from Cíbola they met two other Indians of their own who said that they were the only other survivors of Estevanico's party of over three hundred men and many women.

But if Cíbola could not be taken, it must still be seen, and Friar Marcus went to complete his mission by looking at it from a discreet distance. With some of his Indians he moved cautiously ahead until he came within view of the town which he saw rising from a plain of brush and rock "at the base of a round hill." (It was the old pueblo of Zuñi, later abandoned.) Beyond it in the distance he could see six other settlements. They lay in a green valley "with very good soil." Smoke from many fires rose from the houses, which, as he had been told, were all made of stone, "with terraces and flat roofs," as it looked to him on his distant hilltop.

As for its size, it was, he said "larger than the city of Mexico," which then had about a thousand Spanish inhabitants. Indians told him that Cíbola was the smallest of the seven cities, even so, and that the city of Tontoneac was the largest and best, with "so many houses and people" that there was "no end to it." Farther away the valley was inhabited "for many days' journey to the east." (He was hearing of the New Mexico valley of the Rio Grande.) He remembered how he had been told of golden vessels and ear and nose jewels and sweat-scrapers to be seen there. He was "tempted to descend" to the city of Cíbola, but not only his life would be in danger there—that was nothing of consequence. What he really feared was that if he died, "no information would be obtained regarding this land," which he believed to be "the greatest and best of all that have been discovered."

A sacred act remained to be done.

With the help of his Indian people he made a cairn of stones in which he implanted a "small and slender cross," there being no large pieces of wood available in that desert. Then as a process of legal annexation he said,

I declare that I erect this cross and landmark as a sign

of possession, in the name of Don Antonio de Mendoza, Viceroy and Governor of New Spain, for the Emperor, our Lord, in accordance with my instructions.

—An act which forestalled any claim to the northern lands which might be made later by the Lord Marquess, with his charter. Friar Marcus concluded,

And I take possession of all the seven cities and of the kingdoms of Tontoneac, Acus, and Marata—he named the whole land the kingdom of Saint Francis after his holy father and patron—which I am not going to visit in order that I may return to give a report of what I have done and seen.

And then, he said in his report,

"I turned back with much more fear than food," and "with all possible haste" made for Compostela in New Galicia, where the Governor, Don Francisco Vásquez de Coronado, met him and took him on to the city of Mexico and the Viceroy.

ii.

THE GENERAL AND THE MARQUESS

BORN IN Salamanca twenty-nine years ago, Governor Vásquez de Coronado was an aristocrat who had emigrated to New Spain in the suite of the Viceroy, and had already come a long way in his young career.

Of pleasing appearance—blue-eyed, with dark blond hair, mustaches, and beard, and elegant in figure—he successfully commanded a mission to suppress a minor provincial revolt in the mining district of New Spain. In 1538 he was appointed to the city council of Mexico by the Viceroy—a post he would hold for life. He gave himself to good works, notably the organization of a charitable society to aid female orphans. Through marriage with a virtuous and wealthy young woman—whose paternal grandfather through an illegitimate connection was thought to have been a late King of Spain—he acquired great estates. When affairs in New Galicia needed stabilizing after the cruel and corrupt rule of Nuño de Guzmán, Coronado was sent by the Viceroy to assume

the duties of governor. In four years this well-born but penni-
less immigrant had already made his mark.

Was this a matter of destiny?

He might think so, for in younger days at home in Salamanca, a mathematical friend who had mysterious powers
once spoke to him like a seer.

He said he saw that Coronado would one day find himself
in faraway lands. (This much was true now, for he was in
New Spain.) Moreover, continued his friend in that fateful
conversation of earlier years, he would command a high position and hold much power. (Now at twenty-nine he was a
governor, and even greater things seemed to be readying for
him.) But finally, said the prophet—if it was unfortunate he
must still tell what he knew—one day in the future Coronado
would suffer from a fall from which he would never recover.

As to the third prediction, nothing had come of it. What
immediately concerned him was the question of the command of Viceroy's expedition to conquer the northern kingdom, which was at once set into preparation upon the report
of Friar Marcus of Nice.

A number of officers wanted the captaincy-general of the
enterprise. Chief among them was the Lord Marquess, who
believed he alone had a royal commitment to it, but the
Viceroy would never give it to him. Another claimant was
Pedro de Alvarado, his old lieutenant, but he was otherwise
engaged. Another was Nuño de Guzmán, the Lord Marquess's old enemy. But he was now in jail as a result of
Cabeza de Vaca's reports of his savage treatment of Indians
on the northern frontier. There were other possibilities, but
the officer whose name was sent to the King was Coronado,
and even before his commission was formally issued to him,
he set to work preparing the expedition, sending out scouting
parties, and marshalling a great force—"the most brilliant
company ever assembled in the Indies to go in search of new
lands."

In all the stir of preparations, with rumors flying, and the
idle, adventurous young men of the city crowding to enlist,
the Lord Marquess, waiting at Cuernavaca, was ignored. True,
the Viceroy had sent him a copy of the report made by Friar
Marcus, but he dismissed it with the remark that he himself
had given to Friar Marcus most of the information it contained; and once again he offered to cooperate in any penetration undertaken in the north.

Even if he was fifty-four years old, and lame from a lance

cut suffered years ago in a tournament, and somewhat crippled by a broken arm that had not been set properly, how could his great experience, knowledge and powers of command not be recognized once again and given their proper play? He was as keen as ever, and his thirst for great deeds would never die.

But when there was no official response to his latest proposal, he left Cuernavaca for the capital and went to call upon Coronado, who was well known to be occupied in the Viceroy's preparations for the northern campaign. To the young General, not even thirty years old, who was not yet officially appointed to the command, the scarred old conqueror proposed himself to lead the army to the conquest of Cíbola.

Coronado had no power in the matter, but he loyally reported the furious veteran's proposal to the Viceroy, who chided him for dealing with the enemy, and proceeded, on January 6, 1540, officially to commission Coronado in the command, ordering "that no impediment or hindrance whatsoever be placed in your way in the discharge and exercise of the office of captain-general in said lands. . . ." The expedition would be ready to march in February.

The Lord Marquess of the Valley of Oaxaca did not wait to watch it go—that great column of two hundred thirty cavalry, thirty-two infantry, four friars, a surgeon, a thousand Indians, a thousand horses, six hundred pack animals, six bronze field pieces, twenty-seven harquebuses, nineteen crossbows, the whole commanded by General Vásquez de Coronado wearing a helmet with plumes and a full suit of armor overlaid with gold, as became a young, handsome, confident field commander.

If there were justice left for him anywhere, the Lord Marquess once again must return to the royal source of it. He sailed for Spain from Vera Cruz in January, 1540, and paused at Havana on February fifth. Once again, though it take all his resources, he must travel in style, for pride required him to arrive at court with a great show. When again he should meet the Emperor Charles V to plead for suitable treatment and great new duties, he must present a proper state.

But during the next seven years despite unceasing effort and hope he reached the Emperor only once; and then only for a moment. One day in the street—so the story went—he saw the royal carriage approaching, and in desperation he threw himself upon it, clinging to its straps and calling to its occupant.

"Who is this man?" asked Charles V.

"I am the man," cried Hernando Cortés, "who brought to Your Majesty more kingdoms than your father left you towns!"

The coach swept on. Cortés was swallowed up by the street crowds. There was nothing left. He had only one home to go to—the New World. In December, 1547, he set out for Seville to sail for Vera Cruz. At the age of sixty-two, without again reaching the sea, he died on the way.

iii.

CÍBOLA IN FACT

TO DISCOVER and take the unknown lands north of New Spain, Viceroy Mendoza sent his expedition out in two forces.

The main one of these was the land force commanded by General Vásquez de Coronado, which would be guided to Cíbola by Friar Marcus of Nice. The other was a sea force under the command of Captain Hernando de Alarcón, consisting of a ship and a sloop, which was to go north by sea and keep abreast of the land march, if contact could be maintained. Perhaps supply of the army and future travel to the new kingdom could be managed by shipping.

The army was mustered in full at Compostela, the capital of New Galicia, in late February, 1540. The Lord Viceroy was present, having come from the city of Mexico for the grand departure of his troops. One by one the soldiers—General Vásquez de Coronado first, cavalry next, infantry last—passed before the royal notary, gave their names, the number of their animals, and the nature and extent of their armor and arms. Many were fully armored, others listed only a helmet or a coat of mail, some carried Spanish guns and swords, and many more only "native weapons"—lances, or bows and arrows.

"When these people," recorded the royal notary, "had been seen, reviewed, and examined by His Lordship," the

commander and his chief officers asked that they be permitted
to take a solemn oath "in order that they might more ef-
fectively do their duty as faithful vassals and servants of
His Majesty," as was "fitting to his royal service." Thereupon,
by the Cross and the Holy Gospels, each in turn with his
hand upon a missal held by a Franciscan friar, they gave their
honor to their cause.

A tiresome affair had to be disposed of in the next few
days. It seemed that gossip had reached to General Vásquez
de Coronado saying that "some persons ill-disposed towards
this expedition" had been going around in the capital with
the unpleasant statement that the expedition was to be traced
to his own notions, and that its members had been enrolled
solely through his own "request and urging," and that because of him and his recruitment of the army, the city of
Mexico and other towns would be "left with but a few
people," which might "result in serious difficulties."

It was infuriating that such talk should go about, when the
truth was that the expedition had been organized by the
Viceroy "in the name of His Majesty," and further, declared
the General, out of the whole army only a "very few" were
residents of New Spain, and furthermore, they were not going
to the north because they had been "attracted or induced" by
him, but were going "of their own accord," and finally such
a handful would "not be missed in New Spain." The General
asked that witnesses be called to examine the newly written
muster rolls, and to testify about the composition of the
army, in order to put down scandalous talk. Who knew where
it had come from? The Lord Marquess of the Valley of
Oaxaca had sailed for Spain, but what if he had expressed
himself before leaving?

In any case, a number of reliable witnesses settled the
matter.

Were they present at the mustering of the army on Sunday,
February 21, 1540, in this city of Compostela?

They were.

Did they see or recognize any residents of the city of
Mexico in the ranks or on the roll?

Only one or two, including, of course, the General.

As for the members of the expedition—all witnesses said
they were going of their own free will, and one said they
were "the happiest people in this land that he ever saw going
on conquests and expeditions," and another said one man
was being sent to the war by his father "because of his

mischievousness," and several witnesses, lifted by the spirit of the occasion, declared that actually, the capital would be better off without some of those who were leaving—it would be "one of the greatest blessings that had come to this New Spain" to see the departure of "many of these people, as they were mostly single and dissolute men without anything to do . . . but eat and loaf," who, in any case, "would have had to go to Peru and other places."

Sworn and notarized, the proper character of the expedition was established on February 27, 1540, and a month later, the army was at the frontier at Culiacán. It had to travel at the pace of a heavy baggage train with many cattle, and the General was held back by such slowness. He organized a light scouting force, put Captain Tristan de Arellano in command of the main body with orders to follow him when they could, and struck out ahead with Friar Marcus as his guide. They took the minimum in field rations and the General allowed each man to carry only one pound of "other necessary articles." They expected to live off the land, and they thought they had a vivid and accurate image of it in mind, after all the talk in the city of Mexico which repeated what Friar Marcus had told about it—green valleys, passable trails with no obstruction greater than "one small hill, half a league long," a road which in its early stages was only five leagues from the coast of the South Sea, and finally a city larger than Mexico with great stone houses trimmed in turquoise —and which in the repetition grew into a picture of what the Spaniards wanted to find.

All too soon, scratching their way northward over barren land with a small flock of sheep, the General's scouting party learned the hard truths that lay behind rumor.

They came to mountains which they could not pass through in fewer than four days. Two or three wretched villages of huts yielded up no information about what lay beyond. "The whole company felt very displeased at this," said the General. Would all the rest turn out this way—all the excited promises heard in Mexico? The General heartened them as well as he could, telling them that the Viceroy had always declared that this part of the trip would be "effort wasted," but that the real interest awaited them all at Cíbola.

"All marched cheerfully," then, though along "a very bad trail," which again "troubled the soldiers not a little, seeing that everything which the friar had reported turned out to be quite the opposite." Instead of the gentle hill half a league long, the truth was they had to cross mountains where even with the best of trails there was great danger that the horses might fall away into canyons below. The trail was so rocky that many of the sheep lost their hoofs picking their way along. A dozen or so horses died of exhaustion. Some Indians and Negroes in the General's party deserted.

And the sea coast—this lay fifteen leagues away, not five, and it took Indians in the region ten days to reach it. Friar Marcus was wrong again, and "all felt great anxiety and dismay to see that everything was the opposite of what he had told," said the General. He heard, too, that the ships of Captain de Alarcón had been seen, and he could only hope that they may have "discovered something good."

On the Eve of St. John—June twenty-third—they entered the last desert before Cíbola, and here more horses died, and the way was harder than ever, with wasteland, mountain and glare. As for living off the land—there was food for neither man nor animal. A Spaniard, several Indians and two Negroes, in their hunger, ate of a pestiferous weed and died of it.

But if the way was "very bad" for perhaps a hundred miles, at the end of it the scouting party at last found a promise of ease. "We found cool rivers," said the General, "and grass like that of Castile . . . ; we found also many nut and mulberry trees . . ." and soon came Indian messengers from Cíbola, which lay two days' march ahead. Several exchanges followed, avowing peace on both sides, but before the last night on the march, the General sent his chief of staff to observe whether there might be a strategic place where the Indians could take a stand and fight.

"He went, and found a very bad place in our way where we might have received much harm. He immediately established himself there with the force which he was conducting."

At night the Indians also came to take up a position there. When they found the soldiers already in place, they attacked, "like valiant men." The soldiers were ready and in a little while an Indian "sounded a little trumpet as a sign of retreat" and the skirmish was over with no harm to the Spaniards. Word of this encounter was sent back to the General at once. Indian signal fires sent news of the army across the valley. With daylight the General ordered the march resumed, for he thought they would all die of hunger if they had to wait one

more day before coming to the city where there must be
stores of food.

The army drew into a wide valley with rolling floors of
olive green bush and grass. Where the earth showed through,
its color was a dense pink, and in the same color, striped
with bands of dusty ochre, on all sides rose grand mesas. In
their great receding perspectives they looked like mighty
palaces empty of all but elegance and grandeur, and in the
color-washing light and wavering air of midday in summer,
their façades took on an opalescent glow. Deep in the valley
along a low-domed hill was a cluster of houses. It was
Cíbola.

The General came in sight of it seventy-seven days after
leaving Culiacán, and sent officers and monks ahead to read
aloud the Requirement of 1513, which in this instance "was
made intelligible to the people of the country through an
interpreter."

In reply, arrows flew, and one cut through the robe of
one of the friars. Bringing up his own party, the General
ordered the attack, closing against the city of Cíbola in
mounted formation, with the battle cry of Lord Saint
James. Indians were massed against him in the open fields
before the many-terraced town. Their order soon broke under
the mounted assault. They turned and ran for the "terraces
and corridors" of their houses, and many of them were killed
before they reached the walls. Once home, the warriors took
up the defense on their rooftops.

The General deployed his horsemen about the base of the
city while he led the foot soldiers to the walls. These looked
very high. His crossbowmen and harquebusiers were ordered
to fire at the Indians edging the roofs, but the "crossbowmen
soon broke the strings of their crossbows and the musketeers
could do nothing, because they had arrived so weak and
feeble that they could scarcely stand on their feet."

Among them the General in his golden armor was the
prime target, and twice he was knocked to the ground by
"countless great stones" which the Indians threw down
from the roofs as he tried to mount the walls by a ladder.
Only his well-made helmet saved him, for one rock came so
hard that it made a dent in it. He bore two small wounds
in his face and many bruises on arm and leg, and an arrow
struck him in the foot and stayed there. As he was felled for
the second time, the chief of staff came and threw himself
over the General to protect him, failing which he must have

been in much greater danger. He said long later that he was removed as one dead from the field and placed in a tent where he "remained unconscious for a long time."

When he came to, he was told that the Indians had withdrawn, and the city of Cíbola had fallen, and there, said a soldier, "There we found something we prized more than gold or silver, namely, much maize, beans, and chickens larger than those here of New Spain, and salt better and whiter than I have ever seen in my whole life."

Two or three other soldiers were wounded, and three horses were killed, and seven or eight hurt. But soon all were "healed and well," and the General could report that "all these gentlemen and soldiers bore themselves well, as was expected of them," and he now looked about at the kingdom he had entered, and of which Friar Marcus had given the first extended news.

"Not to be too verbose," wrote the General to the Viceroy about the friar's report, "I can assure you that he has not told the truth in a single thing he said, but everything is the opposite of what he related, except the name of the cities and the large stone houses."

But even the houses, if they were "good," failed to match the report, for they were not made of stone, and their doorways were not ornamented with turquoises. The great Seven Cities were "seven little villages," and now it became clear that Cíbola was the name not alone for the first of them, but for all of them together. In honor of the Viceroy's native city, the General named the first one Granada, and established his headquarters there while he sent exploring parties out over the country.

He was obliged to say that so far as he could judge, there seemed little hope of "getting gold or silver." Still, he added, "I trust in God that, if there is any, we shall get our share of it, and it shall not escape us through any lack of diligence in the search." He sent descriptions of the people, their foods, their animals, their beliefs, and he added examples of their handiwork, some of which did show scraps of turquoise. He dated his report August third, 1540, and sent it by messenger, with armed escort—the only return trip of which there is record for that summer. If so it was, then Friar Marcus of Nice, his usefulness as a guide at an end, travelled to the city of Mexico in the small company.

iv.

WINTER QUARTERS

FROM GRANADA Pedro de Tovar led a party north and found the Hopi pueblos. López de Cárdenas scouted westward and discovered the Colorado River and the vast work it had made through ages—the Grand Canyon. In the early days of August the General had visitors—Indians from a town to the east who had heard of his coming. They lived on a red river and a little way farther on a great country of plains opened out. There ranged immense herds of strange cows—the visitors showed how their short horns curled, how tight was their curly matted hair, how massive were their bodies, how short the legs of the bison of the plains east of the Pecos River. It was information which should be acted upon, and the General dispatched Captain Hernando de Alvarado with twenty soldiers and a chaplain to explore the eastern country and send a report within eighty days. The Pecos Indians guided them on their way, while the General awaited the main body of the army to overtake him at Granada.

It arrived in November, in good order, but with a disappointing report about the fleet under Alarcón. It seemed that a detachment of the army had gone looking for the ships, and had heard reports of them from Indians, that they had sailed up a wide river. Hurrying to see, the soldiers found only a tree on which was written, "Alarcón came this far. There are letters at the foot of this tree." They dug for the letters, and read how Captain de Alarcón had searched and waited for the General or his men, and then, fearing that the ship and the sloop were becoming unseaworthy through rotting, he had been obliged to write his letters, bury them, and sail homeward.

But if this was disappointing news, the General heard better from the east. Tovar sent an enthusiastic report of his discoveries, and advised that the army come to take up winter quarters where he now was. He was in a town among many towns on the banks of a great river called the River of

Our Lady, for he had so named it in honor of its discovery on her feast day. (It was the Rio Grande in its central valley in New Mexico.) The people there received him with flute music and little ceremonial marches, and gave him food, skins, blankets. They were good people, who would rather farm than make war. They raised chickens and grew corn, beans, and melons. The houses were made of mud and rose two stories, as a rule, though some were higher, and one (Taos), was "well worth seeing." In all he estimated there were eighty towns in the river country. He placed crosses wherever he went, and the people blessed these in their own way with dustings of sacred meal, and climbed upon them to fasten flowers and feathers to the wooden arms. It was much the best country Alvarado had yet seen, and he sent the General a map of it, and many examples of Indian dress, and a buffalo head, and strongly advised that the whole army come there to take up winter quarters. The province was called Tiguex, and could be reached in a march of eight days from Granada.

The General decided to go.

Once again he rode out in advance of the main army, taking with him thirty horsemen, and striking eastward as winter came down from the continental north. There were three days when he had no water, but just before reaching the river he found towns and turned northward to join his advance party. After the brush deserts and rocky passages of the march, he now came into the rich valley of the great river, with its easing glades of cottonwood and willow, and its fields of corn by the earthen towns. On both sides of the immediate fertile valley the desert reached away, and in the distance blue mountains were always visible.

The General found everything in good order. On his first evening in camp he received Alvarado, who had just returned from a look at the eastern cattle plains, bringing news of much promise, and a strange creature who was the chief source of it.

This was an Indian prisoner whom Alvarado called the Turk, because he "looked like one." The Turk had come into his possession at Pecos, telling many stories of the wonders to the east. He had, he said, once brought a golden bracelet from the east. The General pricked up his ears and sent for him this evening at the encampment on the Rio Grande. Questioning followed:

The Turk came from the plains?

Yes, replied the Turk.

What was that country like, of which he spoke, east of the big cows?

So: a river six miles wide full of fish bigger than horses. And?

On the river were rowing boats with sails, holding forty oarsmen. Golden eagles were fastened at the prows. Great lords reclined at ease under canopies in the stern. The king of that land spent his siesta under a great tree whose branches dripped with little golden bells which rang in the breeze.

Did he know what gold was, really?

Of course he knew. It was *acochis*.

The General showed him an object made of tin and asked if this was gold.

The Turk smelled of the tin and replied that it was not gold, for he knew gold and silver, and did not care for other metals.

So there was also silver in that country?

Oh, quantities. The table service was all of silver, and great vessels, too.

Where was the Turk's golden bracelet of which the General had been told?

It had been taken from him and was hidden at Pecos. If they would let him go alone he would find it and bring it back.

He was taken away under custody.

The images he raised in the mind were all implicit in the questions he had been asked. He knew only a little Spanish. The Spaniards turned his answers into their own terms of treasure and wealth. The country which the Turk kindled alive in the Spanish imagination was called Quivira. Spring could not come soon enough for the soldiers to find it and from it take their fortunes. The General questioned him another time, and the wonderful answers streamed on:

Gold—there was so much of it that it would take not pack animals but wagons to haul it. The king's canoes had golden oarlocks. Beyond Quivira were other, even richer lands—Harahey and Guaes, and the king there was called Tatarrax who prayed out of a book to a lady who was Queen of Heaven.

How could the Turk know all such things? He was a man of marvels, and on one occasion he was a man of holy terror, for without ever leaving his cell or talking with anyone else, he told the guard who kept watch on him how many Spaniards had been killed in battle against a certain Indian town in the third week of February, 1541. The guard understood where such powers came from when one day he saw, he swore under oath that he saw, the Turk talking to the Devil who was enclosed in a jug filled with water. The books of learned chroniclers at home were full of creatures like the Turk, who must be dealt with carefully, but whose knowledge was not to be dismissed.

v.

QUIVIRA

THE MAIN ARMY arrived at the river on a day of heavy snowfall and found the garrison putting itself in order after a battle which they fought on the day before. At first peaceable, with little flute songs and gifts and corn meal blessings, the pueblo people had changed their view of the newcomers, and the General had gone to war against one of their towns.

The grievances of the Indians were many. The soldiers had required Indians to abandon a town so that the garrison could live in it as the autumn turned to winter. A soldier had attempted to violate an Indian woman. The General had levied an assessment of clothes from the Indians so that soldiers would be kept warm, even though Indians, with only the clothes they wore, should freeze.

The Indians came by useful information—they learned that the soldiers were mortal, and that their horses were also—those chief sources of superior power to move about fast and overwhelm people who walked. One day the Indians stampeded the Spanish horse bands, killing many horses, driving others away, and locking others inside a pueblo enclosure, to be slaughtered at will. The soldiers recovered most of their mounts, but the Indian revolt had spread, and in the valley towns arose the spirit of war.

The General held a council of officers and chaplains, and with utmost gravity all aspects of the perilous situation were weighed. It was decided that peace must be proposed to the

Indians, and if they refused, then battle must follow. The offer was made. Defiance met it.

Two pueblos were at once designated for destruction—Arenal and Moho, up the river from the army's winter quarters at Alcanfor. The first was taken by the river garrison, with arms, battering ram and fire on a day of snow. After the arrival of the main army the second was besieged for fifty days before it fell. Other pueblos fortifying for rebellion were reduced and one was burned. The surviving people of all the towns in the immediate valley abandoned their dwellings and fields rather than remain near the Spanish invaders. The soldiers were left with the shell of a conquest by the river, which was now frozen solid all the way across.

But as the individuals of the army saw it, their purpose was greater than to live in mud houses, as they called the pueblos, and grow beans and corn. Quivira beckoned, and when winter slacked off, and just before the ice could turn to spring freshets, the entire force of fifteen hundred people, and a thousand horses, and five hundred cattle, and five thousand sheep, left Alcanfor on the west bank and crossed over to the east bank on the ice to set out in late April, 1541, for the buffalo plains. There, insisted the Turk, who went along as a chained guide, untold riches waited to be taken in the land of the river six miles wide. (In the same month, Hernando de Soto, marching from Florida, reached the Mississippi, and a few weeks later, on a Sunday, Francisco Pizarro was assassinated while at lunch, after Mass, in his palace in Peru, calling out "Jesu!" and drawing a cross with his finger in his own blood on the floor.)

For many weeks the great column toiled eastward over flat plains while Quivira remained always beyond the horizon. The Turk guided the army now one way, now another, and searching for the fabulous, the marchers saw only natural marvels—seas of grass, a hailstorm so violent that the stones dented armor, great canyons of red rock, vast herds of buffalo running across the plains like cloud shadows. They met an old blind Indian who told how he and his village, wandering in search of food, met four great doctors several years ago, one of them a Negro, who healed the sick, blessed food, and asked how to go toward the setting sun. In this memory the wandering soldiers recognized Núñez Cabeza de Vaca and his companions, whose reports had started the whole enterprise by which a Spanish army was now come to these empty and profitless plains.

By early summer they had found nothing, and if much more of the summer must be spent in returning to the river, they should go at once, to gather stores before another winter which, as they now knew, they must endure among the pueblos.

The General, explaining how necessary it was to protect the army's future, ordered all the main body to the river except thirty-six cavalry and six infantry who would remain with him. He would go forward to find Quivira fast and alone. When he found it he would send word after the army and they could all turn around and join him to take the riches of the east together.

Many soldiers objected, declaring that they would choose to die with him if need be rather than go without him to the river, but in the end, all did as he ordered, though they won his permission to wait for two weeks on the plains in case he should send for them. He moved out with his escort until he vanished into the blur of light and distance which was all that defined the plains.

The army saw or heard nothing of him until in autumn he returned to the pueblo on the river, and then all were eager for his news.

In brief, he had no news—no good news.

Quivira?

Only a succession of endless plains under the summer sun.

Gold? The river six miles wide? The royal canoes?

No sign of gold. No river. No canoes.

But King Tatarrax?

If the General had seen King Tatarrax, he was a naked ancient wearing a copper bangle—his whole wealth—around his neck.

But the Turk, who knew where the gold was?

The Turk was dead, by order of the General, for he had proved to be a lying traitor who had even schemed to betray the army to enemy Indians. Even to the very end he had continued to make his promises and to waft his visions of Quivira.

And nothing of these was true?

On the contrary, in Quivira you lived off small game and cow meat and nuts and berries, and if you had to cook a meal, you scratched together a little heap of dried cow dung and lighted it to make a fire.

But perhaps Quivira had not actually been reached? Perhaps it would all come true in the end?

Perhaps. The General agreed that, since he now knew so much about the plains, he could lead the garrison out again in the next spring, and then, farther to the east than he had been able to go this time, he might at last show them the kingdom they believed in.

Meanwhile, winter was here again in the river pueblos, and there was enough to do to keep alive.

vi.

The Undiscovered

THE GENERAL, a keen horseman, enjoyed exercising his string of twenty-two mounts. Two days after Christmas in 1541 he went out riding. With him was one of his young officers, Captain Rodrigo de Maldonado, who had distinguished himself in the destruction of the rebellious river towns. As they rode side by side, the commander and his aide broke into a race. Both rode hard. The General pulled into the lead. Suddenly he fell from his seat and landed directly in the path of the captain's horse. It was too late for the captain to turn. All he could do was to gather his horse for a jump. The horse took to the air, but one of its flinging hoofs struck the General's head, knocking him down.

He was carried to his quarters where for days he lay close to death. How could he have fallen? They found that his saddle girth, long neglected and rotting, had broken. When slowly he began to recover it seemed that his confidence was gone. He awakened to word of danger which had developed far to the south toward Mexico—Indians had rebelled and had attacked a Spanish way station. The homeward route was threatened. When he heard the news, the General took to his bed again.

Now in his weakness he was full of thoughts of home, and he remembered the prophecy of the mathematical seer in Salamanca—how many years ago now?—who had promised him a faraway land, and power, and a fall from which he would never recover. Was the prophecy now all fulfilled? If so, then the General told his attending doctor that he wanted to die at home, surrounded by his wife and children.

When the doctor repeated outside the sickroom what he had heard there, the garrison fell into two camps—those who longed to go home and those who insisted on reaching, once again, for Quivira. The question was argued as winter broke into spring, but in the end, the power of command had its way, and in April, 1542, the army lumbered away westward from the river of the pueblos, carrying the General, on his bad days, in a litter. Four Franciscans, a Portuguese soldier, a Negro and a Mexican Indian stayed behind, and two of the Franciscans later found martyrdom in the northern wilderness. Otherwise—it was a record of which the command could be proud—only twenty men, including Spaniards and Indian allies, were lost on the two-year expedition. (Far to the East, in that same April, Hernando de Soto, having explored as far west as part of Arkansas and Oklahoma, died near the Mississippi and was buried in its waters—the Turk's vast river which the General never found.)

As for the great northern kingdom, a soldier who went there with the General wrote some twenty years afterward, remembering the passion and promise of Cíbola, ". . . And thus the name of these seven cities and the search for them remains until now, since they have never been discovered. . . ."

In 1545 the presiding judge of a royal inquiry in the city of Mexico reported to the Emperor at Madrid, concerning the General,

"Francisco Vásquez came to his home, and he is more fit to be governed in it than to govern outside it. He is lacking in many of his former fine qualities and he is not the same man he was when Your Majesty appointed him to that governorship. They say this change was caused by the fall from a horse which he suffered in the exploration and pacification of Tierra Nueva."

Granted honor, the General remained an invalid until at the age of forty-four he died in the city of Mexico on September 22, 1554, and was buried under the altar of the Dominican church. If his expedition went and returned without establishing any lasting settlement, it still served the best of all uses in its time which was to gain knowledge of new lands.

V

FRUITS OF CONQUEST

A conqueror was a name
of honor.

—*Thomas Gage, 1625.*

i.

The Nature of Man

FOR HALF A century after the return of Coronado the northern wilderness rested undisturbed, though Quivira was not forgotten, nor was the South Sea, "where there were pearls."

But if new expeditions were in the making, they did not come to readiness before 1550, and then, on April sixteenth of that year, a royal order at Madrid suspended all new conquests across the Spanish world until a question of the utmost importance could be explored to the satisfaction of the Crown.

In effect, the question was, what is an Indian?

It had been hotly debated for many years, and the opponents in the issue were passionate in their convictions. On one side were the missionary clergy, led by the Bishop of Chiapa, Fray Bartolomé de las Casas, who held that the Indian was a human being, who possessed an immortal soul, and who was capable of enjoying freedom and of being educated. On the other were the great landholding conquerors who found it useful to quote Aristotle in their contention that the Indian was a "natural slave" set aside by nature to serve masters who were born for a rich and comfortable life. The argument split the Spanish world down the center, though odd mixtures of fellows were found on each side of it.

The great principle, aside from humanitarian feeling, which moved Fray Bartolomé and his adherents was enunciated by the highest authorities. Queen Isabella the Catholic had long ago declared that the Indian was a "full and free citizen," and Pope Paul III in his bull "Sublimis Deus" had responded to the discovery of whole new populations in the New World with this judgment:

"The said Indians and all other people who may later be discovered by Christians, are by no means to be deprived of their liberty or the possession of their property, even though they may be outside the faith of Jesus Christ . . . nor should they in any way be enslaved."

Fray Bartolomé insisted that the Indians could be favorably likened to people of ancient classic civilizations, and far from qualifying as Aristotle's "natural slaves" actually met his requirements for "the good life." The Temples of Yucatán seemed to Fray Bartolomé to be as wonderful as the pyramids of Egypt. In "all the sciences, arts and crafts that they have been taught," especially in the study of liturgical music, Indians impressed their missioners as intelligent and able people. "No one is born enlightened," declared Fray Bartolomé, and continued with love and fury to say, "From this it follows that all of us must be guided and aided at first by those who were born before us. And the savage peoples of the earth may be compared to uncultivated soil that readily brings forth weeds and useless thorns, but has within itself such natural virtue that by labour and cultivation it may be made to yield sound and beneficial fruits." How was this to come? By "the method that is proper and natural to men . . . namely, love, gentleness and kindness."

The first bishop of Mexico, Juan de Zumárraga, in the twenty years of his reign (he died in 1548) shared the view of Fray Bartolomé. Believing that the Indians were rational beings whose souls could be saved, he worked to educate them. He founded an academy for Aztec boys and another for girls, and fostered the writing of books to teach them. Sending for a printing press—the first to be brought to America—he hoped to spread knowledge abroad, not only for Spanish colonists but for Indians. Policies like these, derived from churchmen in positions of power, and permitted expression by the Crown, vastly enraged the conqueror soldiers and lords of the captured lands and peoples.

Why had they fought and risked all if not to gain ease, riches and slaves to the end of their days? What happened to a soldier taken by Indians? They had seen the atrocities —hearts dug out of living men with stone knives and all the rest. They were glad to have the support of a learned canon lawyer in Spain, a certain Sepúlveda, who declared that the Indians were and, under Aristotle's doctrine, should remain, the "animate possessions" of the conquerors, who were their lords by nature.

The atrocities that followed under this conviction were seen by many men, and recorded. The noses and hands of Indian prisoners were cut off. Governor de Guzmán, on the northwestern frontier of New Spain, abused his captured slaves so dreadfully that rather than procreate children who might grow up to be taken by him, Indian parents were known to have denied themselves the act of conception. A witness stated that he had seen Spanish lords, "long after the conquest," ride to the hunt with their hounds, with Indians as the quarry, and do this either for the sport itself or merely to train their killer dogs. An English priest in the early seventeenth century remarked upon "the chiefest of all the islands of this New World, which is called Hispaniola and formerly by the natives Haiti, which lamenteth the loss of at least three millions of Indians murdered by her new masters of Spain." A few generations after the Lord Admiral Columbus found his "very gentle" people, not one person of their populous Carib nation survived. In Peru, the Spaniards behaved so cruelly that they seemed quite of another order of being than human, and, as Indians explained, must therefore have been spawned by creatures of the sea.

"Surely," wrote Fray Bartolomé in his last will and testament, "surely God will wreak His fury and anger against Spain some day for the unjust wars waged against the American Indians," and elsewhere he bitterly said that "the Christians let it be seen in the Indies that gold was their God."

Charles V abdicated in favor of his son Philip II in 1556, with the argument still unresolved. In practice, it never was precisely resolved, though in 1573 new regulations were imposed on the terms of colonial conquest and administration which in principle, at least, granted to the Indian his humanity.

The King by his orders declared that he had made justice real in the Indies. He made it possible "for the Indians to go safely by all roads and to carry on their civil pursuits peacefully." If the royal wish were tantamount to achieved action, the King had freed Indians "from all burdens and servitude." More, he had bestowed upon them the valued knowledge of such earthly goods as "bread, wine, oil, and many other foods, woolen cloth, silk, linen, horses, cows, tools, arms, and many other things from Spain," and he had "instructed them in crafts and trades by which they live excellently." In sum, all such advantages were to be enjoyed by Indians who would "embrace our Holy Faith and render obedience to our King." If Indians must pay in labor for such advantages, it seemed officially suitable, since their employers the Spanish landholders to whom they were "entrusted"

must guarantee their safety, their well-being and their nourishment. And if armed action should have to be taken against
Indians, this must come only upon specific approval by ec-
celesiastical authority. It was a solution carefully planned in
Madrid, thousands of miles away, where an official recom-
mendation on paper seemed to administrators like an accomplished reform of the poor realities which still persisted
in the colonies of New Spain—all the old habits of Spanish
greed and Indian retaliation which continued to demonstrate
the polarities of human nature, no matter what king might
command or church condemn.

Through the decades of the sixteenth century the argument lost its violence, the enterprise of colonial lords recovered itself, and once again the frontiers of the New World
continents were pushed farther out against the unknown lands.
Effort at the perimeter of empire was given constant renewal
by a highly organized ocean trade which linked the Old
World and the New, while slowly, inevitably, the New World
learned how to belong to itself.

ii.

THE OCEAN TRADE

IN THE SIXTEENTH and seventeenth centuries, sailing for the
New World was still the experience which called most strongly to people of the Old.

The natural dangers of the voyage and those added by
piracy made it advisable for ships to cross the ocean in fleets
rather than singly, with armed convoys taking them past the
traffic lanes of European commerce.

Two fleets were dispatched each year from Spain. One of
these took sail in late spring bound for the Gulf of Mexico,
and was commonly referred to as the *flota*, or merchant fleet,
to mark it off from the other, which sailing in mid-summer
for South American ports, was called the *Galeones*, or galleons. Cádiz was the active trans-Atlantic port, and much
of its seagoing life was observed and recorded by Thomas

Gage, an English Dominican friar who sailed for Mexico in 1625.

Forty-one ships of the galleon class made ready in the Bay of Cádiz in early summer of that year. During the afternoon of July first, the Admiral Commanding, being notified that the ships were ready, ordered a signal fired by cannon to warn "all passengers, soldiers and mariners to betake themselves the next morning to their ships." Given to the wind the next morning, the ships with their towering masts and sails "went out one by one, crying 'Adios, Adios,'" and from shore came the reply for each one, "Buen viaje, buen viaje."

An armed convoy of eight galleons escorted the fleet to defend it against possible attack by Turks or Hollanders, "whom the Spanish dons shake and tremble at," on its course set for the Canary Islands along the great Atlantic curve of upper Africa. The convoy stayed with the fleet as far as the Golfo de Yeguas, which the Dominican said was so named because its waters acted like "Kicking Mares—the swelling surges did so kick our ships that we thought they would have kicked our St. Anthony's gilded image out of our ship."

From the Canaries, the fleet set westward before a "pleasant and prosperous gale, with a quiet and milken sea." The ships were now powered by the Lord Admiral Christopher Columbus's wind before which he had gone to find the Indies. Even in its mildness, the heavy ships with their blunt breasts and towering castles went "floating and reeling" on their way.

If the danger all abroad on the sea was too large to fit the mind the whole time of the voyage, life within the ship was trying in many lesser ways which passengers made note of. A legal officer—a judge—going out to serve in the colonies wrote home of conditions which he and his wife and children found on board. Their cabin was hardly high enough to stand in and was only five feet square. They slept on the deck, using thin mats stuffed with dog hair and blankets of goatskin. Rats and cockroaches were busy all about them, especially in the darkness of night, and it was next to impossible to avoid lice. The castles at prow and stern, loosely and elaborately built up on the hull, shook so in even moderate winds that the judge wondered if they must be taken off by harder weather. If anyone was seasick—most were—there was no comfort or ease to be had. The smell of the bilgewater was sickening by itself—"foaming like hell and stinking like the devil."

In health, the passengers were either lying down or sitting day and night, for there was no place to promenade. Their food was monotonous and revolting—hard tack, a few hens while they lasted, salted beef and mutton, a few spices. Sailors had been known to eat rats and chew upon the leather fittings of the rigging to vary their diet. There was no water for washing except that of the ocean when the ship was becalmed, when men could jump overboard to swim. But not all could do this, and all sought comfort and patience in the chanted prayers of the cabin boys which marked the hours, and spoke their own devotions and considered the mystery of man's life, which came from Almighty God, and so often found itself in odd or precarious circumstances, yet the while remaining attached to Him.

The bowl-shaped hold of the ship carried such cargo as wines, figs, raisins, oil, olives, kerseys, linen, silk, iron, and for use in the mines of Mexico at Zacatecas and elsewhere, quicksilver, to "fetch out the pure silver." Certain voyages brought horses and cows—though many animals died of the confinement and strangeness of shipboard—tools, arms, and "a thousand kinds of seeds as well as plants" carried in large earthen jars. Most of the items in the cargo had never been known in the Novo Mondo before the entry of Spain, and many new crafts, skills and trades were implied by these objects. Within a few decades New Spain had developed ocean traffic with China, Japan, the East Indies and the Philippines. Much of the cargo from Europe would be taken overland to the Pacific ports of Acapulco and Mazatlan for shipping on to the Orient, and returning to Spain, the Atlantic fleets would bring oriental cargoes to Europe.

To beguile the time of the long voyage, the passengers created their own entertainment. They sang songs to the accompaniment of the guitar, and watched cockfights on deck so long as there were birds that had not yet gone into the stew, and played at bullfighting, and gave impromptu plays, and there was always someone to dance. Otherwise, "we much delighted and sported ourselves," said the English Dominican of his own voyage, "in fishing many sorts of fishes." In 1605 westbound passengers were reading a book just published which would never thereafter be out of print. It was *Don Quixote de la Mancha*.

Sometimes the ship ran into weather so hot that no one

could remain below in the stifling cabins. "Such a day," said the Dominican, "was no pleasure unto us, for the repercussion of the Sun's heat upon the still water and pitch of our ships kindled a scorching fire, which all day distempered our bodies with a constant running sweat." They could only cast off most of their clothing and wait for night, but even then, it was too hot below for sleep, and they stayed on deck wearing only their shirts. Some swam to be cool, but this was dangerous, for a swimming sailor was taken by a shark.

If a ship named for a saint met the saint's day during the crossing, it was an occasion for excitement and joy, well prepared for during the days of the voyage. The ship was "trimmed around with white linen," while her flags and topgallants depicted the saint. A festive dinner was served, and at nightfall, "at least 50 shots of ordnance" were fired, and then came five hundred squibs of fireworks. If the weather was calm, the "masts and tackings were hung with paper lanterns having burning lights within them." In one such fiesta, said Thomas Gage, the ship's company of soldiers, passengers and "some of the younger friars" acted "a comedy out of famous Lope de Vega." Carried away like any amateur watching home theatricals, the Dominican declared that the play "was as stately acted and set forth both in shows and good apparel, in that narrow compass of our ship, as might have been in the best stage of the court of Madrid." And "the waits ceased not from sounding, nor the Spaniards from singing all night."

And when the *flota* came to the first islands of the New World, those making the passage for the first time marvelled at how the "naked barbarians who with great joy do yearly expect the Spanish fleet's coming" still painted themselves red all over, as they had been reported to do by the Lord Admiral Columbus more than a century before. But by now islanders knew more of their visitors, and there was an occasional incident, as when an Indian shot a friar with a poisoned arrow, so that he died at sea four days later after the ships had resumed their way, and was buried overside, "his grave being the whole ocean."

Havana was of interest to the ocean passengers as the treasure station of the Indies. There, "commonly in the month of September," reported the Dominican, "is joined all the treasure, as I might say, of America, all the King of Spain's revenue, with as much more of merchants' goods," which in the year he was there "were thought to be in all worth thirty million," carried in fifty-three ships. Havana was a strong-hold, impossible to conquer, with its deeply protected harbor, and its two fortress castles, one at the mouth, the other inside. In the outer castle were "twelve pieces of ordnance of brass, exceeding great, which they called the Twelve Apostles."

Enemy navies or pirates were not so foolish as to come within range of the Twelve Apostles; but other approaches to the treasure fleets might be managed, and one time an admiral of Holland, whom the Spaniards called Pie de Palo for his wooden leg, waylaid a homebound fleet from Mexico with six or seven millions of cargo and drove it up the Matanzas River, not far from Havana. The Spaniards found the river "too shallow for their heavy and great-bellied galleons, and so ran them aground." The Dutchman captured almost all the treasure, even to a chest containing gold chains, diamonds, pearls and precious stones which a Spanish Jesuit hid under his habit. The Spanish Admiral Don Juan de Guzmán y Torres, said the Dominican, finishing the story, was imprisoned on reaching Spain, went mad, and was beheaded.

It was in itself a long voyage to sail from Havana across the great Gulf of Mexico, and there was a lift of feeling when at last the travellers heard the cry of *"Tierra, tierra, tierra!"*—and "we with full sail running to embrace it." Now with their goal in sight the ship's companies were able to abandon frugality, and contrive a grand supper, using up all provisions which they had guarded carefully while the voyage yet lasted. Lying offshore at night the better to land safely by daylight, the Dominican and his fellows lighted "hallowed wax candles," and knelt to Mary, pouring forth hymns, litanies and prayers of thanksgiving.

In the morning, by the sparkling sea light of the coast, the ships drew into the harbor of Vera Cruz through the blue gap in the white reef, while cannon salutes were exchanged between ship and shore. The city had been removed from the Rio Antigua in 1599 to be permanently resettled upon its original site opposite the protective island of San Juan de Ulúa, and was now a town of wooden houses set in the sand dunes, with a large church. The friars went in procession with crucifer to the cloisters prepared for them, where cups of chocolate were offered to all.

Dinner followed, and the Dominican noted by the way how those who ate and drank too greedily of the fruits and water of that new land were taken suddenly by "dangerous

fluxes," which hastened death "to those newly come from
Spain to those parts." After dinner seats were set up in the
church for the new arrivals, among whom was the new Viceroy of Mexico, and there they saw a comedy played, "which
had been on purpose studied and prepared by the town for
the entertainment of the new Viceroy." When presently it was
time to move overland to the city of Mexico, they found
the sandy road to be "as wide and open as is our road
from London to St. Albans." Indians along the way, well-
instructed in advance, welcomed the travellers at every town
with flowers, music, the Te Deum, and refreshments.

iii.

COLONIAL WAYS

BEFORE SAILING from Cádiz, the English Dominican had
spent an evening with a Spanish colleague in holy orders
who gave him supper, washed down with sherry wine. As
the evening wore on, and the sherry flowed freely, the
Spanish friar—a century after the conquest—was lifted with
visions about the nature of the New World, which he had
never seen, and to which his English friend was going before
him. He gave him, in a persistence of the fantasy which
Europeans had held before the discovery of America, an
eloquent description of what he would find across the world.

"The Indies," he fancied, were "paved with tiles of gold
and silver, the stones to be pearls, rubies, and diamonds,
the trees to be hung with clusters of nutmegs bigger than
the clusters of the grapes of Canaan"—for the first wealth
dreamed of there was spices—"and the fields to be planted
with sugar-canes, which would so sweeten the chocolate that
it would far exceed the milk and honey of the land of promise. The silks of China he conceited so common that the
sails of the ships were nothing else, and finally he dreamed
of Midas' happiness, that whatsoever he touched should
be turned to gold."

The friar's paradise watered by the wine of Jerez resembled the real world of the colonies in only one particu-

lar—there was wealth in the Indies. But it remained in the hands of a few—the lords of the government, the church, the Crown. The rest of the small Spanish population of New Spain knew a hard life.

During the sixteenth century the yearly emigration from Spain to the Novo Mondo amounted to no more than a thousand to fifteen hundred people. The first census of New Spain, compiled in 1560, showed a Spanish population of about twenty thousand, of whom perhaps eight thousand lived in the city of Mexico. About twenty years later, fifteen thousand lived in the capital. The royal fiscal officer of New Spain estimated that of these about four thousand were unemployed, and the Viceroy said that "every morning in (the city of) Mexico there arise eight hundred men who have nowhere to eat."

In mid-century, Friar Toribio de Motolinia wrote to the Emperor Charles V, "Spaniards are poor and indebted (in New Spain) and there are many idle people eager to . . . rob the natives because they say the Indians are rich and the Spaniards poor and dying of hunger."

It was a shameful spectacle, and he added a word about the greedy and contemptuous use which many colonists made of their wonderful new land. "The Spaniards who have anything are trying to make their fortune and return to Castile . . . Royal officials as well as merchants and rich men are going away laden with gold and silver and the poor remain in want."

In immediate consequence, crime increased, and the idle often had no choice but to live as vagabonds. But a further consequence, which would take centuries to come to full power, was the growth of the idea of restored independence which the original owners of the New World could only feel in the face of their exploitation and treatment as mere conveniences in the imposed structure of the conquering society.

But those with authority and riches—church and state— from the beginning of the colonial establishment, worked to recreate in the new lands all the marks of style which supported life in the old. Chief of these was religion. The Holy Faith, uniting all expressions of life, as it did for the European Latins, on whom the Reformation and its divisiveness had little effect, remained in New Spain as the great motive power of society. In its name education was immediately and widely fostered. Indians were taught Latin before they were taught the Castilian tongue, and friars learned native languages immediately the better to communicate their sacred truths to the people whose souls they sought in honor of the love of God.

In a general climate of education, books were wanted, and Bishop de Zumárraga imported the first printing press in America and issued from it in 1539 its first production, a catechism printed in both the Nahuatl and Castilian languages, a century before the first printing press was set up in Boston.

All other marks of a cultivated life rapidly took form, and within a quarter century of the hard physical triumph of Cortés, New Spain was giving value and expression to the works of the spirit and the mind. The ocean trade brought a steady stream of books, many from the house of the publisher Jacob Cromberger, who had set up his presses in Seville in 1500. It was his son Juan who contracted to establish the Bishop's press in Mexico in 1539. More than seven hundred works were printed at Seville during the sixteenth century and thirty thousand volumes of general books were brought into New Spain during the last quarter of the sixteenth century, in bindings of flexible vellum laced and tied with thongs, or bound in wood covered in calf or velvet. If many of these were works devoted to theology or other aspects of religion, many thousand others were works in philosophy, poetry, drama, history and prose romance. In the growing city of Mexico in the first Spanish century there were fifty booksellers.

The need and love of learning called forth the establishment of the University of Mexico, which enrolled its first students—four brothers named Castilla—on June 13, 1553. A schoolbook, published in the following year, which set forth in a series of exemplary dialogues a description of the city, included information about the new University.

It was patterned after the old school of the Lord Marquess, the University of Salamanca. The beadle carried a silver mace and wore a robe which reached to his ankles, and the students went dressed in long cloaks, and square caps that touched their ears. On all days except holidays, "continuous lectures and interpretations of authors" were given. The University was situated in the great plaza. When passersby heard raised voices coming from open windows, they recognized the sound of students "shouting at the professors."

The type for all colonial cities was the city of Mexico. Gazing upon it from the heights of Chapultepec, the author of the schoolbook had to write,

"O immortal God! What a pleasing spectacle is displayed from here! How beautiful, how pleasing to eyes and mind, how delightful in variety! . . . The whole is situated on an extensive, level plain completely exposed to our gaze on all sides."

His rhapsody continued with recognitions of the towers of Spanish houses, the domes of churches, the Indian quarters "in the suburbs," and far beyond, a backdrop of stony ridges, timbered mountains, and cultivated hills, with here and there the haciendas of great families.

Of the great plaza, the schoolbook cried,

"Good heavens! how level it is and how spacious! How gay! How greatly embellished by the superb and magnificent buildings that surround it on all sides! What order! What beauty! What a situation and location!"

Here, ever since the conquest, the general market was held for all goods and commodities. The cathedral—erected by the Lord Marquess with stones of the Aztec temple it displaced—could not call forth the elevated style of the schoolbook, which only called it "so small, so humble, so lacking in adornment." A larger, more spacious church was to take its place in after years.

The Spanish colonial style brought with it a certain air which the conquerors gave themselves in the capital and elsewhere.

"At the rebuilding of this city," remarked the English Dominican, "there was a great difference betwixt an inhabitant of Mexico and a Conqueror; for a Conqueror was a name of honor, and had lands and rents given to him and to his posterity by the King of Spain, whereas the inhabitant or mere dweller paid rent for his house. This hath filled all those parts of America with proud Dons and gentlemen to this day, for everyone will call himself a descendant from a Conqueror, though he be poor as Job. Ask him what is become of his estate and fortune, he will answer that fortune hath taken it away, but it shall never take away a Don from him."

In the tradition, then, of the *hidalgo*—the "son of a somebody"—in Spain, the new owners of the colonies saw themselves as often too noble to work. Wealth and consequent position had been acquired rapidly in the beginning of the colony, and the dream persisted that these must always be ready to come to the following generations, without effort. Work? Work was for natives, and natives did most of it, not for their own benefit, but for that of their enlighteners. "Had I wanted," said the Lord Marquess of the Valley of Oaxaca in his great days, "had I wanted to plough the land myself, I would have stayed home."

If at home in Spain, the idea, the honorific of *caballero*, had been acknowledged in only a relatively small number of courtiers or persons of position, the colonials, in their disdain for work and the superiority which they maintained over the natives, took generally to themselves the air and honor of *caballero*, in a state of society which differed greatly from that at home.

For already the colonial life was a society of many colors —white, red, black, and the varying shades produced by the marriage of the Old World to the New. Where most other colonies about the world were settled by families—men and women already united and productive of children under the ways of their parent culture—the Spanish conquest of America was carried out by men who came without their women. From the very beginning—as with the Captain General and the beautiful and gifted Doña Marina who was given to him in courtesy by her Indian father, and all the countless other gifts of Indian women offered to lusty soldiers—the creation of a new people, with all its vast potentialities, was inevitable. Spanish ladies emigrated later to the colonies, and some families took pride in trying to keep their European blood unmixed. A curious observation about the distinctive characteristics of the mixed colonials included an attempt to identify the particular odor of racial strains. The white was said to smell of the *pezuño*—the hoof of cloven-footed animals; the Indian of *posca*—a mixture of water and vinegar; the Negro of *grajo*—the strong sweat of his armpits. A realism as unrelenting as his ceremonial grace abided within the Spaniard.

Of that grace the most eloquent colonial illustrations remained in what he soon proceeded to build—his churches, palaces, town houses, and public plazas, and parks, and haciendas. In many of these, the arts of the conqueror and the conquered commingled. As the conquered Moor had modified certain details of the Spanish style, so the conquered American of the Indies gave his character to the colonial. In the Americas the Spaniards found a civilization capable of expressing its whole nature in powerful, direct and wonderfully skilled art. They gave it no respect, but, because its evidences were inseparable from a mythology and a system of life which spoke to them only of soulless abominations, they destroyed as soon as possible after their triumph as many of its monuments and masterpieces as they could reach.

But when they came to build, Spaniards must employ Indian artisans and craftsmen to carry out in new colonial towns the richly encrusted style of the Spanish baroque, with all its memories of Rome, North Africa and Iberia. The result was that another memory was added to these in Mexico through the acts of the native workers—the memory of their own pre-Columbian style in architectural, ornamental and sculptural form.

Colonial palaces, monasteries and convents carried crenellations like those on the great wall of the Aztec plaza, and the scroll, so often seen to unite parts of a design in Aztec painting and carving, became a common device in the baroque of the conquerors, along with countless other stylistic details. But it was in the larger vision of a church, or a great house, that the new land gave its nature to the designs of the old—some heavying of proportion, a certain coarsening of craftsmanship, a more earthlike sense of the mass, which seemed to imply the very weight and spaciousness of Indian earth, and which unmistakably altered the character of the lighter, more delicately ornate Iberian idiom. To the Novo Mondo the Spaniards brought glory enough in their arts—and there the conquered peoples added glory again, out of the richness of their humanity and its ancient understanding of the earth which was their home.

In every city and town, as these spread outward across the land with the rapid settlement of new colonial centers, the abiding piety of the Spaniard built church after church. Coming across deserts to a city or over a mountain and into its cupped valley, the first thing seen was the airy salutation of the church—its towers and domes. These spoke of haven, of home, safety in the present and the crown in eternity for anyone who would seek it.

As for the worldly life, the English Dominican recalled that "It is a byword that at Mexico four things are fair; that is to say, the women, the apparel, the horses, and the streets."

In his time the streets were wide enough to accommodate

three to six coaches side by side, and were cleaner than "the streets of Christendom." He believed there must be fifteen thousand coaches there, of every degree of richness, and as for the saddle horses of gentlemen, these were tricked out not only with bridles of silver and silver studded saddles, but with horseshoes of silver.

In the center of the city, not far from the grand plaza of the cathedral—ancient site of Montezuma's Sun Temple—a great park served as a sort of outdoor drawing room for the society. It was the Alameda. Trees of every height and pattern of formal planting in aisles and walks let in light at different angles and made pools of shadow which eased the eye. To this "pleasant shady field," as the Dominican called it, came every afternoon about four o'clock "the gallants of this city, some on horseback, and most in coaches—" about two thousand coaches, he thought, "full of gallants, ladies, and citizens, to see and be seen, to count and be counted."

It was a lively spectacle.

"The gentlemen have their train of blackamoor slaves, some a dozen, some half a dozen, waiting on them, in brave and gallant liveries, heavy with gold and silver lace, with silk stockings on their black legs, and roses on their feet, and swords by their sides. The ladies all carry their train by their coach's side of such jet-like damsels . . . who with their bravery and white mantles over them seem to be, as the Spaniard saith, *mosca en leche*, a fly in milk." But bravest of all in the magnificent throng was the Viceroy, who went often to the Alameda in such state that his train was said to be as grand as that of his master the King of Spain.

During the decades of the rebuilding of the city after the conquest, "it was a wonder to see the people that resorted thither, hearing of liberty and freedom." Native laborers did most of the job. "Their pains were great, for they bare on their backs," said the Dominican, "and drew after them stones, earth, timber, lime, brick and all other things necessary in this sort. And little by little Mexico was built again with a hundred thousand houses, more strong and better than the old building was."

So great a growth required more land than water to support it, and in 1607 the draining of the lake was begun, so that solid streets could replace canals. The work continued for generations, using at first a tunnel through a mountain to take away the lake water, and later a great drainage canal. Cloudbursts causing flood, and the general volcanic origin of the Mexican land with its banked fires or unclosed fissures below ground which made earthquakes a commonplace, threatened the city periodically, but without affecting its growth. Except for the encrusted towers of the churches, it was a flat city, for houses were not built above three stories high because of earthquakes, and the streets were made wide and spacious so as not to interrupt the winds, for, said the schoolbook of 1554, it was the winds and the sunlight which must "disperse and drive off the pestilential vapors which the neighboring swamp emits."

In the high colonial times, the city was rich and its economy—its Spanish economy—was fed by native labor. The very land of the Indians was acquired from them by the conquerors through superior guile, and with three or four little plots together which each served an Indian family, a colonist was able to make himself "one good and fair house with gardens and orchards." Money was minted in Mexico, using the precious metals taken from the newly developed mines in outlying districts to the north, of which the first to be exploited was Zacatecas. Fortunes grew, and the Dominican heard of a resident of the city who kept chests full of gold bars and wedges of silver.

The wealth of citizens was reflected in the splendor of the churches, for a rich communicant might give of his great substance to do honor to God and hope for the forgiveness of his sins, while the poor people were permitted to offer their pittances for the same purposes. Gold beaten to thin leaf covered complicated carvings in altars and screens, and the high round arches of transept and chapel were picked out in gold leaf, so that light ran along ribbonlike curves of gold, and gold and silver ornaments, vessels and even furniture enriched the effect.

All these, observed the Dominican with an edge of wryness —he later apostasized to become a Puritan pastor in England and so modified much of his earlier joy in the Roman church—caused "admiration in the common sort of people," and in turn admiration brought on "daily adoration in them to those glorious spectacles and images of saints," many of which, in their clustered niches rising in gilded ranks above the altars, cost so much that "a common price" for them was "twenty thousand ducats." In any church, all the rest, "copes, canopies, hangings, altar cloths, candlesticks, jewels belonging to the saints, and crowns of gold and silver, and tabernacles of gold and crystal to carry about their sacrament in procession, would mount to the worth of a reasonable mine of silver, and would be a rich prey for any nation that could make better use of wealth and riches." The disaffected friar could not understand the total piety of a people whose temperament called them to an outpouring of both substance and spirit in their worship.

New Spain feared attack neither from without nor within. The conquest had been so complete that in the city of Mexico there was no fortification of any sort, and if Indian attacks harried the northern boundaries in the mining country, local garrisons, maintaining vigilance, managed to meet these. Enemies from the sea were confidently faced with only the fortification of San Juan de Ulúa in the harbor of Vera Cruz. The colonial of the powered class was comfortable—and more.

The Dominican considered that "both men and women are excessive in their apparel, using more silks than stuffs and cloth." They went heavily jewelled—"a hat-band and rose made of diamonds in a gentleman's hat" was common, and even a tradesman could wear a hat-band of pearls. The female mulattoes of the city outraged the Dominican—so much so that he studied them closely, and reported that "a tawny young maid and slave will make hard shift, but she will be in fashion with her neckchain and bracelets of pearls, and her ear-bobs of some considerable jewels." Such young females showed attire "so light" and "carriage so enticing" that many Spaniards even of the better sort (who were "too prone to venery") disdained their wives for them.

He described their silken petticoats almost as though he fingered their fabrics, and their ribbons with silver or gold tags, and their laces, and their bodices, skirts, and girdles "stuck with pearls and knots of gold," and the mantles they wore over one shoulder, "swaggers-like . . . that they may the better jog the right arm, and show their broad sleeve as they walk along," behaving, he said, "more like roaring boys than honest civil maids." Their shoes were high with many soles, and some were covered with silver, and had silver buttons. Most young women, he stated, were, or had been, slaves, "though love had set them loose, at liberty to enslave souls to sin and Satan."

It was an odd thing to realize, but slowly he came to do so, that the fruits and foods of the New World did not seem to stay hunger, no matter how much he consumed. "Our stomachs ever and anon were gaping and crying, 'Feed, feed,' " but without much continued satisfaction. "In Spain," he said, "and other parts of Europe, a man's stomach will hold out from meal to meal . . . but in Mexico and other parts of America we found that two or three hours after a good meal of three or four several dishes of mutton, veal or beef, kid, turkeys, or other fowls, our stomachs would be ready to faint." He finally consulted a doctor of physic about the matter, and was told that "though the meat we fed on was as fair to look upon as in Spain, yet the substance and nourishment in it came far short of it." The reason was this: the pasture in Mexico was drier than in Europe, and soon withered away, and animal feed was insufficient.

"As in the flesh we fed on," he wrote, "so likewise in all the fruits there. These are most fair to behold, most sweet and luscious to taste, but have little inward virtue or nourishment at all in them, not half that is in a Spanish *camuesa*, or English Kentish pippin."

He was moved to philosophy by this disappointment to appetite.

"And as in meat and fruit there is this inward and hidden deceit, so likewise the same is to be found in the people that are born and bred there, who make fair outward shows, but are inwardly false and hollow-hearted." He was persuaded of this view by Spanish colonials with whom he talked. From them he heard a story which had for him the virtue of coming from his English home. It seemed that when presented with a gift of "the fruits of America," Queen Elizabeth of England, glancing at the tribute, promptly declared "that surely where such fruits grew, the women were light, and all the people hollow and false-hearted."

The New World would need long years in which to find its own real character and make it known to the Old.

iv.

STATIONS ON
THE WAY NORTH

AFTER THE CONQUEST, the colonial Spaniards rapidly came to comprehend the great physical characteristics of their new land. The Pacific coast, curving from south to north, soon yielded up its secrets, and the first ways to the north were those which the Spanish explorers followed parallel to the South Sea, with inland cities of the west used successively as staging points—Guadalajara, Compostela, Culiacán.

The vast isthmus of Middle America, was, they then found, ribbed with two great mountain ranges running from north to south, one on the east, which they called the Sierra Madre Oriental, and the other on the west, the Sierra Madre Occidental. Between these, as they came to know during the half-century following their victory in Mexico, reached an immense, arid, interior plateau, for the whole length of the land. Vast enough to contain secondary mountain ranges which were scattered about intermittently as survivors of huge convulsive incidents of the land's making, it presented to the slowly toiling traveller over and over again the same sequence of earth features—desert, mountain, valley, and again desert, mountain, valley, for as far north as any Spaniard from Mexico would ever go to live.

As go they must—for exploring from the capital the northern interior, where Indian towns remained to be subdued, and Indian raiders to be fought off along the trail, the colonials found wealth. It was not the sort they wanted—they already worked golden treasures of Mexico. It was of a sort they must work for themselves—precious mineral in the mountains, principally silver. Prospectors and miners followed the explorers, and made the beginnings of a road to the heart of the interior. With the growth of this way to the north, the road along the South Sea was no longer the main path of northward exploration. For many generations the upper Pacific coast remained *terra incognita*—California was said to be an island, and information about it would come not from coastal travellers but from followers of the new path to the northern mines and beyond.

It took them across the lake north of the capital through the town of Tenayuca where they saw still standing a sacrificial pyramid surrounded by a cordon of huge stone serpents. Each slope of the pyramid was studded with fifty-two carved snake-heads. Soon the road opened out upon empty plains, with mountains always in the distance which in the end must always be met, and passed through or around, to enter upon more plains, broken by an occasionally winding valley whose flat riverbed more often showed dry white stones than water.

After a passage of perhaps fifteen days at the pace of oxen with carts, travellers came to an Indian town which in 1531 they defeated and colonized. It became the town of Querétaro, the first important station on the interior way north. Ringed about with mountains, it lay in a wide rolling plain open to the sun. From there, as more mines were found farther to the north, roads went direct to Zacatecas, and later to San Miguel de Allende, and Guanajuato.

In 1546 the greatest silver lodes of all were found at Zacatecas, which lay distant by about three weeks of travel from Querétaro. The further trail was made through dry plains which turned into the dust-grey deserts of Aguas Calientes where white, glaring rock showed wherever the surface was broken. In the far distance mountains were like fainting mirages, and all along the way, colonists had to fight off attacks by Chichimeca Indians. Distance itself was a hazard, when only five or ten miles a day went past, and the objective lay weeks if not months away. Like other dangers, this was met with all that was implicit in the shrug of the Spanish people—their acceptance of life as it was, their patience, their sense of fatality enclosed by their faith in God. To go north, over that hard road, and meet the chance of every day? *Qué importa?* Chance was all about, anywhere, every day. All that was certain was Heaven or Hell, with their defined conditions. Gird and go, then, they seemed to say. However hard this earth, eternity would be either far easier, or quite clearly harder. *Mula!*—a word of urging to the pack animals.

Drawing close to Zacatecas, the way lifted into easing mountain meadows, and presently found the mines which created in 1549 a "silver fever" among the colonials. "Thousands of adventurers" hurried to Zacatecas, despite Indian warfare along the road. The mining camp was settled and grew, to become the most important colonial town, after the city of Mexico, in the second half of the sixteenth century and the early decades of the seventeenth.

Vital to the economy of New Spain, the long road north from the capital—close to five hundred miles in the mid-sixteenth century—was protected by forts and garrisons set up along the way.

In 1561, Indians of the region of Zacatecas loosed warfare more fierce than ever before against the whole northern commerce, and until it was suppressed by troops in 1562 the Spanish settlers lived in a state of "constant dread." Presently certain garrisons became towns, such as León and Aguas Calientes, and mines were found even further north than Zacatecas and the road pushed on into open wilderness marked by cactus groves and dry red earth. Its character was somehow expressed in the name later given to a village north of Zacatecas. It was The Corpse—*El Muerto*.

Passing through a barrier of low mountains where scattered scrub pines dotted the slopes, travellers saw a butte with rocks on top so formed that they made a great monkey face which anyone could recognize. It was the sort of place which became a landmark and a reference point. Hot winds blew, and whirling funnels of desert dust appeared out of nowhere, danced along, and vanished. Cicadas raised their piercing high drone to the zenith. Rarely, and at far intervals, an occasional surcease from the hot sky and the crusty earth appeared in the form of a small river whose trickle fed an arched tunnel of trees. Their inky shade cooled travellers just to see it.

After a month's travel from Zacatecas, settlers gradually confronted a long, rocky, bare mountain ridge which reached from east to west as far as the eye could see. There, on the dusty plain leading to its southern face, they founded the gold, silver, and ruby mines and the town of Durango in 1563. Beyond the ridge they would find a great iron mountain, all the color of rust red, where, in even greater wealth than the silver mines yielded all across the north, iron ore would be taken for centuries.

In the following year, silver was again discovered in the Valley of San Bartholomé, farther north by a month and a half on the trail, and the mines of Santa Barbara were established. With its mine works, its dwellings, and its little garrison, Santa Barbara was the point of departure for new enterprises which again reached out at the end of the century for Cíbola and the plains of Quivira, all but forgotten since their abandonment by General Francisco Vásquez de Coronado in 1542.

VI

THE NORTHERN
KINGDOM

Since the success of the undertaking
depends on the appropriate and effective
means which God our Lord may be pleased
to dispose, it is just that you labor to
avoid giving any public or private offense
to Him by members of the expedition. . . .

—*Instructions of the Viceroy to
Juan de Oñate, 1595.*

i.

The Known Road

IN THE 1580s and early in the following decade, four small expeditions, one of them unauthorized, made the great tour of Cíbola and the plains, though without establishing outposts there. Two of these enterprises set out from the mines of Santa Barbara. In 1595 a colony was authorized for the far north, and at last, in the kingdom to be called New Mexico, the living heritage of the conquistador was to take root in North America.

To prepare and command the enterprise, a resident of the city of Zacatecas offered to the Lord Viceroy Luís de Velasco his "services for the discovery, pacification, and conversion of the said provinces of New Mexico."

He was Don Juan de Oñate, a man of circumstance in his middle years. Spoken of as one of the five richest men in New Spain, he was the son of a former governor of New Galicia. The father, who was one of the discoverers of the Zacatecas mines, was called "the refuge of soldiers and poor gentlemen in this kingdom," and the son of this tradition had even more nobility on which to look back in his family, for his wife was not only a granddaughter of the great Lord Marquess of the Valley of Oaxaca, she was also the great-granddaughter of the Emperor Montezuma.

In the first proposals he made, "I offer," he wrote in his request for the contract for discovery and conquest, "to take at least two hundred men, furnished with everything necessary, including provisions sufficient to reach the settlements and even more, this all at my cost"—for he was a millionaire—"and that of the soldiers"—for he was also counting on men ready to make their fortunes, which might require a certain investment on their parts, and he was able to emphasize for King Philip II that His Majesty would not be "obligated to pay them any wages besides what I may willingly give them from my estate," which would favorably dispose in his favor a home government already suffering the effects of inflation brought on by the flow of immense, and then dwindling, riches into the economy of Spain. Further, proposed Don Juan, he would at his own expense supply necessary food, animals, raw materials, manufactured implements, rations for the troops, and his own personal equipment, which would include great herds of horses and mules with saddles, two coaches, two carts with iron-rimmed wheels, and sets of armor, with weapons of every sort, by the half-dozen, and "six buckskin jackets," all of which he would have "assembled at the town of Santa Barbara," which was "the last place in the conquered territory, as soon as possible, trying to have it by the end of March, 1596."

His offer up to this point was accepted, but he was required to be ready not by March, but by January, 1596.

He then cited those necessities for which the Crown would be expected to pay, which included six friars and "six bells of the usual size," and all else that new churches would require. The Viceroy again approved, but substituted a lay brother for one of the friars and reduced the number of bells to four. Throughout the long contract, his requests were approved in general, but with reduction in the numbers of many items—instead of six cannon, three, and of two dozen coats of mail, one dozen, and of two dozen harquebuses, none, as these were "not available at present."

He required the granting of property and hereditary authority in the new lands, and the power and the right to organize civil and military government, and to appoint men to office, and for himself an annual salary of "eight thousand ducats of Castile," and the title of Captain General and Governor. The title he was to receive at once, but no salary until the expedition began its march, and then not eight but six thousand. Since he considered, with other educated men of his place and time, that New Mexico reached to the South Sea, where there would of course be harbors, he asked and was granted permission "to bring two ships per year, free of taxes and import duty, to provision the land and exploit the mines that may be discovered." The contract was as detailed as foresight crossed with duty could make it.

In June, 1595, in the extensive rhetoric of legal government to which he gave his days and nights with quill and inkpot, the King wrote to Don Juan, ". . . Trusting in you and that you will carry out this discovery and pacification in a Christian spirit and with complete loyalty, I appoint you as my governor, captain general, caudillo, discoverer, and pacifier of the said provinces of New Mexico and those adjacent and neighboring." Bearing in mind the passionate mid-century debates about the nature and rights of Indians, the King wrote further,

"You will endeavor to attract the natives with peace, friendship, and good treatment, with which I particularly charge you, and to induce them to hear and accept the holy gospel." And finally, he wrote, "I command the soldiers, civilians, and servants who may go with you to accept you as their governor and captain general, to obey and execute what you may order them, including the rewards or sentences that you may impose on them; I grant you full power, as is legally required in such cases, to punish any rebels and to proceed against those who disobey, punishing them according to the usages of war, to do whatever else may be suitable for this purpose. . . ."

Five months later the Viceroy added his own supplementary instructions to accompany the royal appointment of the Governor, the first of which declared that "Your main purpose shall be in the service of God our Lord, the spreading of His holy Catholic faith, and the reduction of the natives of the said provinces." On his own account he emphasized how the Indians were to be treated—they were not to be "compelled to serve against their will," and they were not to be forced to work in the mines, which would cause them to run away and depopulate the land, "which," said the Lord Viceroy, "is the opposite of what we are trying to do."

At the city of Mexico three months later, on December 16, 1596, Governor de Oñate formally accepted his commission in a letter to the King, and four months afterward it was "examined" in the royal offices at Madrid.

But even before that, a new Viceroy arrived in Mexico to take office, and all business contracted for under his predecessor must be reexamined, including the northward contract for the northward settlement. Governor de Oñate was at work making his final preparations, creating the material and immaterial strength which the enterprise would need in the unknown north. People and supplies were gathering, and he began to advance on the known road beyond Durango, when to his dismay the new Viceroy, the Count of Monterrey, after reviewing his contract, sharply curtailed its privileges, including the right to recruit troops for more than the present occasion, the right to make the appointments in his own provincial government, and the right to bring two ships each year to the ocean harbors he expected to find in New Mexico. Contemplating the years of correspondence and wrangle with the Crown government which must pass before any of these rights might even possibly be restored, the Governor could only submit and proceed with his immediate efforts.

He began to collect his forces at the Nazas River between Durango and Santa Barbara—a fast, wide, deep-rolling stream the color of gray jade, sailing through a broad fertile valley. Mesquite groves grew in the open, and willows along the river. There the Governor received an official letter in September, 1596, suspending his northward march until further orders. It was a hard blow. He wrote in courtly fury to the Viceroy.

The letter had come, he said, just as he was about to cross the Nazas River, "the most difficult crossing before reaching the provinces of New Mexico"—which though he did not know it were still a thousand miles away—"with most of the people in the expedition and all of the cattle, provisions, and necessary equipment which I am obliged to take." His rage ran over, and he said, "Even here we were pursued by the obstacles and hindrances which the devil, as the enemy of all goodness, used to impede and delay the benefits that this expedition was to bring to this multitude of souls"—the Indians waiting in the north—"who are under his spell and who are eager for the bread of divine teaching . . ." The letter from the King, he said, "and the threats it carries have so touched my feelings that I am quite beside myself with grief." He could only hope that the next *flota* would bring permission to proceed, and in the meantime, he did, of course, like a loyal subject, put the King's letter upon his head to indicate that it was above him and that he accepted its commands.

But the effect of these upon his people was almost disastrous—where once they had been full of energy and hope, they were now "hanging by a thread," and the difficulties which arose were too many to describe.

What he did not know was that in Spain another candidate for the northward command was petitioning the Crown and was being heard—old Don Pedro Ponce de León, who had been out to the colonies twenty years before. His pretensions, and various reports of the Governor's inadequacy for the post, caused the King to reconsider.

Waiting at the Nazas, the Governor thought to prove that

his preparations had fulfilled in every respect his contract with the Crown. Accordingly, he officially requested four times that a royal inspector be sent to examine his whole command. Moving his train across the Nazas and making camp at the mines of Casco thirty miles further north, he waited for the inspection.

It came in December and January, 1596 and 1597. The camp on the forward trail was examined, with a full mustering, and also the supplies and equipment gathered already at Santa Barbara farther north. The Governor's claims were fully supported—indeed, he was found to have surpluses in a number of items specified in the contract. Notarized reports of his excellent showing went to Mexico, and then to Madrid, and time went by, and still he must wait.

Meanwhile, the King, who suffered from a scrupulous nature, had reason to become uncertain now about Don Pedro Ponce de León. Telling the Council of the Indies in Madrid, who had the New Mexico affair under advisement, to hold Don Pedro "with good hopes" of a decision in his favor, the King ordered them to tell the Viceroy with the utmost haste and secrecy to give Governor de Oñate permission to move out with his expedition, if all was still in readiness; if it was not, the Viceroy was to make a further report.

By a combination of ambition, a stern sense of duty, and personal honor amounting to pride, the Governor had held his people faithful to his command; and when the welcome news finally came north in the summer of 1597 that he was after all to take to the road, he believed he had all still in readiness. It only needed now a final royal inspection to determine this.

The inspection was begun three days before Christmas where "the army of New Mexico" was now encamped near Santa Barbara. It was conducted by a royal inspector in the presence of the Lord Viceroy, the Count of Monterrey. Maize and wheat; goats, oxen, sheep, rams, colts, mares, hogs, cattle, mules and jackasses; tools, anvils, raw iron and steel, lead, quicksilver, nails; footgear; paper; wine; oil; sugar; clothing; medicines and surgical supplies, including Toledo treacle, rose vinegar, and twelve lancets; jerked beef; flour; bellows—the inventory was long, and its items brought to mind familiar ways of life which would be recreated in unfamiliar lands.

The Governor's personal belongings included clothing, arms, armor, and equipment, with twelve saddles, one of which "had blue and gold velvet trappings and silver trimmings; another had a green and gold velvet caparison; another had caparison and trimmings of crimson velvet; still another was of black velvet, and two were of cloth and ocelot skin." He declared also his "two state coaches, one completely equipped, the other without wheels; he said the latter had broken down and was being repaired."

He had gathered forty-two lots of "articles for barter," among which the royal inspector found in addition to the usual glass beads and bangles, and hawk's-bells, a number of "ordinary combs," and butcher knives, and scissors, thimbles, rosaries, fifty-six "Tlascala tassels for rosaries," amulets of badger bone, whistles of Texcoco clay, a jet headpiece, "nine small hats, very poorly dyed, seven of them without lining or fringe," and—for children—"six small flutes," and "one lot of Paris trumpets."

The troops were mustered, and declared themselves before the inspector and the royal notary, listing their arms, armor, animals, servants, clothing, and other possessions, which ranged from the magnificent to the very poor. One soldier said, "I, Diego de Medina, come before your grace and say that I have no arms or other things to declare, except myself, and as this is the truth, I so affirm and swear by God and this cross. Since I do not know how to write, I asked Rodrigo Belmán to sign for me, as witness." The witness signed. The inspection took a "month and six days." On January twenty-sixth, 1598, the train began to move out for the north. With its hundred and thirty families, eighty-three wagons, and seven thousand head of stock, it reached along the trail for four miles.

ii.

THE UNKNOWN ROAD

AN ADVANCE of five or six miles a day was gratifying; ten or twelve, very fast.

Earlier trails had gone from Santa Barbara to the Conchos River, which could be reached by wagons from Santa Barbara after a week of travel northward, and had then followed the Conchos to its confluence with the Rio Grande del Norte, whose valley they had then used as their northward passage.

But this meant a great deviation to the northeast, and the Governor proposed to find, if he could, a way directly to the north which would save many weeks of travel. He struck out for the Conchos through range after range of mountains of which he must find the passes. One mountain reminded the eye of dead fire—it shaded from cold pink to clinker green and ash grey. The land ahead looked generally flat and vacant, except for dust that rose in whirls or on long sky-wide draws of wind. With the first of February the army came to the Conchos, stayed a week to hold a final review and to take leave of the Viceroy and the royal inspector, who were returning to the capital from there. The Conchos flowed to the northeast, and showed a brisk current which made the crossing somewhat difficult.

Three days later the column was at the San Pedro River, a smaller stream, and there made camp to remain for a month, until the chaplains of the expedition, Franciscan friars, could overtake it. The long wait was put to another purpose, too, for here the Governor sent an advance party, under the command of his nephew, Vicente de Zaldívar, who was his second in command, to find the unknown road direct to the north, with seventeen soldiers.

On March seventh half of the advance party returned and on the tenth, the remainder. They had had a hard time, but they had found how to go due north to the Rio Grande. This was astonishing, for they told how none of them had possessed any astronomer's knowledge of the heavens by which to set a course, and there was probably not one among them, who "once the sun had set, could say with any certainty, 'There is east, there is west.'" Their way was dusty, and water was hard to find, and they told how they had been captured by Indians who took pleasure from making them afraid, but who released them.

The next day, the soldiers attacked the camp of their tormentors, and captured two to serve as guides. But after a few days of comfort arranged by the guides—deer meat, badger, rabbit, herbs and roots—the guides escaped, and again the soldiers were trapped in the vacancy of the desert. Then it rained—poured—for a week, and water became a nuisance where it had been the greatest treasure. And when the rain stopped, the soldiers were brought to thirst again almost at once. For five days they went without water and were in an extremity of hunger and thirst when late one April morning they saw trees ahead—groves of willows—and knew from how these grew along a line that there must be a water-course where they grew, and with renewed effort they urged themselves forward, and came to the river.

It was the Great River of the North.

How they behaved—their friends in the main column would not believe what they did when they saw the river. They lost their senses, threw themselves bodily into the current, horses and men both, and two horses were borne away downstream beyond rescue, and two other horses drank so deeply that their bellies burst and they died. The men played the water against their mouths and faces, and drank and drank, until they were hardly able to drag themselves from the water to go to the deep shade of the river bank where they fell down bloated and deformed. One soldier said that they were like drunkards left on the floor of an inn, and that they looked more like toads than men.

For a day or so they rested at the river, fished and hunted —there were geese and ducks going north—and then returned with their good news to the camped army, and knowledge of where to take them on the road ahead.

Again moving, the colonists trudged and creaked their way through one mountain barrier only to see in the distance another that must be opened and passed. On April eighth they entered a desert of dunes—hummocks dotted with mesquite, cactus and chamisa, where the sand pulled at marching feet with every step and cart wheels with every turn. But at last on the twentieth they came to the Rio Grande and rejoiced like their comrades before them. It was all true—it was a great river, larger than either the Conchos or the Nazas, with much vegetation, and trees, said the log of the journey, and fish. They rested there by the river for a week, and then began to follow its bank upstream.

On Ascension Day, 1598, April thirtieth, the Governor, with his every word and act recorded by the royal notary, formally took possession of the new kingdom for his Lord and King, Philip II, in the name of God, and with honor to the Mother of God, and to St. Francis, and with reference to three Franciscans martyred in New Mexico after one of the expeditions of the 1580s, and with a rapid historical outline of the genealogy of God and the history of His church, leading to an account of the legitimate authority deriving from St. Peter and resting on the Spanish monarch. For the King, said the Governor, reading from a legal document carefully prepared,

"I take and seize tenancy and possession, real and actual, civil and natural, one, two, and three times, one, two, and three times, one, two, and three times, and all the times by right I can and should, at this said Rio del Norte, without excepting anything and without limitations, including the mountains, rivers, valleys, meadows, pastures, and waters. In his name I also take possession of all the other lands, pueblos, cities, towns, castles, fortified and unfortified houses which are now established in the kingdoms and provinces of New Mexico, those neighboring and adjacent thereto, and those which may be established in the future, together with their mountains, rivers, fisheries, waters, pastures, valleys, meadows, springs, and ores of gold, silver, copper, mercury, tin, iron, precious stones, salt, *morales,* alum, and all the lodes of whatever sort, quality or condition they may be, together with the native Indians in each and every one of the provinces, with civil and criminal jurisdiction, power of life and death, over high and low, from the leaves of the trees in the forests to the stones and sands of the river, and from the stones and sands of the river to the leaves in the forests."

The immense solemnity and weight of his legal act was now moved into another dimension of human work, as he begged the blessing of God upon what the army and its people had come so far to achieve. Taking a cross, he went to a tree in the grove, and nailed it to the tree, and falling down to his knees, he prayed aloud before it, speaking for all the others words which were formal, and yet which contained hope so great that it could be felt as passion.

"O, holy cross, divine gate of heaven and altar of the only and essential sacrifice of the blood and body of the Son of God, pathway of saints and emblem of their glory, open the gates of heaven to these infidels. Found churches and altars where the body and blood of the Son of God may be offered in sacrifice; open to us a way of peace and safety for their conversion, and give to our king and to me, in his royal name, the peaceful possession of these kingdoms and provinces. Amen."

With this he rose and planted in the soft river earth the staff of the royal standard of heavy yellow silk which showed on one face the lions and castles of the royal blazon, and on the other the image of the Holy Mother of God in her character as Our Lady of Remedies. Trumpets sounded a fanfare, volleys crashed forth from the harquebuses, a chaplain preached a sermon, a feast appeared from the supply stores, and, amidst the parked carts and wagons, the colonists enacted a comedy, specially written for the occasion by one of their number, the captain of cavalry, Don Marcos Farfán de los Godos, from Seville. It was an edifying piece showing how the army came to possess, pacify and convert the new land.

With the very next day, the march upriver was resumed, and in four days, the army came to a place where the river flowed toward them from between two mountains. The expedition called it El Paso del Norte, the North Pass, a name it would always bear.

Indians of the region came to meet them.

"Manxo, manxo," said the Indians, and *"micos, micos,"* meaning, "peaceful ones," and "friends." Here the army crossed the river to the east bank. The Manxo Indians helped them and told them how they would find Indian towns six days later up the river. They travelled on in the wide level valley of the river with outlying mountains parallel to their course. There was shade. There was water. Some oxen strayed away. A child died and was buried. Two horses were drowned in the river. Soon the army saw how mountains thrusting themselves down to the river made travel impossible along the bank, and how they must go around the mountain and leave the river, trusting to come back to it when the mountain had been passed.

"We were exploring and feeling our way," said the log of the journey, "for the first time, and we suffered a great deal because of not knowing it."

Their suffering was extreme in the next many days, for they now entered into the kind of country which they called a *despoblado,* an unpopulated place. When a chronicler—Núñez Cabeza de Vaca, Marcus of Nice, Coronado—spoke of entering a *despoblado,* the laconic statement gave no notion of what he really saw and endured in the desert—the hard rocky passage which seemed to lead nowhere, thirst, punishing light, the vision of distance which seemed never to contract, the sense of time halted.

The army now went north in a vast waterless plain lying east of mountains which barred it from the Rio Grande—a stretch of country later called the *Jornada del Muerto,* the

Dead Man's March. They passed nights without water. It was a great event when one evening a little dog of the expedition trotted into camp with his paws darkened and caked. Captain Gaspar Pérez de Villagrá, a bachelor of arts from the University of Salamanca, noticed the dog, examined his paws, and saw that they were muddy. Mud—there was water nearby. He searched and found a spring. Another soldier found another. The army drank, and named the place El Perrillo, Little Dog, in honor of its explorer.

They went on, with the great train stretched out and divided, for the horsemen were ahead, the carts to the rear by a long interval. During the first fortnight in June, the Governor received word that "the cart train was in trouble." The soldiers in command of it were quarrelling, and all were in misery from thirst. He rode back from the advance party to the carts, "smoothed everything by his tact," and returned to the head of the column bringing provisions from the carted stores. His return gave the advance party "new life." Two Negroes strayed from the line of march and died in the desert.

But at last the mountains on their left dwindled into the earth and the river was free to the army again, and very soon they saw an Indian town on the west bank, where they were received kindly. They called it Soccoro—Succour. Going north again, they came almost every day to Indian towns. Some were deserted, but Indians stayed, their meeting was friendly, and there seemed to be a promise of peace in the kingdom, if the Indians would not abandon their homes and leave the colonists with Coronado's hollow victory.

These towns—pueblos—were the settlements of which Friar Marcus of Nice had been told on his way to Cíbola, and which General Vásquez de Coronado had seen in the valley of the Great River. All were similar. They were built of puddled earth and withes, and their rooms were clustered together like the cells of a hive. Some of the clusters rose one, two, stories above ground in set-back terraces, and even, in Taos, the pueblo farthest to the north, seven stories. The rooms were entered through doors in the terraced roofs, to which the Indians ascended by ladders. If the ladders were drawn up, the pueblo was a fortress without entrance from below.

Fields of corn grew near the pueblo irrigated by ditches with water from the river. The people, when they wore anything, wore cotton mantles. They made their own pots and decorated them with complicated designs. There was no sign of gold, or of turquoises set about the doors, and indeed, there were no doors which could be seen from below.

Now and then the army met with curious recollections of soldiers and friars who had been there before them, a few of whom had stayed in the north, never to be heard of again, until now. In one pueblo, an Indian said to the newcomers in Spanish, "Thursday, Friday, Saturday and Sunday." It was astonishing. "Thomas and Christopher," he added. From this clue, the Governor learned that two Mexican Indians named Thomas and Christopher had remained in the kingdom from the expedition of Castaño de Sosa which had marched eight years before to attempt a colonization but which had not succeeded. Thomas and Christopher were now living in a town up the river, and the Governor determined to use them as interpreters. When a day or so later he found them, he added them to his service.

Visiting in another town he saw with his staff in a pueblo room a wall picture thinly whitewashed over in which he could detect how two Franciscan friars had died after their decision not to return to Santa Barbara with the expedition which they had accompanied to the north seventeen years ago, but to stay and work amidst the pueblos. The wall painting showed them perishing under stones and arrows. The Governor and his staff pretended to notice nothing, but accepted quarters in the pueblo for the night. After dark, when all was quiet, as though in sleep, the Spaniards took their way out of the silent town and hurried away to the river camp of the expedition.

Advancing upriver, the forward party came on July seventh to a great pueblo which they called Santa Domingo. Here the Governor met "a general council of seven Indian chieftains of different provinces of this New Mexico, and each one in the name of his province voluntarily pledged obedience to his majesty."

On August eleventh, 1598, the Governor and his scouts came to a fine place in the valley where another stream— the Chama with its red water—entered the Rio Grande. Two pueblos faced each other, one on the east bank of the Rio Grande, the other on the east bank of the Chama. There were groves of willow and cottonwood in the river bottoms, and the banks rose gently to earth terraces where fields of corn grew, and the desert stretched beyond to blue mountains, and the air was clear, and in the shade all was cool. It was a place to found a temporary capital, and the Governor chose the town on the east bank of the Rio Grande for his, and named it San Juan de los Caballeros—St. John of the Knights. Here he planted his flag, and set men to work.

The first municipal need to be met was a proper water supply, which here could be managed by running a great ditch from the river. On their first day there soldiers of the advance party went to work on the ditch. On the eighteenth, the worn and hungry remainder of the long train of carts, families and animals arrived at the new river capital, and the expedition was reunited. Then the next task must be undertaken—one that met the requirement of a royal decree. Since the third voyage of the Lord Admiral Christopher Columbus, the first structure to be erected in a new town was, by order of the Crown, the church. On August twenty-third, "the building of the church was started, and it was completed on September seventh. It was large enough," said the log, "to accommodate all the people of the camp."

iii.

THE CAPITAL

THE LITTLE rooms of the pueblo were put in order. Corrals for animals and storage rooms and bins for supplies were built, and gates for the four quarters of the town defenses, and as the dry summer wore on—it was a summer so dry that Indians lamented together with great cries—the colony did what it could to create a sense of home.

Though for some, the work was too hard, the expected wealth too far to seek. Almost at once a revolt was threatened by forty-five soldiers and officers—"the worthlessness of some soldiers who organized a conspiracy was made evident," said the log.

Under the clearly placed powers and responsibilities which the King had laid upon him, the Governor, acting swiftly, arrested the leaders and condemned them to death before they could steal supplies and run away to New Spain with their followers, leaving an example which might prove disastrous for the colony. Other settlers believed—some bitterly —that he acted with excessive harshness. They pleaded for clemency, and the Governor yielded to their prayers. Pardons were followed by a week of games and celebrations, the climax of which came on September eighth when the first Mass was sung in the new church of the capital city of St. John.

To bring them a sense of community, and also to demonstrate the Spanish power of arms, the Governor sent invitations to the heads of all the Pueblos to attend the celebrations. All came except the chief of Ácoma, that ancient town to the west which was built on the flat crown of a rock mesa four hundred feet high. Some said that he refused to come, others that he had not received the invitation. In any case, he did not attend, but instead, sent spies who were lost among the Indian throngs and who noted all they saw which they would report later at Ácoma.

They saw a play written and acted by colonists. They saw a bullfight, and a mounted tournament, and a sham battle reenacting the old wars between Moors and Christians. In these they witnessed salvos of musket fire, and a grand "thunderous discharge of artillery"—all with gunpowder but no ball. With these weapons, Spaniards were said to kill Indians; but now nobody fell dead in the sham battle. How was this? Were the firearms, after all, harmless? If so, Ácoma might find the fact useful. The Ácomese spies observed all.

They were present when the Governor addressed all the chiefs, gave them the news of his Divine Lord, and of salvation, and assigned to certain of them their mission pastors who would go to the Pueblos and there teach them the word of God and educate them in the arts of Spanish life. When the chiefs returned to their various towns, each took with him much news of new ways of life in their land.

Shortly afterward, four soldiers deserted, stealing a band of horses and running away southward to New Spain. The Governor sent two captains, Pérez de Villagrá and Marqués, to overtake them. Then, putting his nephew Juan de Zaldívar in command at the capital, and ordering Vicente de Zaldívar—they were brothers—to explore the eastern plains, for once more Quivira glimmered in mind, the Governor himself in early October led a party into the wilderness westward, with the intention of coming closer to the South Sea and its rumored pearl fisheries.

The next intelligence from his river capital reached him ten weeks later, a few days before Christmas, as he was marching homeward from a profitless venture into the west. Approaching Ácoma, where he intended to spend the night, he was met by a small squad of soldiers from St. John with news he had to hear.

He listened to them while still in his saddle.

What they told him caused him to dismount, kneel down and pray aloud in grief.

Then leading his horse he went aside to his tent where he gave orders to be left alone with a cross lashed together out of a broken brush. There he considered what he had just heard.

iv.

TROUBLE AT ÁCOMA

ON NOVEMBER eighth Vicente de Zaldívar had returned to St. John from his tour of the plains, where he had tried to capture bison but without avail—the grown ones were elusive and any calves he captured "died of rage" almost at once. At St. John, Vicente took over the command from his brother Juan, who then set out with thirty soldiers to join the Governor in his western survey. Juan was twenty-eight—three years older than his brother—and both were well built, with hair and beards of a chestnut color.

The weather was turning cold. Crossing the rocky desert west of the Rio Grande for perhaps sixty miles, Juan brought his detachment to the steep drifts of sand at the base of Ácoma mesa on December first. Rising almost straight above them was the four hundred-foot-high escarpment of rosy sandstone. A trail led up the sandy incline, but only for part of the way, and the final approach to the top of the mesa and the town was a succession of toeholds cut in the stone. Indians used the stone ladder with ease. They swarmed down to greet the soldiers.

Juan asked for food, and was promised what he needed if he would come to the top on the next morning. Meanwhile, let the soldiers camp below for the night. All agreed, and in the morning the armed Spaniards, leaving four men to guard the horses, made the difficult and awkward ascent.

They were received by the chief Zutucupan, who pointed to different houses where they would find the various supplies they had asked for.

Juan gave orders to his men to go, one here, another there, to collect food.

They saw, now that they were on top of the great mesa, that Ácoma was not one rock but two, riven by a chasm. The town was built of terraced earthen houses set in two parallel rows. It was surprising to see how large the area of the mesa was on top. It was not entirely flat—there were depressions which caught and held rain water, and the dusty red sandstone of the mesa top rose and fell away in shallow undulation. At the edge, looking down, the soldiers were astonished to see how high in the air they were. There was a sense of alien removal. It would feel good to be down on the wide brush plain again.

When the soldiers separated to collect their supplies, a heart-turning scream sounded over the mesa top. It came from Zutucupan, calling his people to attack the soldiers.

The answer was quick—Indians swarmed from the houses with bows, arrows, lances, clubs and rocks. Juan shouted out to hearten his men. They stood so well that it took three hours for a thousand Indians to overcome them, but in the end they were overcome. Three soldiers forced to the cliffs jumped and were killed on the rocks below. Juan was beaten down three times but rose again until he was killed. By then only five soldiers were left on the mesa. They ran for the edge and threw themselves off, and one more was killed in the fall, but the other four landed in the sand drifts and were soon revived by three other soldiers who had safely escaped by the trail. Together they ran to the picket line in camp. There they held a hurried council of war.

They divided themselves into three parties—one to ride home to St. John to warn the capital, one to reach the Franciscan missioners in the scattered pueblos and advise them to go at once to St. John, and the last to ride westward to find the Governor. Search as they might, the third party did not find him, and it was a squad sent out by Vicente de Zaldívar who brought him word of the fury at Ácoma.

The Governor marched on the next day for the capital, his resolve made, but still to be submitted to his clergy. Snow fell and his soldiers drank melted snow from their morions. At St. John the colonists awaited him and wept when they saw him. In silence he embraced each, and comforted those who had lost men in the massacre at Ácoma. In the church he led all in attending a Te Deum in thanksgiving for his safe return, and then, obeying the regulations of Philip II, he asked the fathers for their official opinion of his plans.

"What conditions are necessary in order to wage a just war? In the event of such a war, what steps may be taken against those warred upon and against their possessions?"

The assembled friars discussed his question, and on December twenty-second gave him full authorization to make war. He at once publicly proclaimed in the capital his intention to make "war by blood and fire" against the pueblo of Ácoma, and attended a requiem mass for his nephew Juan and all who had died with him in the massacre on the mesa.

Christmas came to the tune of sharpening swords and lances, and the gritty polishing of armor, and cleaning of musketry. Vicente de Zaldívar was given the command of the punitive expedition when the Governor, yielding to demands by his people, decided to remain at home. By his command all men-at-arms went to confess their sins and enter the state of grace before going to war—all but one, "who, despite the urgings of his commander, would have nothing to do with the holy sacraments," for which his comrades called him "an abandoned wretch." Seventy soldiers prepared for battle.

They marched out, taking two brass culverins, on the morning of January twelfth, 1599. The winter valley, and the desert beyond it, were a dry dull gold, and far mountains looked dusty and wan, and the sky was more white than blue, and if the sun shone, it gave more light than heat. The army soon became a little more than points of light, springing off peaks of armor, and presently there was nothing of it to see.

At St. John they could do nothing but wait. It would take ten days for the army to reach Ácoma. Who knew how long it would take for what had to be done there? And then there must come a long march homeward again.

The Governor doubled the sentries at the four gates to the capital and ordered watch fires to be kept all night when he received reports of hostile gestures from the pueblo across the river from his own town. The Indians along the river valley were reported to be gathering themselves for war on the colony. Women at St. John whose husbands were marching to Ácoma went to the rooftops to stand guard, determined to do their share in the defense of their new life. No attack came, and the tenseness of the colony eased off, though not its troubled wondering about what might be coming to pass at Ácoma, a hundred and fifty miles away, down the river and into the western desert.

Though were they told of this in a curious fashion, on January twenty-fourth.

Late in the afternoon of that day, a small, ancient Indian woman, all bone and folded skin, asked to see the Governor. She came with an air of circumstance proper to one so old and so used to the respect given to old age by her people. The Governor received her.

Yes? he said.

There, she replied, westward, far, that flat country, and that great high rock that rose straight up from it, with a pueblo on top.

Yes, Ácoma, what then?

War and battle, around and around and around, men striving against each other, beating, so, and stabbing, so, and killing.

Yes, yes?

Some with swords.

Yes, soldiers?

Some with arrows.

Indians. And then?

The air full of power and fury. One, two, three days of this. The rock was wide and the struggle flowed back and forward upon it. There was death everywhere. In the sky there came something—a vision in light. Then up, waving upward, smoke entered the whole air. And then it all ended.

When? When did it all end?

Today. Just today. The war was over.

Over? But who was victorious?

Swords. The soldiers were victorious.

How he would believe her if he could. He thanked her and let her go, hoping she knew the truth.

v.

ANOTHER TROY

NINE DAYS LATER, all she had told came true, and of course much more, when the quartermaster Diego de Zubía rode into St. John from Ácoma bringing two prisoners, and a story full of wonders.

Vicente de Zaldívar had sent him to tell the Governor how the army came to the rock of Ácoma in the settling twilight of January twenty-first. Along the rim four hundred feet above danced the warriors of Ácoma, naked, wild with defiant cries. In the last daylight Vicente sent officers forward to read the royal requirements of surrender and peace. They were repulsed with rage. The army made camp at a safe distance for the night.

In the morning Vicente divided his forces, sending the larger part to march in full view against one end of the mesa while with eleven men he went under cover to scale the other. He reached the top and there established a foothold, which was all-important even though his rock was divided from the other rock of Ácoma by the chasm which cut a wavering course, now wide, now narrow, between the two. Soon he was found and attacked by four hundred Ácomese, but with his handful of men he stood them off. In the fight he saw an Indian dressed in the clothes of his brother Juan, and killed him in grim virtue. Indians along the rim were picked off by musketeers below, and fell to their deaths in the rocks, "leaving their miserable souls up in their lofty fortress," as Captain de Villagrá put it later. After a day of skirmishes Vicente, ordering his squad to stay on their lofty platform, returned below to make bivouac with the rest of the army on the plain.

On the second morning soldiers from the plain swarmed up to join the squad on the mesa top, bringing with them a heavy timber to serve as a bridge over the chasm. They threw it down in place, and a rush of men crossed by it, and drew it after them in case they should need it farther ahead. The

mesa was suddenly alive with Indians who poured from
the houses to attack the soldiers on their own side of the
chasm. The Spanish force was cut in two. In another moment, Captain de Villagrá took a running jump and landed safely across the chasm, seized the timber, threw it
back into place as a bridge, and called his comrades to
cross and join in the attack of the pueblo. The soldiers' bu-
gler—a German from Worms—sounded a flourish and the
battle surged back and forth for its second day. Soldiers
set fire to the houses. The brass culverins were hauled to the
top and fired into the Indian ranks doing terrible damage. A
Spaniard—it was the "abandoned wretch"—was shot by ac-
cident when one of his comrades wildly set off his musket.
He called aloud for God's mercy, got himself down to the
camp on the plain, made his confession to the chaplain, and
died. Many Indians threw themselves off the edge of the mesa
to die rather than be taken. Others threw themselves into the
fires of the burning houses. Others hanged themselves. Repeatedly the soldiers cried out for surrender and peace but
were refused. Darkness put an end to fighting but the fires
showed all night and cries sounded.

When the third day came, Indian elders suddenly came
weeping to ask for peace and to offer surrender. Vicente
agreed at once.

Where, he asked, were the bodies of his brother and the
others who were murdered in December?

He was shown a funeral pyre where they had been burned.
There he knelt down to pray, and through his tears said to
his comrades,

"Here is another Troy."

Seventy soldiers against how many thousand Indians—how
had they prevailed? The soldiers could not help wondering.
The Indian elders answered the mystery by asking a question.
They were beaten, they said, as soon as they saw a great
warrior riding on a white charger in the sky above the Spanish army, carrying a sword of fire, and showing a long white
beard, and attended by a lady of great beauty in a blue robe
and crowned with stars. Who were these persons? the Indians asked.

In the name of the Father-Son-Holy Ghost, said the soldiers rapidly, stricken with honor; for it was plain to them
that the war had been turned for them by the patron of all
Spain, Saint James of Compostela, on whom they always
called going into battle, and by the Queen of Heaven herself.

It was, for the Governor, like hearing everything for a second time, for the old Indian woman had been right in her whole knowledge. All that remained now was for the army to return to the capital under Vicente de Zaldívar, bringing prisoners, and to assign punishments to the survivors at Ácoma. For though many hundreds of her people had died in the three-day battle, the Governor now must conduct the customary trial with full legal apparatus, whereby unsuccessful insurrectionists, and any possible imitators, would be discouraged from further acts of rebellion.

Accordingly, in February, 1599, the Governor presided over a process which consisted solely of accusations by soldiers, duly recorded by royal notaries, and which resulted on February twelfth in the announcement of sentences. Whether through clemency or not, the Governor sentenced no one to death, but instead, sentenced all men of Ácoma over twenty-five years of age to have one foot cut off and to give twenty years of personal service—a term which, with its terminal date, was not to be confused with slavery, which was forbidden by law; all boys over twelve and under twenty-five to give twenty years of personal service; all females over twelve to give twenty years of personal service; and sixty girls to be sent to the city of Mexico for distribution among the convents there. In addition, two Indians visiting Ácoma from other towns were sentenced to have their right hands cut off and to be sent home in warning. The colony again knew peace, however bitter its price.

vi.

THE COLONY LIVES

BUT IT WAS NOT an easy peace. A year later the Governor felt obliged to punish a town where soldiers had been insulted. He hanged two chiefs, killed six Indians, and burned part of the town, though, in his own view, he did it in a "tactful and gentle" way.

Again, at Quarai, across the mountains eastward, he sent Vicente de Zaldívar to discipline the town for killing two soldiers. A five-day engagement followed which ended only when the soldiers cut off the town's supply of water which flowed in an irrigation ditch. The town was burned, hundreds of Indians were destroyed, forty soldiers were wounded, and Zaldívar received a broken arm.

Such troubles were distracting for the Governor when he had plans to get on with the main business of his colony, which was to develop homes and farms. The capital had been moved across the river to the more commodious pueblo at the Chama confluence, which was given the name of San Gabriel, and the work of making a Spanish town out of an Indian hive must be done all over again. Above all, the Governor wanted to explore the lands east and west until the great prizes—gold and pearls—were discovered. He had received substantial reinforcements of the colony at Christmas time, 1600, and the capital now contained "more than five hundred persons"—Spaniards, of course, as Indians were counted separately.

In March, 1601, he sent a soldier and the Franciscan superior sent a friar to Mexico on official business. The two travelled together, carrying letters and messages. The Governor wrote his brothers in Mexico. His letters indicated that, while much remained to be done, matters were going smoothly in the northern kingdom. The Indians submitted readily to baptism and some forty or fifty thousand of them were now "peaceful, undisturbed and obedient." They brought provisions to the Spaniards—fowls, corn, calabashes, and game—"palatable and very healthful." The wheat was sown and successfully harvested. A new flour mill was in operation. A preliminary expedition to the east indicated that he himself would do well to go to inspect that land, for reports persisted that the sea was to be found there—the North (or Atlantic) Sea, and ships could be built there to sail between the North and South Seas. He would leave in April to discover this excellent resource. He understood that the land was fertile and rich and "so teeming with numbers" that it quite equalled New Spain and Peru in population. He had found mines but with so few people available he had not yet been able to develop them. The work would, however, go forward even while he was on the inland expedition. The land in general was "level and fertile and the road to it unobstructed and suitable for carts." It was "so safe and peaceful that one or two men without arms could traverse it without danger," just as anywhere in the settled parts of New Spain. His letters were summarized in the viceregal offices, with a notation that the details he gave proved "the greatness of the conquest."

But the same messengers to Mexico carried another report from the Count of Monterrey which told a quite different story. It was prepared secretly for the Viceroy by one of the original expeditioners, Captain Luís Gasco de Velasco, who wrote it because he remembered how, saying goodbye at the Conchos River in 1598, the Viceroy had asked him to give him "a detailed report of all matters that might be in the interest of the service of his majesty." Under this wide, this almost sacred, sanction in the name of the Crown, with its implied permission to report independently of the Governor, Captain Gasco, at great risk if he should be discovered by the Governor, poured forth a stream of complaints and charges. To begin with, he wrote,

"We have been here three years, hoping to discover something of value and importance, which has not been found up to now."

If he dared to demolish the enterprise with such a statement, and to follow it with appalling details, Captain Gasco did so only because he, and in fact the "entire army" knew how "faithfully and sincerely" the Lord Viceroy had always labored in the royal service.

Actually, then, the Indians were wretched and Spaniards made them more so, taking away their only blankets and leaving Indian women to freeze naked in the bitter cold of winter, "holding their babes to their breasts." The weather was either burning hot or freezing cold. Mice, bedbugs and other vermin abounded, and the capital was so miserably poor that nobody burned "lights at night for lack of means." Colonists treated the Indians abominably, entering their houses at will, taking their women, and possessions, and generally alienating them from the Faith by bad behavior. Even if Spaniards said they had been provoked to warfare on the Indians, as at Ácoma, Captain Gasco claimed that the first acts of abuse and aggression had come from soldiers and that Indians had then defended themselves. The punishments inflicted by the Governor against Indian towns were "pitiful" and "cruel," and it was no great credit to a squad of thirty soldiers if they might have conquered all the Indians so far discovered, for the Pueblo Indians were the "most meek, humble, and timid people ever seen." The friars objected formally and energetically to the Governor about how the Indians were used, and when they did so, the Governor "abused" them for their zeal. He seemed to act only "according to his own whim and that of his nephew."

The Governor was no better in his treatment of some of his own people. In the presence of the writer himself, and of several others, the Governor, angry at a certain Captain Aguilar—"a truthful man, very well liked and honorable" —trapped him in his quarters and with the assistance of other soldiers and some servants, murdered him. "The Governor himself thrust a sword through his body," giving him no chance to confess himself, though he begged to do so, "since he was in a state of sin." On a cruel whim, he was condemned to eternal fire.

Another officer, Captain Alonso de Sosa Albornoz, after having asked for the favor of permission to return home to New Spain, which the Governor promised to grant him, had been murdered by the Governor's nephew and some of his followers, without having received the opportunity to confess his sins. His body was buried under stones and "no one dared to look for it," and you could be sure that after this, "the relatives of Captain Sosa did not again ask for permission to leave." If anyone dared to complain of conditions, or show themselves "zealous" of their honor, "and sign complaints," they were "labeled as traitors."

One time four soldiers left camp without permission—so Captain Gasco put it, but they were actually deserters, running away to New Spain—and the Governor sent two officers after them, who caught them, let two go free, murdered the other two without bringing them to a priest, cut off their right hands, preserved these in salt and carried them back to the Governor as proof of duty done.

What respect did the Governor show for the Crown? On claiming this land at the Rio del Norte, he had had the royal standard dipped before him, and before the Host at the consecration. Was the royal standard ever to be lowered for anyone or anything? The Lord Viceroy recently appointed new captains for service in New Mexico and sent his patent of their commissions to the Governor at San Gabriel, who scorned it. The Governor asked whether the one who brought the letter of appointment was being sent by one of the Oñate brothers in Mexico or by the Viceroy. Told that he was sent by the Viceroy, the Governor replied,

"Then tell him to wipe his arse with his patents."

Making a really dangerous charge, Captain Gasco was "amazed and stunned" to hear the Governor addressed by his

nephew as "Your Majesty." Residents and friars heard it—
"did not approve of it." Considering the oppression under
which the colony lived, Captain Gasco wrote, "It is clear that
these gentlemen will act as they please, unless there is someone to hinder them." He fully realized that he incurred
"no slight danger" in sending his lordship "such a detailed
report of events in this land." He was fearful that he would
be found out. Letters had been opened before. Nevertheless,
he put away his fears "in order to fulfill the commands" given
him at the Conchos by the Lord Viceroy, who could bring
the hideous state of affairs to the King—this was Philip
III, who had succeeded his father—in order that, "as the
most Christian prince that he is, he may liberate his subjects from servitude and enslavement."

Knowing nothing of the intrigue against him, the Governor
in June, 1601, with high hopes, was able to lead a hundred
men at arms toward Quivira and the east.

At almost the same time, in response to the secret report
of Captain Gasco, the Viceroy appointed an official of the
royal treasury in the City of Mexico—Don Francisco de
Valverde y Mercado—to question in the capital three men
who had been in New Mexico with Oñate and who had returned to New Spain. What he learned would in due course
be forwarded to Madrid. In the meantime, he was sending the
report of Captain Gasco, and the summary of the Governor's
letters, to the King. "For the present," added the Viceroy, in
his covering letter, "all I can say is that beginnings are often
difficult, and time will soon reveal what we may expect from
this expedition."

Don Francisco's questions seemed to deal mostly with the
various stages by which the occupation of the northern kingdom had been achieved, and with conditions at large of the
life of the Indian people. However, he asked all three witnesses if they thought the New Mexican colonists would be
able to remain in their river capital, or desired to do so. One
said that some did, while others did not. One said almost
everyone wanted to remain. The third said "in general all
were so displeased that, were it not for fear of severe punishment, they would not remain in that land voluntarily."

None of them had anything to say against the Governor or
his nephew. The witness who thought everyone would leave
if permitted had other matters to report which gave a poor
character to the kingdom and its experience. He told how
colonists arriving with the reinforcements of 1600 had been

led on with enticing promises and reports, only to discover in New Mexico that they must despair of finding "enough food to eat or clothing to cover their own nakedness, and that of their wives, children, and relatives." In winter the rivers froze and Spaniards were "always shivering by the fire." Firewood was scarce, and what there was came from the cottonwood tree. It was "so smoky that women and children" were "in tears night and day." The summers were frightfully hot—in fact, the colonists had a saying which declared that in the kingdom there were "eight months of winter and four of hell." There was a plague of field mice, which bred a species of louse whose bite was so vicious that its pain lasted for four and twenty hours. If people grew chili and peppers, and did not harvest their crops promptly, the mice ate these all up. The mice, indeed, seemed mad—they did not eat cheese. Don Francisco's interrogations in Mexico produced little that was conclusive.

But in San Gabriel, in faraway New Mexico, matters were coming to a head. Most of the colonists did not share the high hopes of the Governor as he set out for the east, and after his departure, their discontents and sorrows began to show openly. Complaints and gossip led to argument, and this in turn to a division of the city into opposing parties. Public debates were held about the broken promise of the northern kingdom. Who wanted to scratch a bean patch or make a ditch to bring river to the corn rows? Many colonists felt as most other conquerors felt, including the Governor's grandfather-in-law, the great Lord Marquess of the Valley of Oaxaca. What had he said? "I came to get gold, not to till the soil like a peasant." The only known wealth to be had in the kingdom of New Mexico was that which grew under cultivation by farmers. Life was hard and dangers were all about.

One party of colonists prepared a document bringing charges against the Governor. His supporters—far fewer in number—prepared another in his defense. The papers were sent to the Viceroy at Mexico, and then, in September, most people of the settlement loaded their wagons with their few possessions, and took to the river trail southward to Santa Barbara.

The Lieutenant Governor of New Mexico, who remained at San Gabriel, wrote to the Viceroy on October first, 1601, confessing that he did not know how to account for "the events and changes" in the kingdom. He did not think it just to blame the Governor, who was away "with most of the army in search of new provinces." If he blamed the friars, they replied "with so many texts from the Holy Scriptures to prove" that the settlers could not "in good conscience take food and blankets from the Indians, or very little indeed," and charged them "with mortal sin if they took anything at all." He could only blame bad luck, and the sins which must have called it forth. In any case, he said, "All will be lost if our Lord does not remedy this situation by permitting the Governor to discover something so important that the men may overcome their indifference and lack of confidence in finding anything worthwhile in these lands." He begged the Viceroy to send help and stated outright that if it did not come "within five months" the rest of the colony would feel obliged to abandon the kingdom, as they were "determined to do."

By the same post another report went to the Count of Monterrey. This came from the Franciscan superior of New Mexico, who confirmed the "evils and ruin" all about him, but went on to assign blame. It lay at the feet of the Governor Don Juan de Oñate, who simply was not sufficiently a man of means to be entrusted with the leadership of the colonization. "The result was that soon after he entered the land, his people began to perpetrate many offenses against the natives and to plunder their pueblos of the corn they had gathered for their own sustenance." The Indians had nothing else with which to support themselves, said the Father Superior, and "Here corn is God." He added wryly that any Spaniard who had his fill of tortillas in the kingdom felt as if he had "obtained a grant of nobility." Because of all these conditions, and others which, he said darkly, he was "not telling," the Father Superior and his friars could no longer preach the gospel there, for it was "despised by these people on account of our great offenses."

The courier who bore these dispatches was Captain Don Luís Gasco de Velasco, whose worst expectations had been borne out. He departed in time to avoid facing the wrath of the Governor.

Returning several weeks later, to find only a handful of his people remaining at San Gabriel, the Governor was enraged and grieved. He wanted to send soldiers after them to force the return of the deserters. He wanted to sue them in court to make them come back. But he found no support, for in due time the authorities at Mexico ruled that the deserters need not return to the north, though the colony should continue to exist with what it had.

It had little enough. Quivira had once again proved to be only an empty vastness. Once again the Governor turned his belief to the South Sea. Not only must there be pearls in the South Sea, for the Indians had never changed their story about this, but there must also be ocean harbors from which ships belonging to New Mexico could sail to the Orient, just as ships had been going from New Spain to the Philippines for almost forty years. If only he had enough troops, with the proper equipment, and some skilled shipwrights, and a handful of trained pilots, the Governor was certain he could still bring New Mexico to prosperity, as he had promised to do long ago.

There was only one hope left.

In 1602 he sent his nephew Vicente de Zaldívar to Madrid to beg the Crown for what was needed in the way of men, money, supplies and new colonists. For two years the matter was weighed, while charges against the Governor were secretly examined. The colony was royally abolished at one time, and then royally reinstated. But no further time and money were to be spent on it by the home government, and Vicente returned to report to his uncle with empty hands.

In 1605 Governor de Oñate made his last effort to conquer the South Sea, but returned from the mouth of the Colorado River with nothing new. After the ready glories of New Spain and Peru, which had only to be fought for, the conquering captains who went north seemed to discover only a succession of unprofitable wildernesses whose wealth would not appear for centuries, and then only in response to a new idea of work—Apalachen, Cíbola, Quivira, and the rest.

Another Lord Viceroy was reigning in Mexico—the Marquess of Montesclaros—when Philip III ordered a new examination of New Mexico to determine whether the colony should be abandoned. Montesclaros gathered information, sifted great folios of papers, and found small reason to be enthusiastic. The Governor's samples of ore, he wrote to the King in 1605, were inferior. He went on to report that,

"The light that we have thus far gathered on this expedition reveals that the people are rustic, wretched in clothes and spirit, that they do not possess silver or gold, dwell in straw and grass houses, and live on native fruits such as maize and vegetables, which they say are grown twice a year in places. Instead of cotton, I have been assured that they weave dog hair."

The state of the colony was extremely shaky, and perhaps a royal inspector should be sent to make a final report. If so, he should go on some plausible pretext of a routine nature which would not alarm the Governor, who if he became suspicious might "be driven to some rash action." The inspector could carry secret instructions and a commission to arrest Governor de Oñate if he found, after examining affairs in the north, that this should be necessary. One further thought—armed protection must by all means be maintained in the kingdom and should come from the resources of the Crown itself, for, wrote the Marquess, "if there should be one lone Christian, your majesty would be obligated through justice, conscience, and prestige to preserve him, even at great cost to the royal treasury. . . ."

In the next year, the King ordered the Viceroy to suspend all further exploration of the kingdom of New Mexico, though for the sake of the Christian Indians with their Franciscan fathers, the colony was not to be abandoned. One more thing: "You shall," ordered Philip, "you shall, with tact and discretion, cause the said Don Juan de Oñate to be recalled for some sufficient reason, as seems best to you, so that he may come without disturbance. . . ." Once securely back in Mexico, he was to be kept there, and another governor was to be appointed in his place.

As with most Spanish official processes of the time, the Governor's demotion and recall took several years to bring about, but finally in 1609 he rode away for the last time from his capital of San Gabriel on the northern river. His command was gone, and so was his great private fortune, and he was going home to the usual legal hearing.

But New Mexico was not yet done with him.

Crossing the hard passage of the Dead Man's March his party was attacked by Indians. In the ensuing fight, the Governor's only son, a young soldier, was killed. He left behind him, then, the grave of his heir, and a small community that strove to keep alive the harsh reality, if not the golden vision, of a Spanish kingdom in the unprofitable north.

vii.

THE HEARING

IN THE CITY of Mexico the investigation of Don Juan de Oñate's labors—was he a statesman able to endure all for duty or merely an ambitious ruffian?—slowly took its way through years during which evidence was gathered, many an affidavit produced, gossip sifted, charge made and counter-charge returned. By 1614, it had assumed the formality of a criminal case, with Don Juan "and his officers and ministers" on trial "for crimes and excesses." He was acquitted of a number of grave charges—certain murders, instances of ill-treatment of soldiers and clergy, fraud, self-indulgence, assumption of royal airs (Captain Gasco's old gossip about "your majesty" and the lowering of the King's standard), maladministration of justice.

But there remained other weighty accusations which, to the satisfaction of the current Viceroy, the Marquess of Guadalcázar, and his "legal advisor," Doctor Antonio de Morga, were proven; and the former Governor, who had been imprisoned in his own house during the long trial, heard himself convicted of inhumane severity in the war of Ácoma and the punishment of the Indians who survived it; of having lived "dishonorably and scandalously with women of the army, married and unmarried"; of unjustly putting to death Captains de Aguilar and de Sosa and of imposing the death penalty on others without justification; of rendering false reports about the conditions in the kingdom; of obstructing royal agents in their duties; of disrespect to the Count of Monterrey; and of mocking a certain friar. For these offenses, he was condemned to "perpetual exile from the provinces of New Mexico," and from the city of Mexico, and to pay a fine of six thousand ducats of Castile, and the costs of the trial.

He appealed his case to the Council of the Indies, and for seven years the papers came and went, during which he "suffered much and spent much." The Council recommended clemency in 1622, and in a familiar act the King responded with the notation, "Postpone this for the time being." The petition was renewed, and in 1624 the disgraced old Governor—he was now more than seventy-five years of age— was in Spain, pressing his case in the most urgent of needs, which was the need to recover honor.

At last he was pardoned. His title of *Adelantado* was confirmed for life, and he was restored to public office, now in the position of Inspector of Mines and Lodes in the home kingdoms of Spain. The Council permitted him to "bring six Indian metal smelters and refiners from the Indies," whose skills he required in his work. The other kingdom— New Mexico—which he had settled, continued to survive. There was a new capital—his successor as Governor, Don Pedro de Peralta, had moved it from San Gabriel to found the royal city of Santa Fe in 1610.

Don Juan de Oñate could reflect that through his efforts —now cleared of dishonor—European civilization was at last rooted in the continent north of New Spain, and would remain though, within the century, it was threatened almost out of existence.

It was saved and restored only by the wisdom and valor of the last conquistador.

VII

THE LAST
CONQUEST

I decided to put some trust
in fate.

—Vargas.

i.

HARSH REALITIES

THIS MISERABLE kingdom!"—so new Mexico was described again and again in dispatches sent during the 1670s by a governor at Santa Fe to the Viceroy in Mexico City.

And in truth, ever since the founding of the capital at Santa Fe, the kingdom of New Mexico had seen hardship grow through the seventeenth century. One kind of trouble would have been enough for the thinly settled Spanish colony, with its little mountain capital of fewer than a thousand souls, and all its other villages and haciendas accounting for barely two thousand more. But troubles of many kinds beset the colony. If most of these came from forces which the colonists could not control, one of them—a bitter and acute social problem—lay within their power to resolve if only two strong and violently opposed convictions could find a suitable compromise. But neither would yield, until calamity engulfed them both.

These were the opposed interests of the civil government on the one hand and of the church on the other—Crown and Cross, this world and the next. The civil governors and all their officers bore themselves as deputies of the King in whatever station they might serve. Drawing their power from the Crown, they held material and military command. The civil authorities were also the servants of the landowners and, as such, they regarded Indians—despite the old argument about the nature of man fought over so long ago and far away—as laborers of inferior status whose work, possessions, and even persons, were not their own but rather existed for the convenience of their proprietors.

The Franciscan mission friars opposed this view. They drew their power from Christ who was God, through St. Peter and his successors, and their purpose was to succor and support Indians as human creatures with immortal souls. In this the missioners followed not only the call of simple charity, but also the conclusions reached by the Church at its foundation about the nature and value of the soul in man. It was the reality of this conclusion, visible only through the eyes of faith, which brought the friars so far and so miserably to do their duty in villages of mud where their teachings were resisted and their very lives were at times in danger.

Doing their duty, they must oppose the civil authorities in all matters concerning the control and exploitation of Indians, and oppose they did—loudly, rudely, and at length. They even went so far as to invoke the dread instrument of excommunication against recalcitrant civil servants, citing atrocities against Indians, robberies, dispossessions, even perversions from the faith.

The governors struck back, filling long memorandums of complaint against the clergy—the friars were greedy in their own way, they whipped Indians, they worked Indians in the fields like animals, they were drunkards and hypocrites. Throughout the better part of the seventeenth century the documents of accusation and abuse were sent by creaking oxcart to Mexico where, if they were read at all, they moved no one to action.

The quarrel further weakened the society of the far kingdom, which was already weakened from without by a decision finally taken at Madrid by Philip III and ratified by his successors. New Mexico was to have no further support of any consequence from the home government. The skeleton of a local administration, with a garrison of a few dozen troops, was ordered to survive. But no new energy of imagination, money or colonizing personnel would be assigned to the north by the Crown.

New Mexico was not alone in her decline. As the seventeenth century wore on Spain's power faded.

> *Miré los muros de la patria mía,*
> *si un tiempo fuertes, ya desmoronados,*

sadly sang Francisco de Quevedo, the poet who died in 1645: "I look upon the walls of my native land, once so strong, now crumbled in ruins. . . ."

If Spain was now poor at home, she was even poorer in her farthest colonies. New Mexico's troubles reflected the troubles at the heart of the Empire. Ties with the old land grew weaker as the strength of the new gained power in its own terms. New Spain, rich in gold and silver mines, kept the bulk of their revenue, aside from the royal fifth, and no longer did the colony's wonderful profusion of wealth go home to Spain—increasingly it remained in the new land because its discoverers had descendants now who called the new land home. If exploitation of New Spain continued, it was now done not for the benefit of the parent country, but for the benefit of the new. As one energy declined, the other grew.

It was an energy which had more than its material character. The Indies slowly found their own soul, and as they did so, a character new to the world had to be recognized— that child of the European, the African and the Indian mixture which created a new human factor in the world's peoples. The conquered replaced the conqueror in the land of their passionate encounter. Material and spiritual independence could only be followed in the far future by political independence, and with this would come inevitably the end of empire.

With the advance of the seventeenth century, then, Spain, ruined by inflation, and overcome by defeats in war in Europe, was no longer the chief source of material power for the colonies.

In the far marches of New Mexico, here was yet another irritant in the disagreeable relations between Cross and Crown, the Two Majesties, for it meant that the Franciscan order, not the Spanish government, became the chief source of supply for the needs of the missions—which in effect meant the province.

Not only those objects which contributed to seemly worship, but also food itself were provided by the friars, and agricultural implements, seeds, cattle, and domestic stuffs. So in material as well as ethical affairs the clergy had it all over the governors, and the bitter quarrel raged on in the name of pride, among other things. When reports of it would come to Mexico, the conditions they described were all too familiar, for to some degree the same posed animosities between the civil and the religious had already arisen there.

When trouble of another sort came in mid-century, the colony was in no condition to meet it. It was hunger, reaching, at times, famine. Drought held itself over the whole kingdom of plain and river valley, and colonists and Indians alike suffered its effect. Apache Indians, unable to find their usual food as they roved the plains with the seasons, repeatedly fell upon the pueblos and farms, massacred inhabitants and made off with stored seed-corn and other foods. The garrison at Santa Fe was too feeble to offer defense. In their turn, hungry Spaniards robbed Indians. In 1668 scores of Indians were seen lying dead "along the roads, in the canyons, and in their houses." Four hundred fifty people died of starvation in a single pueblo. In the words of a friar, there was not "a bushel and a half of corn or of wheat in the whole kingdom."

Raiding Apaches stole herds of cattle and sheep, and in some places Indians and Spaniards tried to live by eating leather. They made a stew of animal hide or harness straps, herbs and roots, or tried soaking leather scraps to soften them, and then rolled them in corn meal and roasted them in the fire. In 1671 epidemic disease carried off many of the weakened population, and again the Plains Indians struck, stole, and vanished, leaving behind them desolation compounded.

It was no wonder that Indians were tempted to rebel under such conditions, or that forty colonial families were ready to give up and go home to Mexico. Hunger and drought and conflict between the powers of authority were bad enough, but increasing threats from the Pueblo people, who outnumbered the colonists by more than ten to one, destroyed the last shred of comfort for the Spanish establishment.

The authorities watched the rebellious efforts of a certain troublemaker—an Indian medicine doctor called Popé. He had been arrested and brought to Santa Fe along with forty-six of his fellow adepts, three of whom had been executed, for the practice of superstition in connection with the ritual dances of the Pueblo towns. Along with the others, Popé had been whipped and left in jail. On the petition of seventy Indians who spoke in outright threats, the Governor released all the Indian doctors in 1675.

But Popé was not satisfied. He actively worked, first at San Juan, and later at Taos, to raise the Indians against their starving and divided masters and teachers. Fostering plans for war, he strove to bring all the Pueblos into a coordinated scheme for an uprising against the colony.

Rumors and hints of such activity came to the Spanish residents and added to the misery which was all too evident to the Franciscan Friar Francisco de Ayeta, who had charge of the oxcart train which came from Mexico every three years to bring supplies to the colony. It took six months to come, six to unload and properly distribute the freights, and six to return, along the road which united Santa Fe with Parral, Durango, Zacatecas and the city of Mexico across the immense reaches of the *tierra adentro*—the central interior.

Santa Fe lay upon the edge of a wide plain where it sloped up into foothills which rose against the western face of a noble range of mountains. Snow lay on the rocky caps of the range for three seasons of the year, and when the setting sun shed its light over them, they glowed with such a color that the colonists named the mountains after the blood of Christ—the Sangre de Cristo.

From the mountain a plentiful creek flowed to the southwest across the plain and eighteen or twenty miles away entered into the Rio Grande. Where this creek came out of the foothills the capital had been settled. On the north side was the *Plaza de Armas,* or military square, whose two main features were the Palace of the Governors, a long, low building with watch towers at each end, and a walled patio in back; and the parish church, which, like the palace, and all the other buildings of the town, was made of adobe. It was the second church of the parish, for, as a Franciscan superior of the kingdom noted in 1634, the first one "had collapsed," and during his residence in New Mexico, he said, "I built a very fine church" for the people, "at which they, their wives and children, personally aided me considerably by carrying the materials and helping to build the walls with their own hands."

The houses of the town, all of one-storied earth construction, lay along the creek. On the south side, where the ground rose on a long slope, the Indian servants of the colonists had their own quarter, called Analco, with its own clay chapel, named for St. Michael.

Coming to Santa Fe from across the plain, travellers would see first the smoke of its house-fires, and only by this would know that the flat, earth-coloured cluster of the town was made together by houses, and was not some bare natural oddment of the earth itself. Though this was a royal city, and the seat of a governor, there was no suggestion here of the magnificence which the English Dominican saw in the seventeenth century in Mexico, where a palace was a massive monument of fired brick or stone with sculptured cornices, and immense wooden door panels hung within pedimented and pillared and escutcheoned portals of carved stone, and windows framed in limestone and barred with elegantly wrought grilles of iron. The royal city of the north was closer in style to the towns of the Pueblo Indians than to the viceregal capital, or even the mining towns of the *tierra adentro*, where the royal highway made a wavering scratch in the dusty map of the high deserts.

In 1675–1676 Friar Francisco, the father quartermaster, found the kingdom in a state of peril from within and without. He was appalled that serious affairs had been allowed to fall so low, and he was moved by the sufferings brought by famine, poverty and strife. It seemed to him that the strongest representations must be made to the Viceroy, and he had firm ideas of what should be done to relieve the kingdom. When it was time for him to set out on his six-month journey back to Mexico City, he was urged by the New Mexicans to present their case and persuade the government to send them aid. He left Santa Fe in early spring, and in the following September he brought to the viceregal offices his memorandums of the bitter needs of New Mexico.

Astonishingly enough, his requests were not referred to Madrid, as he had expected, but instead were acted upon at once by the Viceroy. Within two or three weeks the father quartermaster was granted more or less what he asked for —fifty soldiers, a thousand horses, various laborers, including fifty-seven convicts "condemned to serve His Majesty in New Mexico." He was in Santa Fe again by November, 1677, and was received with joy.

But it was soon clear that he had not asked or received enough in the way of food, implements, arms, animals and men to give more than a trickle of help to a parched land that needed a stream.

When again he returned to Mexico (1679) he brought further requisitions for governmental help; but now he was told that since help had been sent, at his request, two years ago, it was hopeless to expect more. Further, his arguments were "not sufficiently convincing," and in any case the matter must be referred this time to the Council of the Indies in Madrid, where, surely, it would be seen as "a useless and unnecessary expense."

All the father quartermaster could do was to go to work loading his wagons with the usual supplies paid for by his Franciscan order, and turn around to go to Santa Fe on September 30, 1679, hoping against hope that calamity could be avoided in the northern kingdom.

Sixteen months later he was once again in the City of

Mexico, and this time he brought a story of terror and sorrow which bore out all his warnings of the past five years.

On his last trip northward, he had just reached the Rio Grande at the North Pass—El Paso del Norte—in August, 1680, where he was delayed by high summer water at the ford, when couriers arrived from the middle valley of New Mexico to say that the Pueblo towns there had revolted. Spanish churches and farms had been burned and families were toiling down the river road to the south as fast as their lumbering animals would let them. They had no news of the upper country of Santa Fe, but they feared that there also all was lost, and the Governor killed, for the fury of the Indians was appalling, and it seemed clear that the uprising had long been planned to break forth at the same time in all the Indian settlements. Refugees would begin arriving in a few days, to seek haven at the mission of Our Lady of Guadalupe at El Paso, founded in 1659, where Father Francisco and his supply train were halted.

Shock and grief did not paralyze him. Too much needed to be done. He helped at once to organize a provisional government, and to prepare corn meal, dried beef and biscuits for the refugees who would arrive in hunger, and he gave arms to a party of soldiers who would march north on the river road—"all are going absolutely raging," he said, adding "I believe under God that each one must be reckoned as ten men"—to take supplies to fleeing families. They also hoped to find the Governor and the people of Santa Fe if any survived. The father quartermaster was so busy that, as he exclaimed, he knew not what he said or did. The provisional governor said he was "more than a father to us." For two weeks he labored to keep heart and organization in the people of the shattered colony who had already arrived at the mission; and then on September eighth, couriers brought letters from the north with word that the colonists from Santa Fe and the northern districts, including Governor Otermín, alive though wounded, were marching south. As soon as they reached El Paso, all the sorrowful details of the calamity would be known.

When at last they arrived, Father Francisco said he had never seen "such great unhappiness and pitiful tragedy, with the need corresponding to the great numbers, and the poor women and children on foot and unshod, of such a hue that they looked like the dead."

Hardly had they come to the mission than they begged

to be allowed to march on, despite their wretched state, to Mexico and home. The colony was ready to disintegrate completely. But with great foresight Father Francisco had already obtained from the governor of New Biscay, the next province to the south, which the marchers would have to cross on their way home, an agreement by which they would not be granted passage or asylum there. The colony must remain under the jurisdiction of the governor of New Mexico, even if he held his government just outside New Mexico in the territory of New Biscay, at El Paso del Norte on the Rio Grande.

"We have come to the point where we must act or abandon completely," wrote Father Francisco. Abandonment was out of the question, for it would "necessarily expose the missions at one blow"—not only the missions of New Mexico but those also of the provinces below. Grieving for those they had lost, the colonists gathered around the Guadalupe mission and its buildings, and tended to their wounds of body and spirit, and bit by bit the father quartermaster learned from them the whole story of their ordeal.

On August ninth the Governor had been told in his earthen palace at Santa Fe by the chiefs of the Pueblos of Taos and Tesuque that an attack was coming. He at once sent warnings to the farms downriver and to other Spanish settlements, and to the friars in the missions. No one paid much heed. They had been listening to warnings all during the decade.

On the next day, going to Mass, Governor Otermín was halted by a breathless Spaniard from the valley north of Santa Fe who told him that the Indian people of Tesuque had just that morning murdered their pastor at the altar.

"What is this, children?" he had cried out under their first blows. "Are you mad? Don't get excited—I will help you and die a thousand deaths for you"—but one was enough.

The Governor returned immediately to his office and called all his people to join him who could. The families in the northern villages and farms converged on Santa Fe, while those in the middle valley below started for the south along the river road. All day long the attacks continued. Priests were murdered, and many churches were wrecked, and houses, and an Indian at Taos said that not a single Spaniard was to be left alive.

A thousand colonists gathered in the palace at Santa Fe,

where a hundred men-at-arms took up the defense for what must come. Farm animals and horses were kept inside the great patio along with their owners. Two brass cannon were stationed at the main gate.

On August twelfth soldiers on the roof saw the Indians breaking through the cornfields around St. Michael's chapel on the high ground of Analco across Santa Fe creek, and the attack came. It was beaten off, but it signalled the start of a siege that lasted a week. The colonists watched by day to see the Indians turn the course of their life-giving water ditch, and by night to see the parish church, and St. Michael's, and the houses of the town, burn hollow. A witness said "the whole town became a torch."

The brass cannon gave what defiance they could, and the muskets of the troops, but it was soon evident that death by thirst and starvation would have to come if the garrison and the colony could not escape. With a mighty effort they launched a counter attack which held the besiegers away, and a few days later the Governor led his remnant of a kingdom out of the palace and through the roofless walls of his capital out to the plain of Santa Fe and down the escarpment of La Bajada to the river road and flight southward. They marched under the heavy yellow silk of Oñate's royal standard, which was still the colony's visible emblem of state.

Hungry, sick and hurt, the population straggled slowly along the valley. One of the strangest effects of the nightmarish experience was that though shock and grief and fear had stricken the colonists like lightning, and still sent their hearts beating fast in terror, they could only pursue the act of retreat at the dragging pace possible to oxen walking, or to women carrying sick children. Hurry, hurry, said the fearful thought; and plod, plod, went the hungry column in the exposed valley. On the buttes and mesas of the valley they saw Indians watching them, and sending signals by fire and smoke along their way.

As they passed by Spanish settlements of village or river farm they saw evidences of the fury everywhere—houses wrecked, churches burned and profaned, sacred vessels flung down and filled with excrement, a crucifix whipped bare of its paint and gesso, carved saints mutilated as though they lived, and the bodies, naked and dishonored, of their own people.

Why had the Indians revolted? An Indian who fled his own town to give news to the Governor said that they were "tired of work they had to do for the Spaniards and the clergy," who "did not allow them to plant, to do other things for their own needs"—in short, denied them freedom; and that "being weary, they had rebelled."

Other reports said that the revolt had been planned for many years. The colonists later heard a report filled with fantasy. Popé, the Taos doctor, long regarded as the chief agent of the revolt, was only the visible head of the plot. Actually, said certain Indians, successfully bewildering their Spanish listeners, Popé had been steadily in communication with the immortal Montezuma through a mysterious spokesman whom the Indians described as a black giant whose eyes were yellow. This giant, who lived unseen like a god in a kiva at Taos, guiding Popé and giving him power, planned the revolt. He was, it might seem, a mulatto from New Spain named Diego de Santiago (or Naranjo) who was long disaffected from the ways of colonial life. Before 1626 he had come to San Felipe in Mew Mexico as a servant to a Spanish hacienda, and there he took an Indian wife from the pueblo. He was once found among celebrants of a pagan orgy in the Alameda parish church. When he established himself at Taos, he was an adept at sorcery and incitement. Popé, himself "a great sorcerer," according to a Spaniard, and, according to an Indian, "a whirlwind," carried out the whole fury of the revolt of 1680 among the Pueblos, following the design of the black giant who spoke for Montezuma.

In the course of the tragedy twenty-one Franciscan friars and three hundred seventy-nine colonists had been massacred. More hundreds escaped southward to Mexico despite the legal barriers of the governors of New Mexico and New Biscay. The remainder began to make settlements for themselves near the mission of Guadalupe. Each family built its dwelling of withes and clay. The Governor held his state in a hut of dried river mud. Friar Francisco de Ayeta, as soon as possible, hurried to Mexico City to tell the Viceroy of the tragedy in the north kingdom.

Too late, too late—this seemed the unspoken motto of Spanish government in the affairs of the colonial empire. In 1680, the year of the Pueblo rebellion, Spain at last executed a humane law for the sake of conquered Indians.

"War," said the law of 1680, "cannot and shall not be made on the Indians of any province to the end that they may receive the Holy Catholic Faith or yield obedience to us, or for any other reason."

And when the father quartermaster reached the viceregal offices in 1681 with his report of disaster and loss, he was handed a royal order dated at Madrid June twenty-fifth of the year before, which decreed that all that was necessary should be done to preserve the kingdom of New Mexico.

ii.

RETURN TO THE NORTH

AT THE Paso Del Norte where the Rio Grande started its course southeastward toward the Gulf of Mexico, the colony held itself together for twelve years. Under successive governors several expeditions into the lost kingdom were mounted. The first of these, in 1681, hoped to find evidence that the Indians were penitent for their crime of rebellion and stood ready to accept the paternal rule of their civil and religious masters. But no such willingness was discovered—the Indians fled to the mountains, or when the Spaniards did encounter them, showed all their old defiance. The soldiers took prisoners and burned some empty pueblos and returned to El Paso. Later expeditions, in 1688 and 1689, brought no greater satisfactions to the exiled colonists. None of the marches had gone as far as Santa Fe, and they could only wonder what now happened there.

But meanwhile, in Mexico, long debates in viceregal councils examined the question of whether or not the northern kingdom should be recovered, even at the cost of outfitting a new military penetration in force.

There were many reasons why it seemed desirable to reconquer New Mexico. One was that if the frontier were contracted through the continued loss of New Mexico—which, however feebly, had extended the military power of New Spain—then the Indians—Manxos and others—of New Biscay and her adjacent provinces would be harder to control. Another was that persistent reports of quicksilver deposits in western New Mexico again aroused hopes of the discovery of new wealth. Another was a persistent sense of spiritual obligation to the converted Indians.

And finally, in the 1680s, the Spanish colonial government learned that the French—LaSalle and other expeditioners—were moving westward from the vast river called "Micipipi" and might soon represent a threat to the whole sweeping dominion of New Spain to the north and west. Even earlier in the century, an alarming concern was voiced in Mexico of which the English Dominican, in his observations there, made note. He speculated that the Spanish lands of the north reached to the English plantations "of Virginia and the rest, being the same continued continent land," and he had heard Spaniards say that they must subdue all those northern parts "lest our English from Virginia and their other plantations get in before them." Indeed, he had heard them wonder why the English had entered "no further into the main land."

If there were firm reasons against the recolonization of New Mexico, the reasons in favor of it seemed in the end more compelling; and on September twenty-fifth, 1690, a new governor of New Mexico assumed his office at the city of Mexico with the three-fold mission of reducing the border Manxos and other tribes to peace, and of recolonizing New Mexico, and of finding her quicksilver deposits.

He was the son of an illustrious Spanish family and his name was Diego José de Vargas Zapata Luján Ponce de León y Contreras. A veteran of the Spanish campaigns in Naples and Italy, he had been in Mexico since 1673, in the service of the government. A fine-drawn and elegant aristocrat, tall, dark and thin, he wore his black hair parted in the middle and swept to his shoulders on either side of his long, oval face. His complexion was smooth in a pale olive color, and his eyes, under level, dark brows, had a calm power of observation and command. He wore his mustaches trimmed in a narrow line and his beard was a mere pencil line on his strong chin. His nose was long and straight and his mouth in repose was level and neither great-lipped nor small. In the heavy velvets of court dress edged with fur and picked out with gold bullion lace, and tasselled at the knees of his short breeches, and bloused in ballooning fine linen, and bearing a velvet hat circled in plumes, he presented a figure of grave elegance; and in the leather thigh boots, armor, and rain-shedding broadcloth cloak of the mounted officer in the field, he carried an air of just and incontrovertible command. He was forty-seven years old on assuming the governorship of the colony huddled at the edge of New Mexico.

Behind him was a heritage of high style and valor. As long ago as the eleventh century his ancestors distinguished themselves, and the family chronicle continued with an unbroken record of distinguished services to the nation in arms, government and diplomacy. There were triumphant general officers and renowned governors and an ambassador and a bishop in the Vargas lineage, and, most exalting of all to the devout Spaniard, two saints figured in the family story. The great patron of agriculture, St. Isidore, brought back from the dead a daughter of the house in the twelfth century, and since the saint was a farm hand employed by the presiding Vargas of the time, a shrine was built to him on the family property. In another flourish of pious glory, the Vargases could claim as a cousin by marriage the gifted and exquisite St. Teresa of Jesus, author of masterpieces of literary mysticism.

Since their splendid public deeds brought great wealth to the family, there were Vargas houses and palaces at Madrid, Torrelunga and Mexico City, along with income-producing properties such as real estate in Madrid and Granada; vineyards and farms and salt works and pasture lands and olive orchards in the country. The Governor's father was a gentleman scholar who wrote twenty volumes of "general information of the period" and a study of the taxation policies lowered upon the population of Messina by the Duke of Osuna. In the church of St. Francis the Great at Madrid the Vargas family altar blazed away with lighted tapers against encrustations of gold and silver. The new Governor brought with him all the comforts of settled belief and inherited assurance.

On February twenty-second, 1691, he arrived at El Paso and assumed his office in the dusty military square outlined by the mean habitations of the capital village. The troops were smartened to receive him—the mounted soldiers were called "leatherjackets" after their uniforms. His intentions were soon known, and the life of the colony quickened at the power of command at last returned to them.

But it was a year and a half before he could start north, for in the meantime there was much to do, which he did efficiently, to put down the brush-fire revolts of the border Indians. But when they were again quiet, under the conviction that it was profitless to rise against such an officer, he was able to complete his arrangements for the return to the kingdom of New Mexico; and on August twenty-first, 1692, he led his troops—it was entirely a military enterprise, without civilian colonists—up the river road. He marched under the banner of Governor de Oñate, which had gone up the river first in 1598 in the foundation of the colony and had come back in defeat in 1680 under Governor de Otermín—that flag of heavy yellow silk which showed on one face the lions and castles of the royal blazon, and on the other the image of Our Lady of Remedies. It was a dual honor to return under its folds to the lost capital.

Evidently the clay palace at Santa Fe was the one building not destroyed by fire in the revolt of twelve years ago. There were gathered a great throng of Indians from the pueblos, to help Popé to enact the state of victorious governor, which he did with mocking imitations of Spanish manners and occasions. But the successes he had promised—rain, abundant crops, the joys of freedom—did not materialize, and his followers once again knew disenchantment under authority. If they had risen in the ways of ancestral fury against outrageous abuses of their being, they seemed to have gained little as a result; and New Mexico lay useless between the ancient proprieties of her native peoples and the rejected ways of her Spanish conquerors.

The Governor and Captain General marched for three weeks up the river as summer entered autumn. All the Indian river towns were empty. It seemed impossible, yet there was no indication that his steady progress toward Santa Fe was observed by the native people. In this there must seem something mysterious, and soldiers wondered, and kept their wits about them, for they all knew what merciless fury the Indians could show.

On September twelfth the troops scaled the sharp and steep trail up the La Bajada escarpment and once free at the top on Santa Fe plain the Governor called a halt until sunset to rest his men and animals. Twenty miles ahead lay the royal city under its noble backdrop of mountains. They moved forward again after dark, and halted again while the Governor issued his final orders. He had with him certain officers who had a knowledge of the stars, and he asked them to let him know when it was three o'clock in the morning, at which time he would take them all forward again until they came to Santa Fe. All were to hold their fire until they saw him signal with his sword. When he gave another signal they were to flow forward against the walls crying out five times "Glory be to the Blessed Sacrament of the Altar!"

What would follow them could only be thought about until it must happen. The column halted once again while the chaplains gave absolution to all. Then using the darkness they went forward again.

And then they were among the fallen houses of their royal city and before the fortified walls of the palace as the mountains began to show black against the pre-dawn light of the cold sky. They gave their cry five times, two hundred soldiers, and at once saw the palace roof alive like a pueblo with the Indians from within. Growing daylight showed "the expression on the face of each one of them," as the Governor said in his diary. They were astounded.

Who are you? they called, and the Governor repeated the *Gloria*.

No, said the Indians in the twilight of dawn, it was an imposture, the invaders were Apaches, or enemies from Pecos.

The soldiers again shouted the *Gloria*.

Very well, said the Indians, if they were Spaniards, why did they not fire guns? Fire a gun, and we will know.

"Be calm," called the Governor. "I am a Catholic, and when the sun rises, you will see the Blessed Virgin on my flag."

No, said the Indians, if they were Spaniards, let them sound a Spanish war trumpet.

Very well—the Governor ordered the trumpeter to sound off, and the drummer also. At the same time he passed the word for the troops to stand fast, guarding all access to the palace, but making no act of war.

Now the Indians seemed convinced by the Spanish war music, and declared that they were ready to fight for five days until they had killed all the soldiers and that none should escape. Saying this, they began "to shout furiously," and continued to shout for "well over an hour."

The Governor let them shout, and heard their insults, and saw them gathering stones and other weapons. Meanwhile he ordered the ditch water flow to the palace cutoff, which produced redoubled cries from the roof.

Come then, he called to them, come down off the walls, make peace, submit, and the water would be released again. He gave them an hour to think it over, and then ordered a breakfast of biscuits and hot chocolate served to all the troops from the field kitchen at the supply camp a little way away.

Presently he brought up his artillery pieces and faced them to the palace and prepared to place mines against the palace walls. Through the foothills came Indians from other towns and he gave them kind words and put guards on them. All day long he saw to the proper military details of preparing for siege, and several times he went with his banner, his rosary and a crucifix to call for peace. He managed everything in calm order and perfect confidence, without flourishes. His soldiers felt his steady nerve, and so, in the end, did the people he had come to recover. Late in the afternoon, the Governor went forward again to call his Indian people to come down and render obedience to the King whom he also obeyed. By the image of Our Lady of Remedies on his flag he promised them peace and pardon. On their reply he would "decide at once whether or not to make peace or war."

Then, they said, let him send all the soldiers to the back to the supply camp; and take away his cannons; and come back himself unarmed, and then they would come down and make peace.

It was perhaps twelve hours since he had begun his conquest. Now it was done. The troops withdrew taking the field pieces. The Governor went forward, dismounted, and embraced the first two Indians who came out of the palace. Two Franciscan chaplains went into the patio of the palace and then more Indians appeared in the plaza "to make peace," which the Governor extended to them "with great love." He said,

"I stood there dismounted, embracing them, shaking hands with them, and speaking to them with tender and loving words, in order to assure them of my good will and of the said peace. I told them to make this known to the rest, who had not come down, although some women, old and young, had done so."

Presently he withdrew to his camp, and there, he said, "I decided to put some trust in fate." In a sort of grandeur of good manners, he ordered all the soldiery stationed about the palace to return to camp, leaving the Indians free entirely. He doubled the guards on his picket lines of horses and mules, and kept two squads armed and alert with saddled mounts at the camp; but the night went safely by, and in the morning, he left off his armor and put on court dress, "in gala," as he said, and alone, with only chaplains, for so the Indians asked him to come, he went into the great patio of the palace and there received the allegiance of the whole town. With all kneeling, the chaplains intoned the "Te Deum laudamus" under the topaz light of the sky of Santa Fe in autumn.

iii.

PACIFICATION
AND PERSECUTION

HE WAS BACK in El Paso five days before Christmas, 1692, after touring the north country and receiving pledges of peace. Again and again he strode alone and unarmed into throngs of uncertain Indian people in their *placitas;* and always, under his strong gaze and calm certainty, they did as he had come to ask. The news of what he called his "happy conquest" was received in Mexico City with jubilations. The cathedral was outlined with lights, the bells of all the churches rang out, and when the official history of his expedition was written by command of the Viceroy, the Governor became known as "the new Cid," and the "Cortés of these times." He had brought with him some samples of a vermilion earth from the Blue Range of western New Mexico in which the rumored quicksilver was supposed to lie; but assays made at Mexico City showed no trace of it, and hopes of wealth from that source died away. An odd little discovery at the domed desert hill of Zuñi—the old Cíbola—reminded the Governor of his family when he found, among sacred objects carefully kept by the Indians there after the revolt, a number of books. Most of them were of a religious character, and one of them was a volume of the works of his grandmother's second cousin, Saint Teresa of Jesus.

His task was of course not done, for he must resettle the colony in the north, now having prepared the way. In October, 1693, he gave the order to march to seventy families, a hundred soldiers, eighteen Franciscan friars, and a throng of Indian allies. They took a thousand mules, two thousand horses and nine hundred head of cattle. Supply wagons and three artillery pieces completed the train. They went up the river with hopeful expectations.

But when they came slowly into the country of the first pueblos in the middle valley, they heard news to chill their hearts. The pledges of a year ago were disavowed, and all the Indian towns but five were again in rebellion against the Spaniards. The Governor took his train safely through hostile country to Santa Fe, and there he once again approached the people with patience. But they defied him for two weeks, while he kept his soldiers and settlers in a freezing camp outside the walls of Santa Fe. Twenty-one colonists died of the cold, while the Governor made repeated proposals of peace. At last he could wait no longer, and opened battle against the royal city.

He regained it with the loss of only one soldier, and with the future of his whole colony at stake he punished by death seventy Indian captains. As he took his people into their city at the New Year war messages were rising in smoke over the mesas and pueblos of New Mexico. The heavy task of conquest by arms lay ahead, after all, and while the colony took root again at Santa Fe, the Governor must give himself to the duties of a campaign in the field. If the colony was to survive, the pueblos had to be reconquered one by one, and it was three years before peace settled over the kingdom. And then, turning to the founding of new Spanish towns, and the strengthening of the colony through the arts of peace he was able to write to the Viceroy, "With full sails we forge ahead."

The Franciscan missioners now felt secure in their adobe churches and convents at the pueblos, and once again Indians learned the forms of Spanish worship, agriculture, architecture, certain types of weaving, and cooking—all of them except worship modified by the primitive materials and resources at hand. Farms came up again along the great river. The work of men began to bring that subsistence, perhaps even that content, which the early dreams of immediate wealth did not promise. The Governor's first term was running out before his designs for the future of his kingdom had had a fair chance of realization. He petitioned the Crown offices for a second term; but unknown to him a new governor had already been appointed to take his place—one Pedro Rodríguez Cubero, who arrived at Santa Fe in July, 1697.

Governor de Vargas in all proper courtesy and form honored his credentials and planned to remain at the capital for a little while in order to effect an orderly transfer of authority, and to answer any inquiries posed by his successor. He would, he declared, be grateful if this period of customary collaboration could be as brief as possible, since he had other affairs to pursue elsewhere if New Mexico did not need him any longer.

The answer he received was unexpected.

On October second by order of Governor Cubero he was arrested and imprisoned in a small clay cell at one end of the palace of Santa Fe. No one was permitted to see him. Under instructions from the Governor, the municipal council drew up a bill of indictments against him, he was fined four thousand pesos, and all his local property was confiscated. If anyone appealed on his behalf nothing came of it. Governor Cubero sat in his cabinet, spending his days and nights at his desk, writing whole sheaves of state papers and—it was said—drinking too much wine. The palace and other official properties in Santa Fe went to rack and ruin under him, and still he did nothing but write his memorandums, while his noble prisoner passed three years in a cell at the other end of the palace. The garrison, once so smart and proud under Vargas, turned into a shambling set of half-soldiers. New Spanish towns settled by him and launched into safe and prosperous futures by him were now, lacking military protection, abandoned. If the kingdom could be saved by one man, it could also be lost by one.

Finally in 1700 the Franciscan superior of New Mexico travelled to Mexico to tell the Viceroy of the scandalous treatment of Governor de Vargas. The prisoner was ordered instantly released without bail and before summer passed he was again free and on his way to Mexico where his case would be reviewed.

It was reviewed, also, in Madrid, by the King, and in short order all his old estate of conqueror was restored to him, and in addition, the King created him Marquess of La Nava Brazinas, and reappointed him as Governor and Captain General of New Mexico. He returned, then, to Santa Fe, according to his convenience, and arrived there once again in November, 1703. His successor, hearing what was coming, hastily discovered a reason to march out against certain Apaches, and instead made his way discreetly to Mexico. Just as hastily the municipal council of Santa Fe, upon the demand of the Marquess—"it is justice for which I ask," he said—reconsidered its bill of charges against him and now, capable of boundless indignation in his behalf, contradicted every one of the accusations which they had virtuously thrown against him six years before.

The Marquess inspected the effects of the Cubero administration, and said,

Cubero tried to "destroy all I had done and leave no memory of it."

In consequence, there was much work to restore, and the Marquess set out to restore it.

iv.

THE LAST CONQUISTADOR

HE WAS the last Conquistador, for the need of major conquests by force was no more, and with his fulfillment of duty, a great arc of style and character was completed, from Columbus to Cortés, Núñez Cabeza de Vaca, Vásquez de Coronado, Oñate, and Vargas himself. In 1697, the Jesuits opened a century of missionary settlement in Lower California, and in the following century, the Franciscans built their great chain of missions up the Pacific coast in California, and colonial Spain came with them—but in peace, as she came to Arizona in the 1730s. Texas was given her colonial settlements in the seventeenth and eighteenth centuries. Any strife in those lands thereafter came not from the settled native peoples but from the Indian rovers who lived not in towns amidst cultivated crops, but in whole empires of space, with sustenance depending upon the cycle of the seasons when berries ripened or bison roamed from north to south and back again.

Apaches continued to trouble the farms of the great valley of New Mexico, and in March, 1704, the Marquess of La Nava Brazinas took to the field in command of a light squadron of fifty officers and men to go downriver to Bernalillo forty miles away. There he attached a number of Indian allies to his force and then turned with them to go east through the mountains in search of raiding parties of Plains Indians who had been rifling the farmyards and corrals of the great river farms.

At sixty-one he was still a proper field commander; but the turn of seasons in a man's life was mysterious, and though he kept up his campaign journal, reporting Apache trails along the eastern base of the Manzanos mountains, he felt somewhat feverish and weak. In another day or so he was too ill to make his journal entry, and his troops brought him back to Bernalillo on the river and laid him to bed in the house of the mayor. It was not long until he knew what he must be about.

He sent for his military secretary and began to dictate to him.

"In the name of God almighty," he said, in the changed voice of a pneumonia patient, and then he commended his soul for "a most clear career of salvation," and consigned his body "to the earth from which it was made." He stated his wishes for his funeral, and he then made record, like a man of honor who has yet known desire and frailty, of two illegitimate sons, and to them and to their legitimate sister he left his cash resources equally. Since they could use them, he gave to his sons his armor and his six shirts of Dutch linen, "embroidered with the best of lace." They were to have also his Genoese hose, and his suits of court dress—blue brocade with gold buttons, and white with waistcoat and trousers of brown cloth ruffled in gold and silver, and his hats, plumed, or faced with ermine, and his French cloaks of broadcloth lined in velvet, and his leather thigh boots and his leather jackets, and his pistols and swords. To bring more cash into the estate he asked that his silverware—thirty plates, twelve porringers, two platters, a flat salver, a keg with stopper and chain, a large tankard, half a dozen forks and spoons, a large waiter, two fountains, and six candlesticks—be sold, along with his personal jewelry, which included a pair of earrings with eight large emeralds with pearl drops and two rings with diamonds. His debts were to be paid according to the list he made. Even more than to the present, prayer belonged to the future, and he asked for two hundred Masses to be said for himself. It belonged also to the past, and the comrades who were gone, and for them he asked for three hundred Masses—"the souls of the poor who died in the conquest of this kingdom." The "title ceremonies and privileges of Castile" were to be observed over his bier, and his body was to be covered with "honest woolen cloth," and he

asked to be buried in Santa Fe "at the principal altar under
the platform where the priest stands." Five of his officers witnessed his signature when his will was done. He died on
April eighth, 1704. On the day of his burial in his capital
fifty measures of corn and twelve head of cattle were given
in his name to the poor in Santa Fe.

v.

TOMBS AND BANNERS

CONQUISTADORS KNEW that glory was fugitive, for most of
them even in their own lifetimes were subjected to stern,
sometimes fierce, inquiries which all too often ended in disgrace or even death. Many conquerors of the empire rose
from the humblest conditions, like the swineherd Pizarro,
and an amazing number of them—Cortés, the Pizarros,
Balboa, Valdivia, de Soto, Alvarado—came from the same
province of Spain, Estremadura, which the land of New
Mexico so greatly resembled. If the Spaniard in his essential
character rarely bothered with a sense of caste, it was because he carried within himself, in the castle of his person,
that seed of desire to make his own sign of greatness on
the world before he must perish.

When this personal impulse toward glory and style was
given purpose in the New World which came true out of a
great act of the imagination—the vision of Columbus and
the self-image of those who followed him—then what followed could only be a triumphant conquest of the unknown.
Confidence amounting to genius gave power to the conquistadors. A captain in Peru when warned against attempting
the passes of the Andes in winter declared that all would
be well, for he and his men were those "whom the earth
and other elements were bound to obey and Heaven to favor."
With the most limited material means such men were bound
to overcome continents.

Their motive in the great centuries of their conquests—
which left along the whole vast crescent at the bottom of
North America from Florida to the isthmus to California

innumerable evidences of their coming and their going—were two-fold. The first was individual. In the Spanish youth lived a taste for glory under arms and a swift rise to wealth. To the commander the conquest opened hopes of titles and a posterity, coronets on tombs, and banners above him in the whispering vaults of his honored rest—though even a tomb could be lost, and that of General Francisco Vásquez de Coronado disappeared when the Dominican church in the city of Mexico was rebuilt, and that of the Marquess of La Nava Brazinas was lost under a road that wandered north toward Taos past the old palace in Santa Fe. To the priest the conquest promised that throng of souls whose salvation in Christ he was born to achieve. Beyond these individual desires lay that great impersonal power which enclosed them all—the authority of the Crown, under which they would know the privilege of finding the way to Cathay, and the honor of bringing new lands and peoples under the colors of Spain. In the double nature of the individual and the official powers, the conquistador found all the authority he required to achieve his ends—which all too often he achieved with all the brutality of which mankind was capable.

But if man was fallible, he could keep clearly in mind the essential nature of his highest faculty; no matter how far he might betray it in practice. The Spaniard had a popular saw which he often quoted out of a play by Calderón —"To the king we owe our life and fortune, but honor is the patrimony of the soul, and the soul belongs to God." It told much about how he placed himself in life, whether at home in Spain or far abroad in the New World which during four centuries he held for his king. When Pedro de Alvarado, Cortés's handsome, amusing, vain captain, was dying of wounds given to him by Indians, he was asked where he ached, and he replied, "In my soul."

Acknowledgments

WITH RESPECT and gratitude I record my particular indebtedness to the following works in the preparation of this book: *The Journal of Christopher Columbus*, translated by Cecil Jane; *The True History of the Conquest of Mexico*, from which I drew or adapted excerpts variously from the editions of Joaquin Ramirez Cabañas, of that translated by Albert Idell, and that of Gennaro García, translated by A. P. Maudsley; *The General History of the Things of New Spain* (commonly referred to as the Florentine Codex), by Bernardino de Sahagún, translated from the Aztec by Arthur J. O. Anderson and Charles E. Dibble (Books 1, 2, 3, 8, 10 and 12); *Hernan Cortés, Conqueror of Mexico*, and *The Rise of the Spanish American Empire*, by Salvador de Madariaga; *The Golden Conquistadores*, by Irwin R. Blacker and Harry M. Rosen; *Travels in the New World*, by Thomas Gage, edited by J. Eric S. Thompson; *Aristotle and the American Indian, A Study in Race Prejudice*, by Lewis Hanke; *Tenochtitlan en una Isla*, by Ignacio Bernal; *Estudios de Historia Colonial*, by Wigberto Jiménez Moreno; *Durango Colonial*, by José Ignacio Gallegos C.; and the following volumes of the Coronado Cuarto Centennial Publications, edited by George P. Hammond: *Narratives of the Coronado Expedition, 1540–1542*, by Pedro Castañeda de Náxera, edited by George P. Hammond and Agapito Rey: *Don Juan de Oñate, Colonizer of New Mexico, 1595–1628*, edited by George P. Hammond and Agapito Rey; *Fray Alonso de Benavides' Revised Memorial of 1634*, edited by Frederick Webb Hodge, George P. Hammond and Agapito Rey; *Revolt of the Pueblo Indians and Otermín's Attempted Reconquest, 1680–1682*, edited by Charles Wilson Hackett and Charmion Clair Shelby; and *First Expedition of Vargas into New Mexico, 1692*, by Diego de Vargas Zapata Luján Ponce de León, translated with introduction and notes by J. Manuel Espinosa. For permission to quote intermittently from certain of these I am duly grateful to authors, editors and publishers. A detailed listing of these and other works consulted will be found in the bibliography.

For assistance in various phases of my work in the preparation of this book, I thank my agent, Miss Virginia Rice; my editors, Mr. Robert Giroux (New York) and Mr. Lovat Dickson (London); Mr. H. D. Vursell; and Mr. Donald Berke, Mr. Witter Bynner, Dr. Henry Allen Moe, Miss Lillian Libman, Mr. Joaquin del Valle, Mr. Frederick Adams, Fray Angelico Chavez, O.F.M., Mr. David McIntosh, Mrs. Charlotte St. John Murphy, Mr. Oliver LaFarge, and the Center for Advanced Studies of Wesleyan University, Middletown, Connecticut.

BIBLIOGRAPHY

Aiton, Arthur Scott. *The secret visita against Viceroy Mendoza*. In *New Spain and the Anglo-American west. Historical contributions presented to Herbert Eugene Bolton*. Edited by Charles Wilson Hackett *et al.* 2 v. Privately printed, Lancaster, Pa., 1932.

Bandelier, Adolph F. A. *Historical documents relating to New Mexico, Nueva Viscaya, and approaches thereto, to 1773*. Vol. I. Edited by Charles Wilson Hackett. Washington, Carnegie Institution, 1923.

Benavides, Alonso de. *Fray Alonso de Benavides' revised memorial of 1634*. With numerous supplementary documents elaborately annontated. Frederick Webb Hodge, George P. Hammond, and Agapito Rey. Coronado Cuarto Centennial Publications, 1540–1940. Vol. 4. Albuquerque, University of New Mexico Press, 1945.

Bernal, Ignacio. *Tenochtitlan en una isla*. Serie historia II. Mexico, Instituto Nacional de Antropología e Historia, 1959.

Bishop, Morris. *The odyssey of Cabeza de Vaca*. New York and London, The Century Co., 1933.

Blacker, Irwin R. *The golden conquistadores*. Introduction and commentaries by Irwin R. Blacker. Texts edited by Harry M. Rosen. Indianapolis, The Bobbs-Merrill Co., 1960.

Chavez, Fray Angelico. *Nuestra Señora de la Macana*. New Mexico, Historical Review, v. XXXIV, no. 2, April, 1959.

Coli, François. *L'art des conquistadores*. Photographes de Claude Arthaud et François Hébert-Stevens. Paris, B. Arthaud, 1960.

Castañeda de Náxera, Pedro de. *Narrative of the expedition to Cíbola, undertaken in 1540, in which are described all those settlements, ceremonies and customs*. Edited by George P. Hammond and Agapito Rey. Coronado Cuarto Centennial Publications, 1540–1940. Vol. 2. Albuquerque. University of New Mexico Press, 1940.

Cervantes de Salazar, Francisco. *Life in the imperial and loyal city of Mexico in New Spain and the royal and pontifical university of Mexico as described in the dialogues for the study of the Latin language prepared by Francisco Cervantes de Salazar for use in his classes and printed in 1554 by Juan Pablos*. Now published in facsimile with a translation by Minnie Lee Barrett Shepard and an introduction and notes by Carlos Eduardo Castañeda. Austin, University of Texas Press, 1953.

Cervantes Saavedra, Miguel de. *The first part of the life and achievements of the renowned Don Quixote de la Mancha*. Translated by Peter Motteux. New York, The Illustrated Modern Library, 1946.

Cieza de León, Pedro de. *The Incas . . .* translated by Harriet de

Onis. Edited, with an introduction, by Wolfgang von Hagen. Norman, The University of Oklahoma Press, 1959.

Cohen, J. M., ed. *The Penguin book of Spanish verse.* Baltimore, Penguin Books, 1956.

Colón, Fernando. *The life of the Admiral Christopher Columbus by his son Ferdinand.* Translated and annotated by Benjamin Keen. New Brunswick, Rutgers University Press, 1959.

Columbus, Christopher. *The Journal of Christopher Columbus.* Translated by Cecil Jane, with an appendix by R. A. Skelton. New York, Clarkson H. Potter, Inc., 1960.

Díaz del Castillo, Bernal. *The Bernal Díaz chronicles, the true story of the conquest of Mexico.* Translated and edited by Albert Idell. Garden City, Doubleday and Co., 1956.

——————— *The discovery and conquest of Mexico, 1517–1521.* Edited . . . by Gennaro García. Translated with an introduction and notes by A. P. Maudsley. New York, Farrar, Straus and Cudahy, 1956.

——————— *Historia verdadera de la conquista de la Nueva España.* Introducción y notas de Joaquin Cabañas. México, Editorial Porrúa, S. A., 1960.

Gage, Thomas. *Travels in the New World.* Edited by J. Eric S. Thompson. Norman, University of Oklahoma Press, 1958.

Gallegos, José Ignacio. *Durango colonial, 1563–1821.* Prologo de José Bravo Ugarte, S.J. México, Editorial Jus, 1960.

Hackett, Charles Wilson. *Revolt of the Pueblo Indians of New Mexico and Otermín's attempted reconquest, 1680–1682.* Introductions and annotations by Charles Wilson Hackett. Translations of original documents by Charmion Clair Shelby. Coronado Cuarto Centennial Publications, 1540–1940. Vols. 8 & 9. Albuquerque, University of New Mexico Press, 1942.

Hammond, George P. *Don Juan de Oñate, coloniser of New Mexico, 1595–1628.* George P. Hammond and Agapito Rey. Coronado Cuarto Centennial Publications, 1540–1940. Vol. 5. Albuquerque, The University of New Mexico Press, 1953.

Hanke, Lewis. *Aristotle and the American Indians, a study in race prejudice in the modern world.* Chicago, Henry Regnery, 1959.

Hodge, Frederick Webb. *History of Hawikuh, New Mexico, one of the so-called cities of Cíbola.* Los Angeles, 1937.

Horgan, Paul. *Great River, the Rio Grande in North American history.* New York, Rinehart and Co., 1954.

——————— *The centuries of Santa Fe.* New York, E. P. Dutton and Co., 1956.

Jiménez Moreno, Wigberto. *Estudios de historia colonial.* Serie historia I. México, Instituto Nacional de Antropología e Historia, 1958.

Livermore, Harold. *A history of Spain.* New York, Farrar, Straus and Cudahy, 1958.

Madariaga, Salvador de. *Christopher Columbus, being the life of the very magnificent lord Don Cristobal Colón.* London, Hodder and Stoughton, 1939.

——————— *Hernan Cortés, conqueror of Mexico.* London, Hollis and Carter, 1942.

——————— *Rise of the Spanish American empire.* London, Hollis and Carter, 1947.

Mandeville, Sir John. *The travels of Sir John Mandeville. The version of the Cotton manuscript in modern spelling.*

Mariéjol, Jean Hippolyte. *The Spain of Ferdinand and Isabella.* Translated and edited by Benjamin Keen. New Brunswick, Rutgers University Press, 1961.

Moorhead, Max L. *New Mexico's royal road; trade and travel on the Chihuahua Trail.* Norman, University of Oklahoma Press, 1958.

Morison, Samuel Eliot. *Admiral of the ocean sea, a life of Christopher Columbus.* Boston, Little, Brown and Co. 1942.

———— *Christopher Columbus, mariner.* Boston, Little, Brown and Co., 1955.

Nunn, George C. *The geographical conceptions of Columbus, a critical consideration of four problems.* New York, American Geographical Society, 1924.

Pérez de Villagrá, Gaspár. *History of New Mexico.* Translated by Gilberto Espinosa. Introduction and notes by Frederick W. Hodge. Los Angeles, The Quivira Society, 1933.

Polo, Marco. *The travels of Marco Polo.* Translated and with an introduction by Ronald Latham. Baltimore, Penguin Books, 1958.

Prescott, William Hickling. *The conquest of Peru.* Garden City, Doubleday and Co., n.d.

Sahagún, Bernardino de. *General history of the things of New Spain.* (The Florentine Codex.) Book I, The gods; Book 2, The ceremonies; Book 3, The origin of the gods; Book 8, Kings and lords; Book 10, The people; Book 12, The conquest of Mexico. Translated from the Aztec into English by Arthur J. O. Anderson and Charles E. Dibble. With notes and illustrations. Santa Fe, The School of American Research and the University of Utah, 1950–1961.

Séjourné, Laurette. *Burning waters: thought and religion in ancient Mexico.* New York, Grove Press, 1960.

Vargas Zapata Luján Ponce de León, Diego de. *First expedition of Vargas into New Mexico, 1692.* Translated, with introduction and notes, by J. Manuel Espinosa. Coronado Cuarto Centennial Publications, 1540–1940. Vol. 10. Albuquerque, University of New Mexico Press, 1940.

INDEX

(For the convenient orientation of the reader, entries for towns, rivers, mountains, and other geographical features are followed in this index by modern political designations such as "Mex." or "New Mex." The reader is reminded, however, that during the period of history treated in this book Mexico in its greatest area was known as New Spain; New Mexico received its common meaning in 1598; and the word Mexico generally referred to the viceregal capital city.)

235